Reconnecting Culture, Technology and Nature

Everyday life is increasingly mediated by technology, but most of the literature on the subject talks only in terms of radical changes. In *Reconnecting Culture, Technology and Nature* Mike Michael uses case studies of mundane technologies such as the walking boot, the car and the TV remote control to question some of the fundamental dichotomies through which we make sense of the world. Drawing on the insights of Bruno Latour, Donna Haraway and Michel Serres, the author elaborates an innovative conceptual and methodological framework through which new hybrid objects of study are creatively constructed, tracing the ways in which the cultural, the natural and the technological interweave in the production of order and disorder. This book critically engages with, and draws connections between, a wide range of literatures including those concerned with the environment, consumption and the body.

Mike Michael is Senior Lecturer in Sociology at Goldsmiths College, University of London.

International library of sociology
Founded by Karl Mannheim
Editor: John Urry
University of Lancaster

Reconnecting Culture, Technology and Nature

From society to heterogeneity

Mike Michael

London and New York

First published 2000
by Routledge
11 New Fetter Lane, London EC4P 4EE

Simultaneously published in the USA and Canada
by Routledge
29 West 35th Street, New York, NY 10001

Routledge is an imprint of the Taylor & Francis Group

Typeset in Galliard by
Keystroke, Jacaranda Lodge, Wolverhampton
Printed and bound in Great Britain by
Biddles Ltd, Guildford and King's Lynn

British Library Cataloguing in Publication Data
A catalogue record for this book is available from the British Library

Library of Congress Cataloging in Publication Data
Michael, Mike.
    Reconnecting culture, technology, and nature : from society to heterogeneity /
Mike Michael.
        p.   cm. – (International library of sociology)
    Includes bibliographical references and index.
    1. Technology–Social aspects. 2. Technology–Sociological aspects. I. Title.
    II. Series.

HM846.M53 2000
306.4'6–dc21   00-036887

ISBN 0–415–20116–0 (hbk)
ISBN 0–415–20117–9 (pbk)

For Aneirin Christakis Rees

Contents

Acknowledgements

This book would not have been possible without the aid of many others. As usual, it is impossible to acknowledge everyone who in some way or other has contributed to this text. Various versions of various chapters have been presented at various conferences, seminars and colloquia: to all those who made comments, raised criticisms, or whose silence I could take as quiet agreement, go my thanks. At Goldsmiths College, Les Back, Andrew Barry, Grant Donovan, Mariam Fraser, Monica Greco, David Hiller, Sarah Kember, Celia Lury, Don Slater, Clive Seale, William Walters and Claire Wardell have listened to my ramblings with unusual forbearance; at Lancaster University and beyond, over the years, Hilary Arksey, Lynda Birke, Nik Brown, Steve Brown, Tom Cahill, Simon Carter, Alan Collins, Susan Condor, Gavin Kendall, John Law, Maggie Mort, Neil Pollock, Paul Rosen, Andy Samuel, Vicky Singleton, Kath Smart, Chris Stokes, Floris Tomasini, Jill Turner, Lesley Waite, Sue Weldon and Brian Wynne have all helped me solidify what was too amorphous, and render amorphous what was too solid. Special mention is deserved by those whose friendship and good humour sustained me throughout the writing of this book: big thanks go to Lynda Birke, Rob Briner, Simon Carter, Alan Collins, Susan Condor, Graham Jenkins, Gavin Kendall, Christalleni, Katerina and Marios Michael, Doreen Norman, Vicky Singleton, Kath Smart, Chris Todd, Lesley Waite and Laura Youngson Coll. In their inimitable ways, Aneirin, Bethan, Elvis and H.B. Rees helped me prioritize.

Mike Michael
December 1999

Acknowledgements

1 Introduction
Situating technology and technologizing situations

There are no humans in the world. Or rather, humans are fabricated – in language, through discursive formations, in their various liaisons with technological and natural actors, across networks that are heterogeneously comprised of humans and non-humans who are themselves so comprised. Instead of humans and non-humans we are beginning to think about flows, movements, arrangements, relations. It is through such dynamics that the human (and the non-human) emerges. This book is about the complex processes of such fabrication. It is concerned with the ways in which the human is not simply 'tied to' – that is, an ambiguous product of – the social (however that might be formulated), but also 'tied to' much more – the technological, the natural.

But of course those entities that fall into the categories of the technological and the natural are no different. They are 'tied to' the social: a technology only 'works' because certain configurations of the social, the technological and the natural are in place. Nature's particular recalcitrance, nature's evident bounty, partly and complexly, rest on the conduct of networks of humans and technologies and natures.

Consequently, a key task of this book is to make a small contribution to the unravelling of some of these connections. It is to place the social in a complex, heterogeneous nexus of entities and flows. In addressing an audience of 'social scientists', the (gently evangelical) aim is to show how a number of categories typical of the social sciences are shot through with the technological and the natural.

However, to phrase the issue in this way is to fall back on some of our most well-established concepts: nature, society, technology. This is not necessarily a bad thing. At the very least it hints at the fact that, in order to do justice to the complexity of the connections between nature, society and technology, what is needed is a collective effort at breaching the disciplines (very generally, the natural and social sciences) that serve to keep these concepts distinct. Following in the path of various scholars, I hope to demonstrate how, with a relatively slight shift in perspective, it becomes very difficult to disentangle the traditionally discrete entities and processes of the traditionally discrete disciplines. They flow into each other. As a result, what becomes possible is a rethinking of the categories of entities and processes that might encompass this intermixing, this heterogeneity. Where once, thanks in part to our disciplinary commitments, we contrasted the social, the cultural and the linguistic to the non-human, the natural and the material (often by relegating the latter to the status of 'mere' social constructions), now we are thinking about the ways in which these fold into one another, or dissolve into one another, to produce different sorts of heterogeneous entities and processes.

As is increasingly well known, there is an emergent (although, inevitably disparate) vocabulary that is beginning to address this heterogeneity. Terms such as cyborg, hybrid and monster are increasingly commonplace. In reviewing some of the main perspectives that attach to this terminology, I will compare and contrast a range of concerns that inform them. These include the implied positioning and politics of the 'author' of cyborgs or hybrids, the analytic role of such macro-sociological categories as globalization and consumption, the character of agency and the relative status of culture. In the process, I will develop my own peculiar version of these heterogeneous admixtures and their doings. What will be particular about my versions of hybrids or cyborgs or monsters (what I shall call co(a)gents) is that I attempt to sketch these out in some detail in order to show how they came into being heterogeneously – that is, I explore how specific technologies, bits of bodies, aspects of nature, parts of culture, and traditions of discourse come together in the production of co(a)gents such as the 'couch potato' or the 'road rager' or the 'seeker of the natural sublime'. All of these entities I find 'out there' in everyday life; sometimes they are explicitly articulated in popular culture, sometimes they are in the process of being conceptualized, sometimes they are in need of a little discursive prompting, that is, I need to 'invent' them.

However, over and above this, a key purpose of this text is to follow through the theoretical implications of what it would mean to treat these hybrid entities as the 'objects of study'. Notions such hybrids, cyborgs and monsters have been used, profoundly and rightly, to deconstruct traditional academic categories and to demonstrate the heterogeneous connectedness of entities that we have kept distinct by virtue of our specialist intellectual affiliations (e.g. to sociology as opposed to biology). Thus, entities such as nature, culture, the human body, the social agent, and so on, that were once regarded as discrete and unitary, are now being deconstructed to reveal their distributedness and interconnectedness: nature and culture, corporeality and agency are not distinct, they contribute, in complex ways, to each other's constitution. This is all very important – it is an endeavour to which I will, I hope, be contributing in this book. However, in addition to this, I want to begin to think about what it means when we draw upon or invent particular hybrids (for example, the 'couch potato' as a popular term used to describe people who laze, remote control in hand, on the sofa in front of the TV), and then treat these *seriously*. What work might the formulation of a new hybrid entity do for us analytically? By taking a figure such as the couch potato seriously, what light might it throw on, for example, relations of power within the family, or subcultural identity? More specifically, how does it enable us to explore the variegated roles of mundane technologies such as sofas and remotes in these social processes? In sum, by taking up this strategy, I want to explore the range of otherwise unrecognized connections that contribute to, flow through, and extend from, such hybrids.

There is another dimension to this work that I need to address. Much work on hybrids, particularly the cultural studies influenced analysis of cyborgs (sometimes known as cyborgology), has tended to focus upon what might be called the most 'exotic' of technologies. For example, it is innovations in particular technoscientific domains – information technology and biotechnology are iconic in this respect – that are regarded as crucial in the reshaping of the social, the cultural and the human. Indeed, the exoticism of these technologies lies, in part, in our perception of their present role in changing, in some fundamental way, say, the organization of society (e.g. are there new stratifications emerging?), or our conceptions of ourselves (e.g. are there new models of kinship or cognition developing?). In contrast, those studies of the role of technology that have come out of the tradition of the sociology of scientific knowledge have also focused on more mundane technologies. Here, we can say that 'mundane' refers to those technologies whose novelty has worn off; these are technologies that are now fully integrated into, and an unremarkable part of, everyday life. To study mundane technologies is thus to explore how they mediate and reflect everyday life, how they serve the production and reproduction of local social configurations. In this respect, my work can be said to fall within the emerging field of studies in 'material culture' (see Dant, 1999, for an introduction; also the *Journal of Material Culture*).

Needless to say, there is no clear dividing line between these two endeavours. The distinction between mundane and exotic is, of course, spurious. After all, the mundane often entails the most exotic of technologies in its construction, and vice versa. For example, walking boots may be 'mundane' technological artefacts, but in their design, production, distribution and marketing, the most exotic of technologies are involved. For example, as we shall see later, information technology – such as the internet – serves as a prime medium for the advertisement and assessment of walking boots. Conversely, 'exotic' technologies are realizable – that is, can work – only by virtue of the fact that various mundane technologies are in place: the light bulbs that illuminate the laboratory benches of bio-technologists, the chairs and desks of the information technologists who oversee our servers.

Despite the highly porous boundary between the mundane and exotic, the distinction does serve a key purpose. Exotic technologies (and sociotechnical systems), as we have seen, can be said to be instrumental in the reconfiguration of our conceptions of the social and of nature (out of very many such accounts, see for example, Appadurai, 1990; Gergen, 1991; Strathern, 1992). They challenge our existing understandings of who 'we' are, what society is, the status of expert knowledge, the role of technology, the value of the natural. Exotic technologies can, then, be said to mark epochal cultural shifts. As such, they are the objects of extended academic and popular reflection. In contrast, mundane technologies have lost their novelty and now linger in the background, doing their 'job' largely outside the intense discursive glare that attempts to capture the exotic. Yet it is these very mundane technologies that not only serve in the (re)production of the exotic, but also constitute the 'normality', the 'ordinary', the 'invisible' even, against which is set the strange. Moreover, in the interstices of the everyday where mundane technologies quietly go about their business of sustaining normality, we find all manner of little 'abnormalities'. These mundane technologies do not simply furnish order (against which are contrasted the upheavals rendered by exotic technologies), they also resource disorderings. Thus, our everyday 'habitual' routines that involve these technologies can also encompass little disruptions and subversions that, perhaps, lead to grander changes. Thus, I want to explore how mundane technology, heterogeneously, that is, both materially and semiotically, at once reinforces and undermines the typical arrangements and processes that comprise everyday life. These 'typical arrangements and processes that comprise everyday life' are themselves heterogeneous of course – they entail other technologies. They incorporate social and cultural entities and relations, and they entail the 'natural' – bodies, environments, animals.

In sum, it is in the role of mundane technologies as what Bruno Latour (1992) has called the missing masses that I am interested. As 'missing masses', these artefacts – unnoticed, everyday, always present – serve in the processes of heterogeneous ordering and disordering. That is to say, these mundane technologies, which, let us recall, are heterogeneous insofar as they entail both the social and the material, at once contribute to, and disrupt, the unnoticed, everyday, always present co(a)gents that populate our world. By exploring these quotidian technologies (and mundane hybrids), I am aspiring to follow in the footsteps of Arendt's (1992) version of Benjamin, who is fascinated by the way that the smallest – the least noticeable – enacapsulates an epoch.

Developing technologies

So this book is partly about the role of mundane technology in heterogeneous ordering and disordering. But what of the way that the social sciences have narrated technology? It goes without saying that the stories told about technology are many and complex. Wiebe Bijker (1995a), in his excellent overview of sociohistorical technology studies, ranges over a wide variety of perspectives that he arrays along a continuum. At one pole there are those perspectives that regard technology as determining the social; at the opposite pole there are those that view the social as determining the technological. This continuum assumes that technology plays a key part in the modern social world, enabling some groups, disabling others: it is, through and through, political. However, as Bijker asks: 'How do artifacts acquire their politics? Is it bestowed upon them by their users or is it "baked into them" during their construction?' (Bijker, 1995a, p. 237, also see, for example, Winner, 1985, 1993; Russell, 1986). That is to say, are the politics they do and the discriminations they exercise part of 'what they are', or due to their use by persons? The contemporary answer to this question is, unsurprisingly, 'both'. As Bijker (1995a, p. 214) puts it: '. . . a general pattern can be recognized in which the study of technology and society has been developing. This pattern can, very schematically, be characterized as a sort of slow pendulum movement – a dampened oscillation'. First technological determinism, then social shaping; now, oscillating in the middle are a number of approaches that examine the mutual determination of both these factors. From alternately privileging the social and prioritizing the technological, the role of both is emphasized nowadays: these shape one another in complex knots.

There are a number of perspectives in the sociology of technology that occupy this middle ground where the social and the technological are regarded as mutually determining. I will consider three, examining in detail one. Firstly, there is the systems approach associated with Hughes (1983), secondly there is actor-network theory (ANT), thirdly there is the social construction of technology approach (now developed into the technological frame approach – cf. Pinch and Bijker, 1984; Bijker, 1995b). The first has, in large part, been concerned with the entrepreneurial development of large sociotechnical systems. Its aim has been to unravel the way that technical systems take on a momentum of their own, even while these are thoroughly interwoven with the social, the political and the economic to form a seamless web. Central to this approach is the way that large-scale technologies (e.g. electricity systems) are developed and integrated into these other systems. While these sorts of issues form the backdrop to much that will be addressed in this book, they do not bear directly on the purposes of the current study. Discussion of the second perspective will be deferred until the next chapter – suffice to say here that a core attraction of the actor-network approach has been its willingness to treat the 'natural' seriously, and it is some of the implications of this feature that will be explored in this book. The third of these perspectives is particularly interesting here for it concerns the way that technological innovations are, at least in the initial introductory phase, interpretatively flexible – that is, many of the actors involved, including, sometimes, users, interpret and thus constitute these artefacts in markedly different ways. This increasingly sophisticated approach (which shares a number of common concerns with ANT) is fundamentally concerned with how such flexibility is closed down. In the following discussion, I will consider this process of 'black boxing' or stabilizing the meaning of innovatory technological artefacts in order to draw out further my own concerns.

In Pinch and Bijker's (1984) now classic analysis of the development and estab-lishment of the bicycle as we know it today, a number of relevant social groups are identified (e.g. young men, women, elderly men). For each of these groups, the ordinary bicycle (more commonly known as the penny farthing) was seen as containing a different set of meanings: for young men, it was a splendid racing vehicle; for women it created difficulties for their dress; for elderly men, it posed safety problems. According to Pinch and Bijker, adopting and adapting the dictates of the strong programme and the empirical programme of relativism in the sociology of scientific knowledge (Bloor, 1976; Barnes, 1977; Collins, 1985), it was a different object to each of these groups: there was interpretative flexibility. Pinch and Bijker go on to trace how the variety of meanings was reduced, and how this flexibility was abated. There are two interwoven aspects to this process – closure and stabilization. In the former, which Bijker (1995b) associates with the reduction of technological artefacts *amongst* relevant social groups, interpretations are reduced through such mechanisms as rhetorical closure (say by a redefinition of the problem the technology solves). Stabilization refers to the ways that inter-pretative flexibility was reduced *within* relevant social groups. Through such mechanisms, then, the meanings of artefacts are settled with the result that some survive to be extensively used, while others perish, or are consigned to the museum as technological oddities.

Now, an issue with this sort of analysis lies in the notion of the relevant social group, which Bijker (1995b) directly addresses. On the one hand, there is a political danger of neglecting powerless groups – inclusion of such marginal groups is an interpretative matter of judging what groups and issues are relevant to the case of technological development under study. On the other hand, there is the epistemological issue of the status of the relevant social group: is it an actor's category, or an analyst's? Bijker suggests that there is no simple equation between these versions. Rather, he seems to be saying that there is a need to be judiciously sensitive to the categories of actors: one needs to avoid naive use of actors' categories lest one miss out on relevant social groups that are absent from the histories that such actors deploy. Contrariwise, one also needs to avoid imposing categories lest one produce a distorted account.

We can frame this issue another way. Bijker argues that the interpretations available to relevant social groups are limited. This limitation flows from the technological frame within which such groups are embedded: 'Previous meaning attributions limit the flexibility of later ones, structures are built up, artifacts stabilize, and (technological) ensembles become more obdurate' (Bijker, 1995b, p. 282). The notion of the technological frame is meant to capture the structures that are inherent in interactions among the individuals who comprise a relevant social group: '[a] technological frame is built up when interaction "around" an artifact begins. . . . If existing interactions move members of an emerging relevant social group in the same direction, a technological frame will build up . . .' (Bijker, 1995b, p. 123).

The technological frame is a concept somewhat akin to Kuhn's notion of paradigm: it 'comprises all elements that influence the interactions within the relevant social group and lead to the attribution of meanings to technical artifacts' (Bijker, 1995b, p. 123). These elements include: goals, key problems, problem-solving strategies (heuristics), requirements to be met by the problem solutions, current theories, tacit knowledge, testing procedures and design methods and criteria, users' practices, perceived substitution function (what might a new artefact replace?), exemplary artefacts.

According to Bijker, his concept of a 'technological frame' is designed to capture two dimensions of the relation between the relevant social group and the artefact. On the one hand, there is the social interactionist element: relevant social groups, in attributing different meanings to artefacts, constitute them. In cases of different meanings, there is interpretative flexibility which is closed down when consensus is established (cf. Bijker, 1995b, p. 194). On the other hand, the artefacts them-selves are stabilized semiotically, and in this they are meaningful to different relevant social groups (Bijker cites the example of celluloid which 'speaks to' celluloid chemists, moulders, pressing machine designers and so on). The technological frame is thus ascribed by Bijker a special ontological status as a 'hinge' between social groups and artefacts – it is a means of getting around 'irreconcilable differences between social determinism and technical determinism' (Bijker, 1995b, p. 196).

However, as Rosen (1995, 1993) argues, there are numerous other factors that can contribute to this sort of frame. He notes, for example, that the processes and relations of manufacture (like post-Fordism) can be a key factor in the meaning attributions to innovatory artefacts (see also Mort, 1995). More relevant in the present context is the factor of culture. Rosen shows how the emergence and stabilization of the mountain bicycle is linked to broader cultural shifts (e.g. postmodern culture).

On a less grandiose scale, we can point out that the individual relevant social groups do not simply reduce the meanings of technologies, they are also involved in the proliferation of meanings. This is because – especially in the process of consumption – a relevant social group is a multiplicitous entity. Individuals cut across categories. Indeed, the borders of a relevant social group are highly pliable, and it is part of the aim of technologists to stabilize these (this is what ANT is particularly good at addressing). Conversely, the technological artefacts themselves do not simply, through the technological frame, 'appeal to' certain social groups. Or rather, these technologies are polysemic – as we shall see in relation to the car and road rage, the semiotics of the car are complex and contradictory within individual relevant social groups. Technological development can go in many directions (e.g. more speed; more efficiency; more safety and so on) and the support for these various directions maps, in tortuous ways, onto relevant social groups (for example, people are both users of cars and are pedestrians – these are not necessarily singular relevant social groups, but hybrids shot through with ambivalence).

As an example of this cultural complexity, we can briefly consider Nik Brown's (1998) analysis of the promotion of xenotransplantation (see also Birke *et al.*, 1998). What Brown unravels is that, in the process of promoting xenotrans-plantation (specifically the technologies concerned with the genetic modification of pigs so that their hearts can be transplanted into human bodies), a whole range of cultural resources are mobilized, both by the promoters (biomedical entre-peneurs) and other relevant social groups (e.g. patients and their families, animal rights activists). The technological frame is very quickly seen to spin out to incorporate, or rather interweave with, a broad array of cultural concerns. Thus, there is the issue of hope – the xenotransplantation technological frame tacitly draws upon a long tradition of thinking about the role of hope not just in healthcare, but more generally, in life. This frame also engages with anxieties over the divide between the human and the animal, most obviously evidenced in the 'yuk' or disgust factor associated with such medical procedures (Brown, 1999). These takes on xenotransplantation might be contradictory, but they can coexist within the technological frame. The point is that a technological frame is partly characterized by such broader cultural dimensions, and these enable technological artefacts to constitute and 'address' relevant social groups, and relevant social groups to interpret artefacts in complex and ambiguous ways.

While Bijker's concerns are somewhat different from my own (Bijker is concerned with how emergent artefacts become stabilized, I am interested in how mundane artefacts contribute to processes of ordering and disordering), his approach serves to throw into relief one particular issue that will be addressed below. This concerns the complex role of culture. Manufacturers of technological artefacts, in contributing in one way or another to the culture of users (consumer-relevant social groups), serve in shaping those users' identities, rendering them more or less receptive to those artefacts. But the culture of users, as we have seen, is riven, fragmented, shifting. This point can be further elaborated in relation to those studies that deal with the complexities of technological use – say in the domestic sphere, or within subcultures. It is to some of these that I now turn.

Domesticating technologies

Cowan (1987) has noted that Pinch and Bijker's notion of the relevant social group is hard to pin down empirically. As in the above argument, she points to the 'infinitely expandable universe of relevant social groups' (Cowan, 1987, p. 262). In trying to pin these down she focuses upon what she calls the 'consumption junction'. At this complex node, where technologies are diffused, where technologies are chosen, we face a major analytic problem: 'consumers themselves come in many different shapes and sizes; indeed, any single human being can enter the consumption junction under a number of different guises, depending on what it is that is being consumed' (Cowan, 1987, p. 263). But this is not necessarily a problem; rather, Cowan suggests, it 'reminds us that we must define consumers in terms of the artifact about which consumers are making choices' (Cowan, 1987, p. 263). It also enables us to unpick how these choices are structured – how they are shaped by a set of ostensibly tangential factors that might concern, for example, labour relations, transport systems, other industrial developments. In some ways, Bijker's elaboration of the technological frame captures this; and yet, it is also too constrained, for the relevant factors cannot be identified through specific study only of the technology itself. As Cowan (1987) notes: all sorts of other histories need to be drawn upon – demographic, economic, industrial and, we might add, cultural.

Extremely important as Cowan's formulation is, it does not enter fully into the complexity of the acts of consumption (although see Cowan, 1997). Here, we need briefly to examine some of the ways in which the consumption of technologies has been theorized. Having said this, we do need to be wary of reifying 'consumption': for all its apparent centrality in what is said to be an increasingly globalized world (e.g. Lash and Urry, 1994), historical and anthropological studies show that the introduction of technology into certain communities does not make members of those groups 'consumers' in some universal sense (especially when we are analytically sensitive to the context of cultural difference and colonialism – see, for example, Miller, 1995; Wallace, 1993; Pfaffenberger, 1992a, 1992b).

Lie and Sorensen (1996) provide a sophisticated outline of the ways in which technologies are integrated into everyday life. For Lie and Sorensen, consumers cannot be passive: in integrating technologies into everyday life, we adopt and adapt technologies, we shape, and are shaped by, them. Drawing on the work of Silverstone *et al.* (1992), Lie and Sorensen see this metaphorically as a process of domestication: 'we tame the technologies that surround us in everyday life. This process of taming is characterized by reciprocal change' (Lie and Sorenson, 1996, p. 8). Thus, 'users/consumers make active efforts to shape their lives through creative manipulation of artefacts, symbols and social systems in relation to their practical needs and competencies' (Lie and Sorenson, 1996, p. 9). It follows that consumption is also a process of production. The process of such integration into everyday life routines is at once practical and symbolic: local routines and symbolic codes may be adapted as technologies are domesticated. These changes might be smooth, or they might be agonistic; conflicts might be resolved or they may remain open. But to put it in this way is to underplay the fact that these authors and numerous others (see, for example, Grint and Gill, 1995; Cockburn and Ormrod, 1993; Wajcman, 1995) are deeply concerned with the relationship between technology and relations of power, especially gender. In the context of 'consumption', Lie and Sorensen stress that technology does not map neatly onto pre-existing gender divisions. Rather, they argue, we should 'shift away from viewing gender and technology as pre-determined' (Lie and Sorenson, 1996, p. 20); in the process of domestication, both gender and technology are negotiated. Sometimes, this domestication reproduces existing gender relations, in other instances there is a subversion of these. In other words, we need to get away from seeing the role of technology as merely reinforcing existing relations of power, from analysing technology in tacitly functionalist terms.

The implication of this argument is that we should be sensitive to the likelihood that technologies in the process of domestication will retain a certain ambiguity. They are multivalent – in Silverstone *et al.*'s (1992) terms (drawing upon and developing Kopytoff's, 1986, and Appadurai's, 1986, notion of the biography of things), technologies in everyday life have many biographies. Thus, as the telephone and the car well illustrate, even 'old' technologies can, under certain circumstances, be re-interpreted and re-appropriated (cf. Hebdidge, 1979; Lamvik, 1996; Vestby, 1996). Further, Silverstone *et al.* note that one aspect of this multiple biography concerns the forging of relations beyond the household – what they call 'conversion'. Thus, technologies enable certain users to re-fashion relations not only within the household, but also beyond it. A nice example that can be drawn from Silverstone *et al.* (1992) is that of young people's use of the stereo. On the one hand, it is a means of creating a wall of sound against parental intrusion; on the other, the stereo serves these young people in establishing and reinforcing relations with peers. Lie and Sorensen likewise extend the concept of domestication to technologies beyond the household/home/family (on the non-equivalence of these, see Silverstone, 1994).

Now, this notion of domestication addresses a number of important issues; but in crucial ways, these differ from the ones I wish to explore in what is to follow.

Thus, we can say that the notion of domestication is generally meant to capture the way that new technologies enter everyday life and how, in the process, that sphere at once accommodates to, and reconstitutes, those artefacts. It is often a question of something from the outside moving into an inside – an 'other' being made familiar (which can include both the reinforcement of certain relations of power, and their modification). There is, in other words, a complex mode of integration through symbolic, social and practical reordering and routinization. By comparison, I want to focus upon the already-on-the-inside, routinized, mundane, familiar technologies of everyday life. However, I will also be attending to the way in which such mundane technologies generate a partial disordering – how they are involved in processes of dis-integration and how this operates not only on the symbolic level, but on the practical and material level. To put it another way, I want to look at the way that the inside can go outside, at how the domesticated technology can de-domesticate itself, becoming other, exotic. Part of this involves the fact that everyday life is never purely social – it is always heterogeneously made up of technologies, humans and natures (cf. Crook, 1998, for a discussion of the limits of traditional models of everyday life). These 'cohabiting', co-extensive little societies, technologies and natures (which are themselves heterogeneous – see the next chapter) generate a range of possible trajectories for the uses and 'mis-uses' (or rather, misbehaviour) of technological artefacts – they enable, as it were, some of the unintended consequences of these artefacts.

One of the great merits of the 'domestication' literature is that it explicitly addresses power and gender (amongst other issues such as the status of the public sphere). As I shall argue in detail in the next chapter, at the heart of these power, gender and domestication dynamics is all manner of natures: bodies, environments, animals (cf. Lemonnier, 1993). Semiotically and materially, everyday life – as a process to which mundane technology is crucial – is impacted upon by these natures. My concern, then, is to expand on these accounts of the domestication of technologies by pursuing, albeit in a limited and contingent way, the role that nature plays in the use of mundane technologies to structure relations of power. To reiterate, such uses are highly complex – they entail both the ordering and disordering of everyday life, or, to put it another way, they entail shifting relations of power.

In the studies so scantily described above, the units of analysis – family, individuals, technologies, social processes, and so on – are familiar ones. This book is, in its most hopeful aspect, about thinking through some of the analytic possibilities offered by different units comprised of combinations of humans and non-humans, that is, hybrids, monsters, cyborgs or co(a)gents. Thus, we can explore how these are formed (e.g. in the heterogeneous processes of everyday life) and formulated (e.g. in lay and professional discourse). Indeed, the aim is to go a little further and assume that these hybrid units are simply 'there', contingently real entities that inhabit the social and material world – hybrid units such as the couch potato, for example. By looking at how these are, on the one hand, kept together, sutured, and, on the other, broken apart, sundered, we can begin to unravel otherwise hidden or obscure heterogeneous processes that characterize everyday life. In the process, everyday life becomes conceptually a very complex domain: it is made up of the shifting relations between humans, technologies and natures – relations that often settle into ordered flows, but, sometimes, spin out in little chaotic eddies.

A note on (a)methodology

To talk of heterogeneity in the ways I have been doing is to raise the issue of how we might encompass all the disparate entities, relations and processes that make up this heterogeneity. Given that these various entities, relations and processes have been the 'objects of study' for numerous different academic disciplines, the issue also concerns how we sort through these (see Roberts and Good, 1993). Baldly, we face questions such as: do we favour one discipline over others, slotting into the chosen discipline whatever insights others can furnish, perhaps even using the data derived in those other disciplines (sociobiology comes to mind here)? Or do we try to integrate different disciplines to form a sort of hybrid discipline (examples might include biophysics or biochemistry)? Or do we, more pragmatically, coordinate disciplines around a particular research topic to produce interdisciplinary research? Or do we eschew any disciplinary commitments and aspire to an abstract vocabulary that can accommodate different disciplinary concerns (something actor–network theory has attempted to do, see Chapter 2 here, and Michael, 1996)?

In relation to these choices, my strategy is at once a compromise and compromised – I cannot see how it could be otherwise. On one level, I take up a position that is contradisciplinary. This negative stance is not against disciplines *per se*. Rather, it is meant to evoke the fact that all disciplines are 'impure' – made up of different traditions, containing fragments imported from other disciplines. On another level, the position I take is one that might be called hypodisciplinarity or infradisciplinarity. These signal that 'beneath' and 'before' (although these terms are unhealthily essentialist insofar as they suggest that there are data that 'precede' the categories furnished by disciplines) the disciplinary construction of various entities, relations and processes, there is a movement and interweaving that cut across discipline-bound categories, that, as it were, muddy the domains of expertise. In what follows, in the case study chapters, I use anecdotes as a way of initially, at least, cutting across discipline-bound categories. These little vignettes are meant to illustrate the interweavings of heterogeneous entities (e.g. human groupings, technological artefacts, natural phenomena) and processes (the reproduction of, and change in, social relations, the workings of specific technologies, the operations of nature) before, as it were, they 'become heterogeneous' (after all, what makes them 'heterogeneous' is, to some degree, the way that disciplines, amongst other cultural devices, draw distinctions). In the end, I have to admit that the disciplines I draw most upon are the social sciences. I practise what might be said to be cryptodisciplinarity, even though, especially in the latter portions of the book, I attempt, in common with a number of authors, to develop an abstracted, generalist vocabulary that aims to embrace, more usefully, this heterogeneity.

So, within these disciplinary confines, how do I go about exploring mundane technologies, their roles in processes of ordering and disordering, and their cohesion with cultures and natures to produce hybrid entities? The materials I draw upon in the process of developing my arguments and illustrating my case studies are eclectic. Thus, I draw upon, for example, personal anecdotes, surveys, qualitative empirical studies, popular and professional texts, webpages and official government documents. This eclectic approach is a means, in part, of problematizing formal methodology. If we assume that any method is limited, and that its value lies in its place within an overall narrative structure (for example, the warrant for a particular method rests on a more or less tacit story about the nature of the research issue, a metaphysics of the social and the human, and so on), then the warrant for the present eclecticism is to be found in the narration of my project. As we have seen, my concern is to trace heterogeneous relations, and seek out admixtures of humans and non-humans that can be named in order to see what further associations lie behind their reproduction and transformation. Now, methodology can promise rigour, generalizability, validity, reliability and so on – however, there are always intimations of uncertainty, contingency ('more research is needed' is the archetypal phrase that expresses this conditionality). My amethodology is about bringing together materials that enable a story to be told that is ideally compelling, at the least suggestive, and, above all, always in need of more material through which we can 'nuance' and 'complexify' those stories. Needless to say, nuance and complexity, however accomplished, do not guarantee a good, persuasive story.

But what makes this mosaic of texts compelling? As we might expect, there are many criteria, some well known, others somewhat intangible. Here are a few. Is the work 'rigorous', by which I mean does it speak to a community of scholars with their common parameters of what is to count as 'good work'? Is the work useful, in the sense that it inspires the reader (reinforces their existing intellectual agenda, or enables them to develop an emerging one – cf. Mulkay, 1979, for a discussion of 'usefulness' in the context of scientific reputation)? Does it suggest avenues of research, stimulate exploration, evoke ways of working that are 'productive' (intellectually and institutionally)? Does the text 'evangelize' from a position of certainty, or is it 'modest', wearing its uncertainty and contingency on its sleeve? Has an author engaged in enough promotional labour – say, worked the conference circuit 'appropriately'? These activities and properties might seem extraneous to the notion of methodology but, as the sociology of scientific knowledge implies, they contribute to making effective or potent or persuasive the mosaic of texts (a mosaic that includes sections on methodology) that comprise any academic narrative.

The point of all this is that we are never in a position outside of 'methodology'. What is to count as good 'methodology' rests on, as argued above, a *cultural* 'methodology' of judgement. The present text is an example of what seems to be an emergent academic 'ethnomethod' (Garfinkel, 1967) through which we can conduct our exchanges. The preceding sections that lay out – attempt to render transparent – some of the narrative and methodological techniques deployed in this book do not 'sit above' these techniques; they are a part of them. The claim to transparency, to modesty even, is not a move that is 'meta'; rather, it is one that is rhetorically additional, contiguous (see Chapter 2 for further discussion). That is to say, each admission of 'constructedness' (whether that be in regard of the selection of materials or limited disciplinarity) makes another move in an academic language game of justification and warranting.

There is a related point to make here: every text is performative – it is a means of persuading, of enabling, of inducing and inducting. But it is also a material entity that circulates and connects with other material configurations. In addition to the intertextuality that makes up this book (and makes it more or less potent), there is also its intermateriality. Not only is this book the product of a vast heterogeneous network of connections, it is also ongoingly inter-material – its relations to damp, uncomfortable chairs and animals that chew all contribute to its meaning or, rather, its efficacy. Another aspect of the purpose of this book is, then, to begin to explore how these intertextualities and intermaterialities (and intersubjectivities) interweave. Despite the dangers that attach to this sort of reflexivity (see below), I do make a contingent attempt to practise it later in the book (Chapter 7). More importantly, these heterogeneous connections are explored in detail in the case study chapters (Chapters 3–6).

In a sense, the preceding discussion has been about incompletion: in essence, the methodological and narrative techniques I use simply miss so much. Here is more incompleteness. In this book I have sacrificed depth to breadth. Given the range of substantive topics covered, I cannot see how it could have been otherwise. Amongst the technologies I cover there are, for example, the car, walking boots, the television remote control, dog-leads. Now each entails large historical and sociological literatures not so much concerning the technologies themselves, but rather the sorts of context in which I place them: the body, the emotions, animals, the environment, local government, community, time, new social movements, to name a few. I cannot hope to do all these literatures justice. But, then, the purpose of this book is to begin to frame new questions in the hope that these will contribute something of value to a few of these literatures – at the very least, a reinforced sense of their connectivity to one another, and beyond. The further aim is thus to show how these literatures interlink: the mundane technologies I examine – their embroilments with humans and natures as co(a)gents – suggest new avenues through which we might think of ways that, for instance, in studying the remote control we are also examining the body, gender relations of power, the emotions, community, time and new social movements. To consider dog-leads, we are simultaneously exploring the interrelations between dogs and humans, cultural representations of animals, community, local and central government, the environment and the body.

Confessing about confession

In the foregoing, I have made liberal use of the pronouns 'I' and 'we'. But who is this 'I'? What is this 'we'? Of course, these entities are no less distributed, heterogeneous – in a word, hybrid – than any of the other entities I have mentioned. The implication is that it is important to reflect on how the process, and the author, of writing is itself hybridic, monstrous. In other words, I want to examine how it might be possible to incorporate into my accounts of various hybrids a storying of my own hybridity. However, this is not at all a straightforward task.

Let me begin by noting there will be much more use of the personal pronoun 'I', especially in the personal anecdotes that are used to open each of the case study chapters. For example, in discussing walking boots in Chapter 3, I begin with a description of three visits I made to the Samaria Gorge in Crete. I have chosen to use personal anecdotes for three reasons. Firstly, according to Fineman (1989; see also Boettger, 1998), the anecdote is at once literary (obviously a constructed story) and exceeds this literary status (obviously it is supposed to report or document real events). Thus, it is an openly ambiguous textual form: combining the real and the constructed, holding them in tension. As such, in relation to the broader networks that I wish to investigate, the anecdote allows one to start from an incident and trace out a range of associations without ever seeing this tracing as determinative or exhaustive. Secondly, Fineman argues, the anecdote as a part of a historical record not only reports events but also acts upon them. An anecdote reports an episode, but by virtue of being a particular interpretation of that episode can go on to influence subsequent events. For my purposes, the anecdote can thus serve as a way of constantly pointing to its own performative dimension, to its 'acting upon' the reader. Thirdly, the anecdote acts as a focal point in which a described event adds some flesh to what might otherwise have been the dry bones of an arbitrary example. As a fairly detailed episode, it allows us to glimpse mundane technologies in use, in a particular time and place, and to witness how the meanings and functions of these artefacts are ongoingly negotiated. Further, however, the anecdotes I use are also *personal* ones (as opposed to ones drawn from others or else anonymized). In this they are a means to writing myself into the narrative in order to problematize the authorial voice – again to demonstrate, if not exemplify, the constructedness of the anecdote itself, and the text surrounding it.

There is a danger regarding this warrant for the use of the personal anecdote. While various feminist authors have argued for the inclusion of the personal voice in academic work, as well as valuing the personal voice of experience as 'data' (data that is intersubjectively, collaboratively and responsibly generated – see, for example, Ribbens and Edwards, 1997), the personal voice in my anecdotes is 'ironized'. By 'ironized' I mean to suggest that the 'I' that features in them is not in any simple sense authentic, it is not in any simple sense a unitary entity that spans – is a common character in, and a common narrator of – the anecdotes themselves. The point is to enact how the 'I' that features within and across these anecdotes is marked by distributedness, heterogeneity, flows of materials and signs that escape it/me. There are two issues I wish to take up in relation to this use of the first person.

First, there is the issue of reflexivity. About ten years ago in the subdiscipline of sociology of scientific knowledge, there was a great concern with the way that social constructionist accounts failed to reflect on their own constructedness. Authors such as Mulkay (1985), Ashmore (1989) and Woolgar (1988a, 1988b) pointed out that many such constructionist accounts (which were supposed to bracket any judgement regarding the real) actually depended upon assumptions about the real (for some of the debates around this development see Furhman and Oehler, 1987; Doran, 1989; Collins and Yearley, 1992a, 1992b; Woolgar, 1992). In the case of the anecdote, as Fineman notes, a sense of its constructedness is transparent because of its manifest status as a literary form. A reflexivist response to this point is that this relies on a realist account of what anecdotes are *really* like, as opposed to the fact that this account and warrant of anecdotes is itself anecdotal (say, based on Fineman's stories). This reflexivist process of mapping the interplay of constructionist and realist accounts, however, tends to ascend into some episte-mological high ground. That is, it looks as if one can do this mapping, can show the realist assumptions at the heart of constructionist accounts (the anecdotal status of the anecdote) from on high, a position of everywhere and nowhere (cf. Haraway, 1991a). My use of the anecdote, however, is not simply literary, it is *heterogeneous*. Certainly, as mentioned above, the anecdote is a means of reflecting upon its own textual constructedness, but this constructedness also has another dimension to it. The 'I' that narrates and features in the anecdotes is always already situated and this situatedness is itself heterogeneous (that is, involves the material as well as the textual or semiotic). Moreover, this 'I' is also *emergent* – it is constructed in the textual, but also in the material, as the anecdotes, and the story told across the anecdotes, should make apparent.

Secondly, there is the issue of confession. I admit, that the thought that what is to follow might be read as a confession makes me squirm with embarrassment (of course, this is no less an instance of confession). But again, what makes the use of the anecdote both less and more than confession is that, as noted above, I do not attempt to reveal, or discover, the real 'me'. As Foucault (1981) has taught us, confession is about the constitution of the subject, rather than its uncovering. Here we see the 'I' and 'me' as heterogeneously constructed – the upshot of a range of material and semiotic associations or configurations. Moreover, these 'I's and 'me's are far too distributed, far too heterogeneous, to be contained within a few short pages. This is no boast – we are all this way: the accounts cannot but be partial. Further, this partiality is addressed by using these 'I's and 'me's as common themes that partially connect (Strathern, 1991) the different anecdotes. This allows me to address how certain common actors (and these do not need to be an 'I', they could be any entity) connect, or move from, one hybrid, monster, cyborg, co(a)gent to another. Thus, these 'I's serve as a mechanism for asking how different heterogeneous events and ensembles associate, and how out of these processes of association it is possible to detect a singularity, a unitary entity such as this 'I'. Instead of confession, we have connection. Rather than constitution, I aim for distribution.

Imposing narratives: chapter outline

If the foregoing sections have laid out the key themes addressed in this book, touched upon some of the relevant literatures, and performed a series of warrants for what is to come, this final section looks forward to the rest of the book.

It should be obvious by now that a key point of this book is to consider the heterogeneous and distributed role of mundane technologies in the ordering and disordering of everyday life. Chapter 2 is where I consider the work of a number of key authors without whom this present volume would be unimaginable (at least to me). Specifically, I consider two approaches to heterogeneity and distributedness, namely those of actor-network theory and of Donna Haraway. Along the way, I draw upon the work of Michel Serres, a key influence on the former. In comparing and contrasting these different perspectives I aim to clear a space for my own take on heterogeneity and distributedness, and the development of the concepts of co(a)gency and co(a)gent.

In the subsequent chapters, I flesh out these notions in relation to a number of mundane technologies. So the four chapters that follow entail case studies of, respectively, walking boots, the car, the television remote control (and the sofa or couch) and the dog-lead. A number of concerns tie these chapters together, or at least give them a trajectory. Firstly, over the course of these case studies, I explore the heterogeneity of different aspects of what is taken, common-sensically, to be 'natural'. Thus, Chapter 3 deals with walking boots and their mediation of relations to the 'natural' environment; Chapter 4 examines the heterogeneous role of the car in the 'emotion' of 'road rage'; Chapter 5 considers the body and its construction in relation to the TV, the remote control and the sofa; Chapter 6 explores how dog-leads complexly feature in the 'co-production' of domesticated dogs and human companions. Secondly, as we proceed, from case study to case study, the uses of the notion of co(a)gent are developed and expanded. From an initial intimation of the co(a)gent in the form of the seeker-of-the-natural-sublime, I consider how these hybrid figures are found in popular culture. In the case of road rage, certain combinations of driver and car seem to be identified as particularly liable to this condition. In the case of the remote control, the couch potato is considered as a fully blown co(a)gent that is discoursed in various conflicting ways. In the case of the 'Hudogledog', I manufacture a co(a)gent as a means to developing, tentatively, a vocabulary, a series of metaphors, that can aid in the study of such co(a)gents. In the process, I trace the sorts of analytic advantages offered by populating the world with these hybrid characters and their relations. Thirdly, common across the case studies is my own presence as a part of these (or related) hybrids. As mentioned, each of these four chapters begins with a vignette in which I feature – as a narrative device this allows me to examine, in the final chapter, what is the nature of this 'I' (I call it 'MM') when seen as a component that jumps or flows across these co(a)gents. In other words, it is a means of looking into how MM links these vignettes and the co(a)gents narrated within them. More importantly, as we encounter MM's various manifestations in different co(a)gents, we begin to examine how it is that MM's co(a)gents (country walker, road rager, couch potato) transform into one another, and how, in the process, MM is passed on, acting as a sort of common linking entity. It is in the final chapter that I extrapolate from MM to other entities and attempt to theorize how not only humans but also non-humans constitute such linkages. Putting this more in terms of process, I consider how these entities contribute to the heterogeneous processes of ordering and disordering out of which emerge familiar and novel co(a)gents. In a final reflexive twist, I consider (the value of considering) how, out of these co(a)gents, emerges the writer of this book.

Over the course of the case study chapters, I draw liberally from a range of academic literature. Featuring most prominently are (aspects of) environmental sociology, the sociology of the emotions, the sociology of the body, and the history and sociology of human–animal relations. In each instance, these literatures deeply inform my analyses of the use of mundane technologies. Conversely, these mundane technologies, as focal points in an analysis of the heterogeneous processes of ordering and disordering have also, I hope, enabled me to make the occasional novel contribution to these fields. As usual, the realization of such hopes lies in the hands of others.

2 Theorizing heterogeneity and distributedness

Introduction

In the previous chapter, we considered some of the ways in which (parts of) the social sciences have addressed the role of technology in society. In particular, we have taken note of the emphasis placed on the way that the social and the technological cannot be so easily disentangled or distinguished. As we saw, it is now commonly held that technologies are shot through with social relations, and vice versa. It was suggested, moreover, that in the midst of these entanglements is 'nature'. The implication of these insights, to be elaborated in this chapter, is that a particular technology emerges out of the relations between social, natural and technological actors. So too does a social entity, and likewise a given nature. This chapter draws on a number of theorists in order to outline an array of issues that arise when one wants to engage with this heterogeneity and distributedness (in the sense that what any particular entity is depends on what and how distributed entities and relations have come together). The sorts of questions that I address here include: how might the social be theorized as heterogeneous? How do technology and the natural contribute to the social, while being themselves heterogeneous? What are the sorts of relations into which these social, technological and natural entities enter? What are the sorts of flows that mediate these relations and bind these entities? Can we draw boundaries and borders around or through a nexus of relations in order to identify particular heterogeneous actors, and what might such an identification offer us analytically? To what extent are these heterogeneous entities stabilized or fluid? To what extent do they contribute to identifiable orderings, or to the subversion of those orderings, that is, to disordering?

Clearly, these questions are extremely abstract. In this chapter, the conceptual tools I will review will be, in large part, likewise abstract (although I will endeavour to illustrate some of the key points). The rest of the book is a much more sustained effort to substantiate and elaborate some of the insights and issues that emerge from this chapter. That noted, this chapter, particularly in comparing the work of Donna Haraway with that of actor-network theorists such as Bruno Latour, Michel Callon and John Law, will begin to explore the bearing that these approaches have on a number of traditional sociological concerns. So the perspectives I consider speak, directly or indirectly, to such matters as: the production of knowledge, the positioning of the analyst, the conceptualization of relations of power, the possibility of social (understood heterogeneously) transformation, the nature and status of agency and identity, and the relation between the local/micro and the global/macro. Unsurprisingly, these concerns are not easy to disentangle; they map onto each other in complex ways.

In what follows, then, I will first consider actor-network theorists' analysis of heterogeneity. As we shall see, while this approach has recently been exposed to a number of severe criticisms and major modifications (including some furnished by its leading 'exponents' – cf. Latour, 1999a, 1999b; Law, 1999), it does, nevertheless, provide an important starting point in beginning to unravel the complexities of heterogeneous dis/ordering. Importantly, the exposition of this perspective will be informed by the philosophy of Michel Serres, whose work comprises a key resource in the development of actor-network theory. This will all be compared to Donna Haraway's sustained multiculturalist, feminist analysis of distributedness and heterogeneity. One way of crystallizing the contrast is by focusing on the differing meanings and implications of key figures in Haraway's and actor-network theory's accounts, namely and respectively, the cyborg and the hybrid. As we shall see, while there are notable divergences between these figures (not least in their political implications, in their ontological status, and in their relation to their authors), they also share some common-alities. What will emerge from these critical explications are a number of motifs that will be more fully explored and illustrated in the subsequent case study chapters.

Actor-network theory and the hybrid

In the last 20 years or so, actor-network theory (ANT) has emerged as a major theoretical framework within science and technology studies. However, it has not been confined to that, admittedly huge, multi-discipline. It has begun to feature in a number of areas across the social sciences: social psychology (e.g. Michael, 1996); geography (Thrift, 1996); medical sociology (e.g. Arksey, 1998); manage-ment studies (e.g. Newton, 1996) and economics (Callon, 1998a, 1998b). However wide its application, actor-network theory is still wedded to a key concern of science and technology studies: the production and dissemination of scientific and, more generally, accredited knowledge.

One of the key lineages of ANT is the sociology of scientific knowledge (SSK). This subdiscipline is concerned with demonstrating, through detailed empirical case studies, how the production of scientific knowledge rests on social processes. For SSK, nature does not speak directly through scientists to reveal the 'facts'. Rather, what is to count as 'nature' (or data, or artefacts) is seen to be the upshot of such processes as argumentation and negotiation in which are deployed rhetoric, discourse, representation. We find these resources mobilized at the putative heart of scientific practice – in the laboratory; we find them operating when scientists confront one another in controversies that span labs, disciplines, countries, that are conducted through scholarly journals and in conferences and seminars. We find such resources used to differentiate science proper from marginal science or pseudo-science (e.g. Collins, 1985; Gilbert and Mulkay, 1984; Wallis, 1979; Barnes and Shapin, 1979).

However, numerous sociologists of science have also noted that it is not simply linguistic and representational resources that have a bearing on deciding what nature is. It has also been documented that, in the winning of arguments and the establishment of facts, other resources also have a bearing: funding, materials, equipment, human allies in the form of funders, consumers, legislators (e.g. Knorr Cetina, 1981; Latour and Woolgar, 1979; Lynch, 1985; Pickering, 1995). ANT has been at the forefront of the movement to render heterogeneous the range of resources that contribute to the making of facts.

Now, common to nearly all that goes under the name of SSK is the idea that one should be 'symmetrical' (Bloor, 1976). By this is meant that sociologists must treat what have come to be accepted as 'facts' and what have come to be accepted as 'mistakes' in the same way. Both 'facts' and 'mistakes' should be seen as the upshot of the agonistic processes briefly mentioned above, and thus should be analysed in identical terms – say in terms of social causes (however, for a problematization of this posture, see, for example, Scott *et al.*, 1990; Richards and Ashmore, 1996).

ANT follows and elaborates this general perspective. For ANT, science is explored in the context of society – or rather the differentiation between the two is left open. What is seen to be 'science' and what 'society' is an accomplishment that can only be derived empirically by studying the various heterogeneous actors who impact upon some technoscientific activity. What is studied, then, is techno-science, defined by Latour (1987a, p. 174) as 'all the elements tied to the scientific contents no matter how dirty, unexpected or foreign they may seem'. Thus ANT researchers, in following scientists and engineers, remain undecided about what is science and what is society. They report what scientists and engineers do and see – how in order to establish 'their facts' they do not simply go about deploying arguments, but engage in a process of heterogeneous engineering (Law, 1987) through which they attempt to order and align people, equipment, funds, representations, texts, entities such as microbes, scallops and electrons. This all takes place within a wider network in which other actors – politicians, scientists, bureaucrats – are also attempting to align entities and build networks. Clearly, then, ANT differs from SSK by not privileging sociological explanations. For ANT, what renders a technoscientific endeavour successful rests on many different and disparate entities – human, social, technological and natural (for case studies of this form of analysis, see for example, Latour, 1991, 1996a; Law, 1994; also Hetherington, 1999).

A now classic example of ANT analysis can be found in Michel Callon's (1986a) study of the efforts of Electricité de France (EDF) to promote the electric vehicle. In 1973, the EDF produced a plan documenting the need for an electric vehicle. In order to make this a viable proposition, the EDF had to define a number of key actors. Thus, it represented recent social history in terms of the urban post-industrial consumers and new social movements who attacked the conventional car on the basis of associated pollution and noise levels, and who questioned its pivotal position in a discredited consumer society. Electric propulsion would overcome all these concerns, the EDF argued. In the process, the EDF defined the roles of a range of actors: Renault (who would be responsible for building the chassis); the Government (which would institute favourable regulations and subsidies); electrons (which would behave themselves within the new fuel cells); the public (who longed for an eco-friendly car). Here, the EDF marshalled and aligned a range of heterogeneous entities, attributed to them characteristics and ascribed them roles. In the process, the EDF constituted itself as an 'obligatory point of passage', through which other actors – such as Renault and the French public – had to pass if they were to realize their goals (which, of course, had been newly 'translated' by the EDF). Initially, many of these entities did indeed fall into line – they were 'enrolled' – they constituted the network, acting as they were supposed to, in accordance with the EDF's plan. But then things started to go wrong. The fuel cells did not work properly, they were too expensive, and Renault set about redefining the French public. The point is, that in order for the scientists of the EDF to construct their network – to render the electric vehicle a realizable prospect – they had to draw together many heterogeneous entities. For the actor-network analyst, one can only decide what is relevant to the stabilization (and destabilization) of a new network by looking at what the innovators did: one should not prioritize the social. Indeed, what is to count as social or natural or technological is often a matter of contention – it can only be determined analytically in retrospect (see Michael, 1996, for a more detailed explication of this case study).

This attention to heterogeneity reflects a tenet of ANT, namely the principle of generalized symmetry (e.g. Callon, 1986a, 1986b; Latour, 1987a, 1991; Callon and Latour, 1992). In essence, this principle repudiates any *a priori* distinctions between the human and the non-human, agent and object, the social and the natural or the technological. Thus, what is to count as 'human' or 'natural' or 'technological' is a matter of struggle between various actors such as scientists, policy makers, the lay public and the like. It is a matter of empirical investigation as to what has emerged as 'natural', 'artificial' or 'cultural'. Humans and non-humans alike are interfused with all manner of non-humans and humans (that is, the network) (Latour, 1993a, 1994; for critiques of this principle, see Collins and Yearley, 1992a, 1992b).

So, for ANT, the intermixing of the human and non-human is intrinsic to human society; one of its central interests is, therefore, to develop accounts of how this intermixing proceeds. What ANT provides is a conceptualization of interaction that captures the range of exchanges between heterogeneous actors, say the typically human and non-human. In the process, ANT examines the multiplicity of levels upon which exchanges and interactions between, and mutual shapings of, such seemingly disparate actors are conducted. Akrich and Latour (1992) address this multifariousness by redefining semiotics. For these authors, semiotics becomes:

> The study of how meaning is built, [where] the word 'meaning' is taken in its original nontextual and nonlinguistic interpretation: how a privileged trajectory is built, out of an indefinite number of possibilities; in that sense, semiotics is the study of order building or path building and may be applied to settings, machines, bodies and programming languages as well as texts . . .
>
> (Akrich and Latour, 1992, p. 259)

Of central importance here is the idea of 'building a privileged trajectory out of an indefinite number of possibilities'. The point is that the non-humans are active in such structurings (or orderings) of humans (e.g. their comportment) through a variety of media that are both semiotic and material.

For Latour (Latour, 1991, 1992; Latour and Johnson, 1988; Latour and Strum, 1986; Strum and Latour, 1988), the distinctiveness of human societies lies in the fact that non-humans are necessarily present in all human encounters: 'We are never faced with objects or social relations, we are faced with chains which are associations of humans (H) and nonhumans (NH). No-one has ever seen a social relation by itself . . . nor a technical relation . . . Instead we are always faced with chains which look like this H-NH-H-NH-H-NH . . .' (Latour, 1991, p. 110). Moreover, humans and non-humans share a key feature: both are conceptualized as effects, likewise subject to heterogeneous orderings and structurings; both are networks (assemblages of humans and non-humans) in their own right. A particular human or a human collectivity, a specific technology or a technological system, is the upshot of ongoing configurations of heterogeneous associations.

Now, a key point in this context is that, given their networks, certain technological non-humans come to be highly resistant to resistance; their roles, functions, properties and impacts become 'natural' or invisible, endowed with an automacity that enables them to act in the processes of mundane social ordering. Part of this 'automaticity' rests on the way that non-humans have been used in the replacement of human actors who, insofar as they are potentially unreliable in performing their allotted tasks, would require disciplining, training, supervision, surveillance and so on. Such continuous monitoring is, Latour suggests, inconvenient and inefficient. A more convenient and efficient means of ensuring that certain things get done is to delegate to relatively 'reliable' non-humans (technological artefacts). Latour illustrates this point with an analysis of the operation of the door-closer (or groom – the mechanism that slowly closes the door without slamming). This serves as a replacement for such relatively inefficient and potentially subversive human functionaries as the concierge, the porter or the bellboy (*sic*). Such human functions are thus delegated to technological artefacts. But this is no simple process of 'materialization' or 'objectification' of a human functionary into a mechanical one. Nor do these technological artefacts merely take on the meanings associated with the human functionary. Rather, Latour tells us, this technical translation (the move from human to artefact), that is mediation, is neither purely social nor purely material: it 'resides in this blind spot, where society and matter exchange their properties . . . It is a detour, a folding, a translation' (Latour, 1993b, pp. 14–15; see also O'Brien, 1967). It is both material and semiotic.

However, we need to bear in mind that notions such as 'inconvenience' and 'inefficiency' (and their antonyms) are themselves historically contingent qualities. Under the appropriate economic and cultural network conditions, forms of human servitude are 'more efficient and convenient' than the development and application of technological artefacts capable of fulfilling the same function. In other words, the 'automaticity' and effectivity of these technological artefacts is a complex historical accomplishment. The deployment of door grooms thus rests on the state of the network that would include both local conditions, such as the status of a building into which a door is built (e.g. the Ritz), and more 'epochal' ones (what I will later call 'grammaticized' ones), such as the relative cost of labour.

This noted, and once in place, such technological artefacts contribute to mundane social ordering, that is, the shaping of human users' comportment. For example, according to the strength of its spring and its tendency to slam the door, a door groom would necessitate certain capacities and skills on the part of human users: strength, quick reflexes, ease of movement and so on. Latour (1992) phrases the issue thus:

> . . . neither my little nephews not my grandmother could get in unaided because our groom needed the force of an able-bodied person to accumulate enough energy to close the door later . . . these doors discriminate against very little and very old persons.
>
> (Latour, 1992, p. 234)

In other words, the action of the groom upon the human body serves to shape and discipline the human actor (although see Ashmore, 1993). This can work in various ways: avoiding the relevant doors, enrolling other humans or non-humans to open doors for one, and so on. This process of shaping Latour calls prescription (or proscription, or affordance or allowance): 'What a device allows or forbids from actors – humans and non-human – that it anticipates; it is the morality of a setting both negative (what it proscribes) and positive (what it permits)' (Akrich and Latour, 1992, p. 261). As such, these technological artefacts act as non-human moral agents – they embody a 'local cultural condition' (Latour and Johnson, 1988, p. 301) – which, partly because they are so 'ordinary', invisible even, to the human actors who interact with them, shape human comportment.

However, these structurings or orderings are never absolute: they are always contingent. Under certain conditions, they can be resisted or subverted. So, in counterpoint to successful prescription – that is, subscription – there is also de-inscription, wherein human actors withstand, repulse or undermine the prescriptions or proscriptions of ordering non-humans. However, there is an additional point to be made here. Such non-humans can be seen as the faithful intermediaries of their producers (heterogeneously defined, as usual). An intermediary, Callon (1991, p. 134) tells us, is 'anything passing between actors which defines the relationship between them' and this can include 'scientific articles, computer software, disciplined human bodies, technical artefacts, instruments, contracts and money' (Callon, 1991, p. 134). Such intermediaries compose, order and form the medium of the network they describe: 'they define and distribute roles to humans and nonhumans' (Callon, 1991, p. 137). However, such distribution of roles, such shapings, do not always work – intermediaries are not always faithful to who/whatever put them into circulation. When they break down (Latour, 1993b, uses the example of an overhead projector) we suddenly become aware of their mediating role: all the sorts of work, all the sorts of arrangements that enable them to be ordinary, invisible, become spectacularly apparent. They are mediators, mediating complex, heterogeneous assemblies that otherwise would not be seen, would be assumed, would be 'black boxed'.

Furthermore, however, to 'break down' is a complex, situated, relational process. Latour more recently has acknowledged that technologies themselves, however much their designers attempt to circumscribe their possibilities or potentialities, always seem, much like humans, to escape these circumscriptions: as Latour puts it, 'we are *exceeded* by what we create' (Latour, 1996b, p. 237, emphasis in original). But such excess is also the upshot of networks. Technologies are not simple intermediaries, but also messengers that subtly alter their messages, and this alteration is mediated through the ways in which they enter into, sometimes unexpected, relations with other human–non-human ensembles. In this respect, they 'go wrong'. We shall explore this later.

Consequently, this impact of technologies must always be considered in the context of the broader network. Let me underline this by considering Pfaffenberger's (1992b) answer to Langdon Winner's (1985) question, 'Do technological artefacts have politics?' This question can be rephrased in ANT terms as, 'Do artefacts embody morality?' One answer to both these questions is 'no'. The politics of a technology has to be mediated by the discourses that attach to it. As Pfaffenberger notes, technologies do not have instructions for their use inscribed in their design. Discourses are needed that guide users in their appropriate use. The ANT response to this point would, I assume, go something like this: those instructions are, in part at least, already there in the network. They are present in the pre-existing identities of the actors who, say, desire to get through a wall with as little effort as possible. This is an interest or a goal that is associated with the broader network of, say, people 'getting to work on time'. The use of the door–door groom technologies facilitates this. In having dealings with the door–door groom system, one is drawing upon a fund of knowledge and technique which enables the *design*, as well as the use, of that technology. Moreover, these 'discursive instructions' are not simply discursive: their embeddedness in the network also reflects the operation of other technologies too. The presciption 'get to work on time' that might serve as a (very minor) guiding principle for the *design and use* of doors and door grooms in itself is an imperative shaped by, for example, clock and transport technologies.

Nevertheless, Pfaffenberger has crystallized a crucial issue, one that can be linked to the discussion in the last chapter on domesticating technologies. Discourses that delimit the 'proper' use of an artefact are contestable. They derive, in part, from a cultural domain in which, as we saw, relations of power are central, indeed constitutive. In other words, and as I shall further elaborate below, discursive instructions (albeit heterogeneously distributed across a network) are also deeply cultural, mediating a terrain of struggle and collaboration. What this illustrates is that the cultural dimension of mundane technology has been somewhat underdeveloped in ANT.

To return to ANT's account of heterogeneity, the proponents of ANT have long argued that humans and technological non-humans are thoroughly interwoven. As Law (1994) notes, take away the technologies – telephone, fax machine, computer, but also desk, chair, light – from a manager and they can no longer function in that role. To be human is thus to be hybrid. So, according to Latour (1993a), hybrids are everywhere. Imbroglios of humans and non-humans are becoming increasingly part of our everyday life. Hybrids populate the pages of the press. Yet simultaneously, while we live more or less happily with these mixtures, we are constantly told that the old divisions remain in place: newspapers retain pure headings like science, politics, economy and so on, and the spokespersons of these disciplines reassure us that there is nothing different going on – the traditional, modernist categories are perfectly able to accommodate such hybrid happenings. Now, such heterogeneity is characteristic of the modern condition (indeed, all conditions). Despite our best modernist efforts at denying the 'exchange of properties' between humans and non-humans, this heterogeneous process of mingling continues apace. Thus, in the recent rise of what Latour (1998) calls 'political ecology', 'Lawyers, activists, ecologists, businessmen [*sic*], and political philosophers are now seriously talking, because of the ecological crisis, of granting nonhumans some sorts of rights and some sorts of standing in court' (Latour, 1994, pp. 795–796).

This is part of the insight Latour (1993a) furnishes in *We Have Never Been Modern*. For Latour, we moderns have kept separate society and nature. This very separation has meant that hybrids have proliferated, because we have not paid them the explicit attention they deserve. Latour is keen to impress upon us that the process of hybrid proliferation is not a sort of actuality disguised by false consciousness; yet he also suggests that the awareness of hybrids is something that is relatively recent – the multiplication of strange hybrids (frozen embryos, sensory-equipped robots, gene synthesizers, etc.) have made it increasingly difficult to maintain the nature–society divide. Whereas before we were not in a position directly to address such hybrids, to make judgements about whether they were good or bad, safe or dangerous, this is increasingly becoming an option.

In sum, Latour (1993a) tells us that, in contrast to premodern cultures, modernity has been fundamentally concerned to purify these hybrids (or monsters), to disaggregate them into their ostensibly component, neatly categorized parts. Thus, we moderns have routinely indulged in dualism; for example, we have represented nature as transcendent, while society is seen to be our free construction. Yet beneath all this activity of purification, the hybrids – the quasi-objects – have been multiplying at alarming rates. For example, Latour (1993b) posits the hybrid of the gun-person. For Latour, and contrary to the views that 'it is guns that kill' and 'it is people that kill', it is the 'citizen-gun' that kills. Rather than ascribing essences to the 'gun' and the 'citizen' – each being either good, or bad, or neutral, what Latour aims to do is show how the new hybrid entails new associations, new goals, new translations and so on. As one enters into an association with a gun, both citizen and gun become different. As Latour puts it:

> The dual mistake of the materialists and of the sociologists is to start with essences, either those of subjects or those of objects. . . . Either you give too much to the gun or too much to the gun-holder. Neither the subject, nor the object, nor their goals are fixed for ever. We have to shift our attention to this unknown X, this hybrid which can truly be said to act.
>
> (Latour, 1993b, p. 6)

So, here, what should be policed are not the gun or the person – not subject or object alone – but the combination, the hybrid. According to Latour, we moderns have been singularly inept at such policing, even as we are ever more deeply embroiled in – or rather, necessarily, the effect of – hybrid networks. I will, later, dispute this vision of modernity.

The preceding (admittedly scanty) overview of recent developments in ANT has been couched against the intellectual backdrop of SSK. However, there is also another lineage. A major influence on the evolution of ANT has been the work of Michel Serres. I will now briefly outline a number of his key insights as a means of later unpicking additional themes in ANT.

Michel Serres, Hermes and the quasi-object

Michel Serres has been a crucial figure in the development of ANT. Indeed, after immersing oneself in the literature on ANT, to read his work is to be rocked by the shock of recognition (but it is also, alas, to read his work *through* ANT). His huge oeuvre has covered many substantive topics – the nature of education and instruction (Serres, 1997), human–nature relations (Serres, 1995a), the commonality of motifs in literature and science (Serres, 1982a), the relation between order and chaos (Serres, 1995b). Central to his work, however, are a number of inter-linked themes that he has elaborated across a range of 'studies'. Needless to say, I cannot hope to do justice to this body of work – at most I will aim to extract several notable issues that Serres has articulated and which can serve as additional resources for thinking about heterogeneity and distributedness.

How does one think of the contact and communication between disparate entities and endeavours? How is it possible that the same motifs appear in science and myth? How does a message move from the realm of the natural into that of the social? These are crude renderings of the sorts of questions that Serres has addressed. As Latour (1987b) and Harari and Bell (1982) note, Serres' approach to this process does not entail a dominance of one text or tradition over another – there is no critique or commentary or metalanguage exercised by one over the other (say, science over myth). Rather, there is seen to be what Latour calls a 'crossover', wherein the insights to be derived from myths or fables are no less valuable than those that flow from physics. This project of connection Serres has likened to the search for the Northwest Passage – a journey fraught with difficulty and danger through a labyrinth full of 'dead ends and blocked paths' (Harari and Bell, 1982, p. xxxviii).

For Serres, it is the figure of Hermes, as the sometimes spurious messenger of the gods who gave his name to hermeneutics, which serves to convey the connectedness of thought across different, disparate domains. Furthermore, this figure also embodies the ways in which 'messages' move from the material to the cultural. In the process, these messages are themselves transformed – they shift from being energies, matters, objects, into thoughts, ideas, cultural artefacts and vice versa (see, for example, Serres, 1991). In Serres' view (Serres and Latour, 1995; Serres, 1995c), what is needed is a philosophy of prepositions – 'to', 'from', 'beneath', 'between'.

More recently, Serres (1995c) has began to 'update' the figure of Hermes – the singularity of Hermes (despite his swiftness) can no longer cope with the accelerating multiplicity of messages and movements that modern technology has enabled. Angels in their multitudes are a better metaphor for getting a grip on the circulations and connections of multifarious, heterogeneous entities: humans, knowledges, languages, objects, processes. As Serres puts it in response to the question, 'why should we be interested in angels nowadays?':

> Because our universe is organised around message-bearing systems, and because, as message-bearers, they are more numerous, complex and sophisticated than Hermes, who was only one person, and a cheat and a thief to boot.
>
> Each angel is a bearer of one or more relationships; today they exist in myriad forms, and every day we invent billions of new ones. However, we lack a philosophy for such relationships.
>
> (Serres, 1995c, p. 293)

This is a long way from the 'personalized' angels that guide individuals (Damon, 1997; also see Boyne, 1998). Here, we can see one root to ANT's concern with heterogeneity, distribution, relationality. This is underlined when we consider Serres' concept of the quasi-object.

Of course, whether in their original, singular or their accelerated, myriad form, these message-bearers are themselves mediated by humans, knowledges, objects, processes and so on. These very entities that are put into circulation are also the product and producers of such circulation. In other words, they are constituted in such circulations. When we look at objects, when we think of subjects – we miss out on this heterogeneity and circulation that lies behind them. These are, in Serres' terms, really quasi-objects and quasi-subjects. For Serres, quasi-objects are pivotal in the production of society. What makes the social possible, according to Serres, is the movement of quasi-objects: 'Our relationships, social bonds, would be airy as clouds were there only contracts between subjects. In fact, the object, specific to the Hominidae, stabilises our relationships, it slows down the time of our revolutions. For the unstable bands of baboons, social changes are flaring up every minute . . . The object, for us, makes our history slow' (Serres, 1995b, p. 87). But this movement of quasi-objects is not separate from human relations: 'The relations at the heart of the group constitute their object; the object moving in a multiplicity constructs these relations and constitutes the group. These two complementary activities are contemporaneous' (Serres, 1991, p. 102). Some quasi-objects are like jokers or blank dominoes – they are still underdetermined, they might pass between humans but do not necessarily 'specify' the relations between them. As Serres remarks: 'Our quasi-objects have increasing specificity. We eat the bread of our mores . . .' (Serres, 1982b, p. 232). In other words, the specificity and particularity of quasi-objects become greater and this mediates, and is mediated by, the increasing specificity and particularity of social relations. Indeed, we can begin to think of some quasi-objects as quasi-subjects, so integral are these quasi-objects to the production of the social, and thus of the human subject (see, for example, Serres, 1995c).

In all this, we see that the social and the object-like cannot be separated. But there are also interferences and exclusions in these processes of circulating, mediating quasi-objects. The path between – the relation – is not always clear, it can be disrupted. In exploring this, Serres (1982b) draws on the figure of the parasite. The parasite has several meanings, for example, a beast that takes from its host without giving anything in return, or a disrupter of a signal between communicator and receiver. In all these, for communication in this broad sense to be possible, there needs to be exclusion – a bracketing, a removal of those entities, processes, parasites that would otherwise disturb the connection, and disrupt the communicational flow by introducing noise. This, Serres refers to as the 'excluded third'. Consequently, we also need to be aware of how these circulations entail exclusion (indeed, for Serres, without such exclusion there could not even be the possibility of communication). In light of this, ANT can be regarded as an 'analytic of exclusion'; that is, when one actor translates another – enrols them into a particular association enabled by, and enabling, the easy and routine passage of intermediaries – the enroller must ensure that relevant interference is excluded: old identities must be refashioned, potentially disruptive new associations must be obviated.

Particularly striking are the multiple variations that Serres elaborates of the uninvited guest at the dinner table, who exchanges stories for food. Here, we see how stories (the communicational, the semiotic) are transformed into the material (food, shelter) and vice versa. Serres is addressing the transition from the material to the semiotic (to use terms that Serres does not). This strikes me as a key motif: it tells, for example, how certain material interventions open up the space for new meanings (say, something as simple as the loss of the TV remote control, see Chapter 5). As such, these disruptions and disturbances have the potential for generating more complex orders.

Here, we come to a key concern for Serres, namely the relation between order and chaos. In Serres' ontology, the world abounds with disorder, mixings, movements. Out of this melange occasionally appears order – those regular circuits of movements that signal something akin to a routine flow (Serres, 1995b). Yet, these are never totally secure. As Latour (1987b) notes, Serres' interest is in the interface between chaos and order – the processes of ordering and disordering occur simultaneously. This can be linked to Serres' complex views on time. There is not one time but many – mechanical, cyclical and homeostatic time where a system reproduces itself; thermodynamic time wherein all activity generates waste energy and increases entropy (here there can be no movement back in time); informational time where information organizes matter leading to negentropy, order, structure (see, for example, Serres, 1982a). What we can take from this is the way heterogeneous ordering is accompanied by disordering. The case studies that will follow all explore how this relation between ordering and disordering is played out in the context of particular mundane technologies. First, however, I must turn to the work of Donna Haraway.

Donna Haraway and the cyborg

Donna Haraway is another writer who has focused upon heterogeneity and distributedness. However, her perspective, while sharing certain features with ANT, also comprises a major critique of that approach. While she draws upon science studies, it is located in a complex of other disciplines, most prominently, feminism and cultural studies (although she is highly critical of such academic categories and sees analysis as an embodied, situated process – the writings of activists and science fiction authors feature no less prominently in her writings). So, in contrast to science studies and, especially, SSK which she berates for its political timidity, Haraway's work is through and through politically engaged. But it is also richly textured: not for her the empiricism or social realism of SSK (cf. Collins and Yearley, 1992a). In Haraway's world(s), there are no simple observables: our accounts of nature, society, the future, politics, and so on, entail a profound dose of myth and metaphor.

Central to Haraway's project is nature: nature is, as she phrases it, good to think with – its centrality to Western thought renders it a critical motif through which to interrogate the contemporary world. For Haraway, nature is necessarily a 'topos' in the rhetorical sense – a commonplace that structures our discourse and shapes our processes of argumentation (Billig *et al.*, 1988). But it is also a tropos – a trope: a 'figure, construction, artifact, movement, displacement. Nature cannot pre-exist its construction' (Haraway, 1992a, p. 296). As such, in Haraway's view, nature should be conceived as a 'social nature', an artefactual nature. To the extent that 'the world exists for us as "nature"', this designates a kind of relationship, an achievement of many actors, not all of them human, not all of them organic, not all of them technological . . . it is a co-construction among humans and non-humans' (Haraway, 1992a, p. 297). In this heterogeneity, nature does not become controllable in some simple sense: it is a trickster, a coyote – it retains the potential to surprise us, to play jokes upon us, to knock us sideways. So while nature is deeply constructed, it is also 'beyond'.

Of course, this same heterogeneity characterizes the human and the social – we are the products of associations that are always irreducibly material and semiotic. In addition to intertextuality, we can talk of intermateriality; in addition to subject (human)–object (things) relations, we can talk of object (human) – subject (things) relations. We are the playthings of composite discourses; we are structured by a world of partly shifting signifiers. But we are also materially composite – caught in a network of natures and technologies: we are cyborgs with all the promise and terror that such a condition holds (see Haraway, 1991a, 1991b; Prins, 1995). But we are also biologically composite – our guts are full of useful bacteria, our cells could not function without mitochondria which once were, possibly, symbionts, or parasites even (Haraway, 1995).

With the mention of cyborgs, we come to perhaps Haraway's most celebrated contribution. Inspired by Haraway's (1991a) figure of the cyborg, the editors of the *Cyborg Handbook* write:

> Cyborgs remind us that we are always embodied, but that the ways we are embodied aren't simple . . . cyborg technologies are everywhere, affecting millions of people every day. Some of us may feel like 'cogs' in a machine, but we are really bodies hooked into machines and bodies linked to other bodies by machines. . . . There is no one 'cyborg' and no one benefit or drawback or evil; every person will respond differently to different ways technology invades or caresses her body. Cyborgs are 'situated knowledges' . . . with embodiment . . .
>
> (Gray *et al.*, 1995, p. 7)

This complex passage contains many of Haraway's central themes. The cyborg is everywhere, but it is not simply a 'product'. For Haraway, it serves as a way of articulating a politics that is not shy of the imbroglios of humans and non-humans, that does not yearn for an empowerment of the oppressed grounded in some version of authenticity or purity; for example, the ecofeminist mobilization around the motif of the Goddess. Hence, Haraway's famous comment at the end of the 'Cyborg Manifesto': 'I would rather be a cyborg than a goddess' (Haraway, 1991a, p. 18; although see Lykke, 1996, who argues against the privileging of the cyborg over the goddess – the latter has her uses too).

Rather, the cyborg, which Haraway has identified as a politically situated female entity (although she is also circumspect about the nature and potential of this cyborg-woman in light of the differences one finds in women's circumstances globally – see Penley and Ross, 1991), is concerned with the production of new spaces within the New World Order (that emerges in the bonding of technoscience and transnational capital, cf. Haraway, 1997, p. 7). But this is not inevitable, for the cyborg is deeply implicated in this New World Order, perhaps sometimes even an accomplice. Thus, Haraway writes on the edge, at once practising a paranoia that the New World Order colonizes and constitutes everything, and elaborating a denial of this omnipotence, unravelling those loci when and where the confluences of the New World Order are transfigured, diffracted (for a reflection upon her sometime 'pessimism', see Harvey and Haraway, 1995).

Like the hybrid, the cyborg is embroiled in heterogeneous networks. But what comprises these networks for Haraway is very different to the abstractions of ANT. ANT's perspective is typically micro-sociological. It has thus tended to avoid use of such macro terms as institutions, the state, class, race, patriarchy and so on. This is not to say that it dismisses such 'large actors'; rather, it aims to explicate how these complexes attain coherence, consistency, uniformity across time and space. ANT's purpose is thus the unravelling of large actors in order to show how they are networks that need to be repaired and reproduced moment by moment by their constituent micro-actors (cf. Michael, 1996). In contrast, Haraway is not averse to drawing upon the traditional terms of macrosociology – ideology, multinationals, sexism, racism and so on – although she is always circumspect about these categories (Haraway, 1997). These structures are seen as conditions and products of networks. But getting a handle on these is no simple empirical matter, and they do not impact upon us in some direct unmediated manner.

Our knowledge of the world is 'situated' (Haraway, 1991a). In keeping with her complex conceptualization of the cyborg as a promising monster that can create spaces of transition, situated knowledge (and passionate detachment) is fundamentally about embodied practice. Thus, in contrast to the 'God Trick' of SSK and ANT in which the world is apprehended by a seer who is everywhere and nowhere, for Haraway all knowledge is situated and embodied. (As such, as Morse, 1994, also argues, 'cyborgs' do not entail the masculinist fantasy of corporeal transcendence, where human consciousness is downloaded into the machine.) This situation enables a diffraction of the light generated by the world, not its mere reflection in knowledge. That is to say, the peculiarities of situation facilitate – especially for those situations outside the dominant, hegemonic ones of white, male, Western, bourgeois groupings – a disassembling and reconfiguring of knowledge (here, Haraway very deliberately draws upon an optical metaphor – the fracturing and fractioning of the light from the world causes interference patterns which generate new figurations of knowledge).

Part of this process of diffraction is the acknowledgement that the 'light of the world' is always mediated by a whole array of cultural resources. Our grasp of the 'out there' (as we saw in relation to Haraway's theorization of nature) is always artefactual, social. It is always constituted through myth, metaphor, fiction, fantasy. But it is also constituted through technoscience – its stories, narratives, facts. And interweaving through this are other genres, other discursive fragments: biographies, anecdotes, jokes. In her book *Primate Visions*, Haraway (1989) unravels the way that the discipline of primatology reflects and mediates core themes in Western thought and practice: culture and nature, gender and family, race and colour, Western and non-Western, human and non-human. In doing this, she levels the textual playing field such that the personal (e.g. individuals' biographies or career trajectories) is on the same narrative plane as the structural (ideology, discourse, social position) and accounts of the natural (e.g. the primates and primate groups themselves) are as privileged as accounts of the socially constructed. Now, it might seem odd that the insistence upon the contingency of knowledge can sit narratively alongside realist accounts of things and processes in the world.

However, as we have seen, Haraway works on a knife edge: the New World Order is global constraint (paranoia), but also it is not so all-encompassing, it can also be a myth. It is at once real and it is constructed. As Haraway herself puts it: 'For the complex or boundary objects in which I am interested, the mythic, textual, political, organic and economic dimensions implode. That is, they collapse into each other in a knot of extraordinary density that constitutes the objects themselves. In my sense, story telling is . . . a fraught practice for narrating complexity in such a field of knots or black holes. In no way is story telling opposed to materiality' (Haraway, 1994, p. 63). Here, Haraway contributes to the feminist 'transcendence' of such dichotomies as the real versus the constructed (cf. Rose, 1993). This, of course, is not a transcendence, but a 'holding in tension' – a purposeful 'irresolution'.

This 'irresolution' also finds expression in Haraway's ethics. Prins (1995) has noted that Haraway's figure of the cyborg is a highly ambiguous character. This is because, Prins persuasively argues, the cyborg 'accommodates two different ethical stances. On the one hand, there is the anti-humanist Nietzschean ethic of resistance and self-affirmation as it is celebrated by the cyborgs. On the other hand, [there seems to be] a socialist–feminist ethic of solidarity, a Christian feeling for a suffering humanity' (Prins, 1995, p. 361). In other words, cyborgs are simultaneously a moment of heterogeneous, hybridic expansion and affirmation, and a means of regaining the utopian – that is, socialist-multiculturalist-environmentalist-feminist – human. If the former theme denies human essence and stresses 'becoming', the latter depends upon essence and emphasizes 'being'. These different ethical stances are only contradictory if one operates within a traditional model of coherence. If the Nietzschean cyborg is about the promise of connectivity, and the Christian cyborg is about the alleviation of pain, both of these are read through the collage of myth, politics, technoscience and fiction. They are both constructions and reals, relationally and heterogeneously enmeshed. As such, both ethics can come to prominence, cohabit in the same narrative and practice, or fall by the wayside depending on the configuration of the network.

The foregoing has been, at best, a skimming of the surface of Haraway's rich conceptual brew. What follows is a contrast between ANT and Haraway's work in order to highlight some of the key differences and similarities across a range of key issues. Needless to say, these issues are not separate – they are interwoven in all manner of ways, which will become apparent as the next section proceeds. What will result is the identification and accumulation of a number of points that will be used to construct my own theoretical position, and which will inform the case studies that comprise the bulk of this book.

Parallels and contrasts

Politics and knowledge

ANT takes a microsociological stance, emphasizing the local (re)production of the social in the heterogeneous practices that constitute situated interactions. Central in these processes are the non-humans – architectures, texts, technological artefacts – that, within a given frame (that is to say, network), have an enhanced durability. Thus, for Callon and Latour (1981, for example), it is not possible *a priori* to distinguish between macro-actors such as institutions and states, and micro-actors such as groups and individuals. Their difference in size is a matter of negotiation. The question that follows is: how does a micro-actor become a macro-actor? For Callon and Latour, an actor who makes other actors dependent upon itself, translates their wills into its own language, and renders these translations more durable, has grown in size. But this always functions at the local level through the circulation of intermediaries or quasi-objects (see Michael, 1996, for a more detailed discussion). In sum, ANT does not neglect the 'macro' but attempts to dissect it – to show how it was accomplished, 'black-boxed', rendered durable.

In contrast, as we have seen, in Haraway's perspective the macro is readily deployed, although, to reiterate, she sees the relevant categories as inevitably crude. Haraway has no problem referring to sexism, patriarchy, racism, capitalism, neo-colonialism and so on. These are complex structures that condition the situations of people, even as those situations hold out the promise of critique, of diffraction. The New World Order is real, but it is also shot through with the mythic and the fantastical. Against its cultural icons, figures, narratives and myths, can be counter-posed alternative ones. Here, then, we have a writing practice that is about the provision of alternative, potentially transformative motifs, stories, characters and configurations. One sees the macro, say in the form of the New World Order, and one unpicks it, diffracts it. The macro, complex and constructed though it is, is 'there' awaiting a critique.

This political strategy is seemingly very different from that of ANT. ANT is about disentangling the means by which durable networks came to be in place. The very act of disaggregation can hold out the hope of resistance, and open a vista onto how things might have been otherwise. The historical account of how a network came to be instituted, or happen to fail, serves as a lesson. But it is always a contingent lesson – the conditions that enabled or disabled a network are not universal ones. Hence, Latour's (1988a) preference for throwaway explanations. The macro is always emergent, it awaits unravelling. Having noted this, in Latour's more recent writing (e.g. Latour, 1993a), there is certainly recourse to macro categories, notably that of modernity.

These divergent takes on politics cannot be separated from a series of parallel issues that reflect differing assumptions. For example, in its analysis of socio-technical networks, ANT uses a rarefied, apparently neutral vocabulary. Terms such as actor (or actant), obligatory passage point (an actor through whom others must pass if they are to realize their goals), translation, immutable mobile (e.g. transferable, combinable stable texts – Latour, 1990) and so on serve to give the impression of objectivity. They are terms dispensed from on high – being everywhere and nowhere simultaneously (the 'God Trick' in Haraway's terms). The observer of the network in progress, or science in action, stands outside the network – following her engineers, certainly, but by and large a faithful, external reporter of events. (This is not to say that we are always satisfied with these empirical reports – Callon's early studies are singularly lacking in detail; see Singleton and Michael, 1993, for a consideration of the subtle and ambiguous discourses of respondents in the context of an actor network.) In contrast, while Haraway likewise has recourse to abstract (and indeed, poetic) terms, she develops her analysis from within a 'situation'. Her situation is what allows for the diffraction entailed in situated knowledge. There seems, then, to be a very disparate take on writing and the si(gh)ting of the author.

However, the politics of ANT are not naively 'objective'. As Latour (1988a) has noted in relation to the debate on reflexivity in SSK, it is possible to be reflexive about one's writing without necessarily displaying agency in one's own text, without, that is, entering into a sort of poststructuralist confession in which the author demonstrates and exemplifies the constructedness of his or her own texts (Woolgar, 1988a, 1988b; Ashmore, 1989; Mulkay, 1985). For Latour, reflexivity is a collective process and the more reflexive one is, the more one recognizes that one is engaged in relations of power, that one is inevitably involved in the enrolment of readers, and that one's purpose is to convince or persuade one's audience. Part of this process of persuasion is the enunciation of 'truths', of certainties.

What we have, it would appear, is a contrast between the ostensible 'modesty' of Haraway and the ostensibly (empiricist) 'certainty' of Latour. If the latter has been the predominant style, we might venture that 'modesty' does seem to be an increasingly powerful narrative posture (for an excellent example of the persuasive and enlightening use of modesty in the context of ANT, see Law, 1994). This modesty reflects the key messiness of the situation (or location) which Haraway (1997, p. 37) tells us 'is not self-evident or transparent'. Instead of the clean linear stories of traditional ANT, with their transient triumphs and cruel betrayals, we have complex narratives full of myth, self-reflection, biography, culture.

Now, this 'messiness' or multi-strandedness, as opposed to the linear narratives of ANT, is comprised of various components. We have just noted a few: the interjection of the author and their situation; the role of myth, fiction, stories in the dynamics of technoscience and the 'reality' of the New World Order. However, recently, Latour (1997) has addressed the status of his accounts – for him these are no longer simple transparent accounts of following the engineers as they mobilize heterogeneous entities and relations in the construction of a network. Rather, he now sees his work as the production of 'factishes' – combinations of fact and fetish.

Latour (1997, 1999b) develops this notion in the context of an account of the way that modern critique, insofar as it has been concerned with the debunking of a naive belief of one sort or another, has nevertheless always rested on a '*naïve belief in the other's naïve belief*' (Latour, 1997, p. 81, emphasis in the original). To escape this paradox, Latour suggests that we need new ways of relating the real (the fact on which critique is grounded) and the constructed (the fetish that is ripe for critique). The factish allows us to say 'something else: It is *because* it is constructed that it is so real, so autonomous, so independent of our own hands' (Latour, 1997, p. 69, emphasis in the original). Once our own accounts are rendered factishes, then the sorts of politics that flow from this are somewhat different from critique: 'we are faced with many different practical metaphysics, practical ontologies' (Latour, 1997, p. 78). If what we have are not fetishes to be critiqued, but factishes that are hybrids that have complex effects, then we must exercise caution and care both in relation to critiquing and creating factishes. Indeed, this changes the role of intellectuals: these should now become factishes themselves to '*keep the diversity* of ontological status against their transformation into facts and fetishes, beliefs and things' (Latour, 1997, p. 81, emphasis in the original).

What are we to make of these different politics? I want to retain Haraway's notion of 'situation' – I aspire to do something like diffraction, even if that entails exploring and constructing particular factishes. However, maybe because I am also too much of a modernist, I still want to have, at least, the option of critique, of negativity. Or, to put it another way, Latour's advocacy for the protection of the diversity of ontological statuses is a '*strategic*' oppositional politics comprising a universalizing ethic of caution and care. In contrast, when we come to examine and assess a *specific* factish or hybrid, we might also require a '*tactical*', critical sensitivity to the particular relations of power entailed in it (of course, these relations are not just between humans). In other words, in those urgent cases where *particular* hybrids or factishes generate problematic outcomes, where the immediacy of a situation necessitates swift judgement, then 'care and caution' might be the least useful of options.

Culture and technology

As we have seen, one of Haraway's key resources is cultural studies. In contrast, I have suggested that, in general, ANT has been less attentive to the ways in which the cultural shapes technology–human relations. There is thus the complexifying role of culture to bring into the ANT account.

Let me begin with an extended example of a classic ANT illustration of the process of betrayal of a network, namely Akrich's (1992) study of the provision of photoelectric lighting kits to French Polynesian communities. What Akrich found was that these groups could not adhere to the technical provisions built into the kit. Particularly galling were the mechanisms that cut off the current when the battery ran so low as potentially to reduce its lifetime, or which switched on the current lest overcharging the battery led to electricity leakage that might potentially damage the photoelectric cell. These measures effectively 'groomed' the user, offering 'a set of rewards and punishments that is intended to teach proper rules of conduct' (Akrich, 1992, pp. 218–219). The problem for the users was that there was no easy way to measure the charge in the battery. As such, the 'users felt that its [the kit's] sanctions were arbitrary . . . they denounced it and expressed their displeasure every time the system cut off the current while they were quietly sitting watching television. The electrician, who quickly became tired of doing repairs in the evening, tricked the system by installing a fused circuit in parallel with the control device. When the control device shut off the current, users could bypass it with the fuse . . .' (Akrich, 1992, p. 219).

Here, the over-ruly behaviour of the kit prompted a, perhaps unruly, reaction that was then transformed into a course of ruly action. Although Akrich's details are sketchy, it seems that there was some sort of orchestrated or collective action that yielded a subversive solution. One point is that this 'antiprogram' could be said to emerge in relation to the designers' desire to 'protect' the system (inappropriately realized as it was – 'too draconian' as Akrich puts it).

Now, Akrich's account seems to rely on humanist representations of the process of resistance. There is a recovery of the pure human from the sociotechnical system as an agent that resists. Of course, it is always possible to show the 'networkness' of such agents. However, I would also add that their resistance is not simply a reflection of some sort of 'anti-network' responding to the exigencies of a technology – in the case of the kit, its 'draconian' proscriptions. Rather, it is possible to suggest that this 'anti-network' is partly enabled by the kit–network. Let me rephrase this: the kit makes certain tacit promises – it is, at its most abstract, a technological conduit into the pleasures of Western modernity – pleasures that include uninterrupted television watching. The kit does not simply supply electricity, it supplies or rather it 'promises' the goods and pleasures of its point of origin (Western Europe). In other words, the technology not only disciplines in the 'negative' sense, but it also enables (is productive and positive in Foucault's terms) and, crucially, it 'promises'.

The very obvious point is that nothing simply 'works' – a machine always speaks to a range of 'function-expressions'. By 'function-expressions' I mean that technologies do not just perform practical functions as is often portrayed in SSK-influenced studies of technology. Latour's (1992) door groom is not simply a means of shutting doors, minimizing drafts and halting any chance of slamming. For users (perhaps, the better term is 'consumers' – cf. Lury, 1996) it enables the expression of who one is – it is fundamentally a manifestation of material culture. If one is muscle-bound, one can open the door, stiffened with a door groom, with a muscle-bound flourish or not. If one cannot open the door, one can discreetly recruit relatives or loudly complain to passers-by. Technologies, as articles of consumption and use (and also non-consumption and non-use), are 'opportunities' for the performance of taste and self-identity (Bourdieu, 1984) and, as we saw in the last chapter, for the mediation of local relations of power. To reiterate, the promises offered by technologies address not only the practical but the expressive, indeed indissolubly so. As we shall argue in the chapters that follow, some of these expressive dimensions are enabled (although never determined) by the design of the technology itself.

When we begin to consider the relationship between technologies and users, then, we must see these as inextricably cultural and instrumental. The cultural dimension adds an indefatigable complexity. Early ANT entailed a central heroic character, usually a technoscientist or a group of technoscientists of the ilk of Pasteur (Latour, 1988a) or the three biologists of St Brieuc Bay (Callon, 1986b). But a narrative structure hinged about such heterogeneous engineers, who go about enrolling various humans and non-humans to produce their networks, is nowadays thought to be too Machiavellian a model. Having noted this, it has certainly been argued that these stories are not simple representations of real events – they are 'semiotic'. Pasteur is a textual signifier and Latour's account concerns how this signifier operated in the emerging narrative of the rise and rightness of Pasteurism. However, as Lynch (1993) has noted, there is not inconsiderable slippage between the semiotic and the social: '[Latour's] historical narratives are difficult *not* to read as, for example, realistic accounts of how a person named Pasteur managed to build alliances and proselytize a particular research program' (Lynch, 1993, p. 109, fn. 88, italics in the original). So the ANT story-line of heroic or managerial scientists has been severely criticized (e.g. Amsterdamska, 1990; Law, 1991a). Here, the worry is that, to the extent that the analytic perspective is that of the hero (hence the following of the scientist-hero), marginal or peripheral actors are excluded. Importantly, in the present context these stories of technoscientific heroism can be said to neglect the cultural conditions that resource *both* enroller and enrollee, that bind manager and minions in a more or less common matrix, that simplify *and* complicate their interrelations.

Citadels and strings

This last point has been developed by Emily Martin (1998). As she frames it, ANT seems to operate with something like a metaphor of the citadel. Knowledge is produced within and seeps out into the world, amongst the '"untutored" public' (Martin, 1998, p. 30). In contrast, Martin regards 'both "science" and "society" as categories . . . produced inside the heterogeneous matrix of culture, the missing term in ANT' (Martin, 1998, p. 30). Against the Citadel, Martin posits the imagery of the rhizome and the string. Drawing on Deleuze, she sees the rhizome as a system whose various protrusions can join at any point with one another, can become 'concretized' as bulbs or tubers, can be cut up and fragmented only to regenerate. This image she uses as a way of capturing 'the kind of discontinuous, fractured and nonlinear relationships between science and the rest of culture' (Martin, 1998, p. 3; for related Deleuzian responses, see Lee and Brown, 1994; Wise, 1997; Michael, 1999). Thus, in contrast to the linear stories of ANT, which trace the enrolment of one actor by another through the movement of, for example, immutable mobiles, she notes that immutable mobiles can fail to effect enrolment, or maybe their effect will be partial or beyond the goals of their producers. The regard in which these are held, the ambivalence and contingency with which they are received, will reflect 'the imagery, language and metaphor operating in . . . culture' (Martin, 1998, p. 33). The flow, however, is two-way, these cultural resources also move back into the citadel of science (as Martin illustrates with respect to models of the immune system).

Regarding the figure of the string, Martin draws upon Haraway's (1994) notion of the cat's cradle. By comparison to the war game metaphor of triumph by, and betrayal of, the 'great men of science' that informed early ANT, the cat's cradle is more collaborative. In the building of complex patterns (for which read the admixing of stories, natures, myths, technoscience and so forth), there is a passing on from one person to another: 'one does not "win" at cat's cradle; the goal is more interesting and open ended than that. It is not always possible to repeat interesting patterns, and figuring out what happened to result in intriguing patterns is an embodied analytical skill . . . Cat's cradle is both local and global, distributed and knotted together' (Haraway, 1994, p. 70). But perhaps we should not be so harsh on ANT. Martin, for example, suggests that cat's cradle can sometimes be competitive – as when one waits to see who messes up in the passing of the string. Moreover, the antagonistic metaphor of ANT has had its uses: the centrality of the hero-scientists is, as Law (1991a) notes, a means of exploding the myth of their heroism, heterogeneously deconstructing them, and demonstrating how they arrived at a position of immense discretion. Further, Mol and Law (1994) have suggested an alternative metaphor to that of the 'network'. Examining the changing meanings of anaemia across a variety of settings, they note that this term 'anaemia' invokes very different practices and discourses. For them, it is not the case that its meaning is determined at one central site, say the laboratory, and that this meaning is transferred, through the usual ANT media (Mol and Law, 1994, e.g. immutable mobiles, delegates, intermediaries), into other sites. Rather, there is simultaneously a fixity and a fluidity to this 'entity' anaemia. As they say: '. . . if we are dealing with 'anaemia' over and over again, something that keeps on differing but also stays the same, then this is because it transforms itself from one arrangement into another without discontinuity' (Mol and Law, 1994, p. 664). In other words, the configuration (the pattern of relations and entities that make up something like anaemia) changes, but this is not necessarily an antagonistic process characterized by the enrolment, persuasion and, hence, (partial) trans-formation of the 'receivers' of the configuration. These 'receivers' may themselves take an active part in these reconfigurations.

Mol and Law's and Martin's emphasis upon, respectively, the fluid and the rhizome/string figure should not be seen as a simple privileging of these metaphors over the more 'rigid' ones of network and Citadel. Drawing upon Gilles Deleuze and Felix Guattari (1983, 1988), the sense of liquidity (where things are changing, becoming) should always be linked to that of solidity (where things 'freeze up' – cf. Michael and Still, 1992). Deleuze and Guattari's dichotomies – root/rhizome, territorialization/deterritorialization, molar/molecular, sedentary/nomadic – are not absolute (after all, that would be to practise rootish, that is, binary, thought): 'there are knots of arborescence (rootishness) in rhizomes, and rhizomic offshoots in roots . . . The important point is that the root-tree and the canal rhizome are not two opposed models . . .' (Deleuze and Guattari, 1988, p. 20). In the case study chapters, there will be several illustrations of this flipping between, and co-habitation of, fluid and network, citadel and rhizome.

Agency and boundaries

This brings us on to issues of agency, identity and boundaries. Those who do the enrolling, or who take on the cat's cradle and complexify or simplify its pattern, exercise a certain agency, a 'certain discretion' (as Law, 1991b, calls it). Yet they too are distributed, constituted in heterogeneous relations of power. The capacities (in the broadest sense) of a person who adopts or adapts the cat's cradle are shaped by a knotted complex of technologies, humans, myths, narratives, natures. Haraway's cyborg, as we have seen, can be Nietzschean, but it can also be humbled and muddled.

Now, this attribution of agency raises important issues. For Callon and Law hybrid *collectifs* (their version of hybrids) are 'relations. Links. Interpenetrations. Processes. Of any kind' (Callon and Law, 1995, p. 486). Whatever their 'overt size' hybrid *collectifs* can be decomposed into their multiple heterogeneous components – or, preferably, relations. The extent of this analytic decomposition, the range and number of such connections that are unravelled, is a 'matter of taste' according to Callon and Law. However, they also note that in 'normal discourse' (that is, modern Western), agency is not attributed to networks, interactions or fields, but to singularities. Moreover, Callon and Law conclude that perhaps we cannot 'know' all these hybrids and their agencies. This certainly makes sense given that many of the combinations and interrelations will be complex, momentary and accidental (as I shall argue below).

In contrast to Callon and Law's narrative, or aesthetic, truncation of such networks, we can note Strathern's (1996) empirical version of truncation in which networks are especially prone to cutting by virtue of particular relations of power, namely, property ownership. Such relations of power suggest that certain 'sites of agency' have the capacity to curtail connectedness. As we might imagine, these sites are themselves heterogeneous and distributed. The question that I shall address in the final part of this chapter is: what happens when we begin to think about such distributedness in terms of agency? Can we detect certain knots of heterogeneous relations – hybrid *collectifs* – which are addressed in popular culture? If so, how do these relate to Latour's (1993a) account of the modern constitution in which humans and non-humans are discursively kept separate, are purified? Furthermore, what might the act of seeking out such knots – that is, of drawing boundaries around a hybrid *collectif* proactively, and of ascribing a discrete identity and a degree of agency to rather 'odd' configurations of a limited selection of mundane humans, natures and technologies – yield analytically? Might such a process reveal otherwise unremarked relations and processes?

Exotic and mundane revisited

Haraway's work on the cyborg, on biotechnology and the new biology, and her frequent drawing upon science fiction suggest that the technologies that she is dealing with are somewhat 'exotic'. They are technologies that are epoch making – the global information network (the 'superhighway'), those bio-technologies that fundamentally and very publicly blur the boundaries between the 'natural' and the 'cultural'. In contrast, the work of Latour, in particular, has been concerned with the mundane: door grooms, seat belts, door keys, for example. Of course, what is exotic today, is mundane tomorrow. But, more importantly, the mundane is always in the exotic, and the exotic is not slow to become enmeshed in the mundane. Thus, for example, as Latour remarks in interview

(1997, see http://www.factory.org/nettime/archive/1065.html, 15/07/98), to argue that new information technology means that we are now living in cyberspace, is hype, an absurdity. Access to these technologies is always mediated by the mundane – cables, for example; and, as we shall see, even more mundane technologies. Yet, the exoticism of, say, biotechnology still generates public anxiety as the traditional categories of human and non-human become blurred. What are we to make of the pig with a human gene for a less immunotoxic, more transplantable heart (cf. Brown, 1998, 1999a; Birke *et al.*, 1998)? But these concerns over purity are not confined to exotic admixtures: they also extend to human embroilment with ostensibly mundane technologies. As I shall argue below, where there is too much intimacy with mundane technologies – cars and televisions, for example, then, normalizing discourse can be found. Contra Latour, we can find a sustained, culturally resonant scrutiny of some of these hybrids. These are the hybrids (or what Hess, 1995b, has called 'low-tech cyborgs') that most interest me. However, to reiterate, as we shall see, even for something as seemingly mundane as walking boots, the exotic is central, materially (e.g. literally in terms of materials) and culturally (e.g. in terms of their shifting cultural meanings).

Now, if we are all heterogeneous and distributed, and also, as Latour claims, if we have always been so, what has made us aware of this recently? What makes the writing of this book possible, let alone worthwhile? How are the issues sketched above entering into 'our' history (cf. Elam, 1999, for an incisive critique of Latour's rather limited view of 'our' history)? This is a naive question and it can be answered naively (as Latour has done when he, very circumspectly, suggests that we nowadays cannot escape representations of hybrids, especially in the media). But who is this 'we'? Cyborg, hybrid, heterogeneous, distributed? Latour has expressed concern that we moderns have failed properly to scrutinize the production of new admixtures of humans and technologies – new hybrids – and, as a result, we are in danger of being overwhelmed by their proliferation. As I have hinted above, 'we' moderns do sometimes police such hybrids. Furthermore, this 'we' is not comprised of 'pure humans'. Rather, such 'policing' can itself be mediated by hybrids. It can entail coincidences or collusions between technologies and cultures that serve in the disruption of certain hybrids. These collusions might be accidental, stochastic, but they might also be clues to the strange agencies that, Callon and Law (1995) suggest, 'we' never get a grip on. Following Serres, we can begin to trace the odd movements of quasi-objects, which are sometimes jokers or blank dominoes, sometimes parasites and which sometimes reinforce, and other times perturb, the hybrid *collectifs* that populate and 'structure' everyday life.

Prospecting

ANT, Serres and Haraway provide the intellectual backbone to this book; they shape fundamentally the analyses of the different mundane technologies that feature in the next four chapters. But these analyses also invoke concerns that have recently emerged in other arenas of the social sciences. Thus, I also draw upon treatments of emotion (e.g. rage, pain), the body, identity, nature (animals and environment), risk, need and globalization.

In its simplest form, my argument is the nowadays mundane one that mundane technology in everyday life constantly shapes humans, and humans shape it. It enables and constrains various modes of comportment. Latour has argued that, as moderns, we have been particulalry resistant to picturing this heterogeneous relationality, this hybridity. What I will argue is that in some cases we can be very adept at such scrutiny. There are numerous discourses and practices that have emerged to 'surveille' and 'police' this hybridity. In seeking these out, we can look to popular culture. The 'worry' that underpins this surveillance seems to be that the relations entered into with technology are pathological in some way or another. Often, although not always, it is assumed that the human is the problem. Contact with certain technologies renders them deficient in some way, for example prone to rage or to indolence. However, I shall argue that these 'pathological' conditions are crucially tied up with the history of the technologies themselves, as well as the cultural and social, indeed, heterogeneous, circumstances into which these technologies are 'received'. When the technologies are also viewed as material culture, when we unpick some of the cultural assumptions reflected in, and mediated by, the technologies, we find that they play a pivotal part in 'problematic' human comportment. Thus, as we shall see, the physical design of the TV remote control at once contributes to the production and dissolution of the 'couch potato'.

As such, technologies do not uncomplicatedly serve in the building of orders. They are not mere intermediaries; sometimes they verge on being jokers, involving only diffuse orderings; sometimes they are parasites, disrupting and transforming the messages that flow between designers and users, and amongst users. Now we can begin to think of technology in its ambiguity – not only does it contribute to order (is part of the missing masses as Latour has suggested), it also resources disorder. Technology is implicated in the patterning of order and disorder.

What the preceding sections have articulated is a sort of programme of heterogeneous deconstruction. We unravel the heterogeneous, distributed complex of relations to show unseen interdependencies. Yet, this 'deconstructionism' (even the present heterogeneous variety) has arguably become commonplace. It is no longer as much hard work as it used to be to show how a person like Pasteur (Latour, 1988b) or a technology like the Aramis transit system (Latour, 1996a) is constituted out of heterogeneous relations and entities. The conceptual toolkit for this sort of analytic work is now in place. Of course there are refinements and innovations, but, in large part, the nature of the task has been settled and we have the 'right tools for the job'.

However, there are problems with this process of deconstructive unravelling of heterogeneous relations. As Graham Button (1993) has pointedly asked: where does the list of entities and relations end? This list is potentially infinite. Button's point is that the choice of entities and relations is arbitrary, not empirically based, because actual practices and actions are rarely studied in typical ANT accounts. In his argument in favour of an ethnomethodological approach to technology, Button thus advocates that close empirical study would reveal the limits of participants' heterogeneous work.

Yet, as we have noted, Callon and Law (1995) clearly recognize this point when they comment that the extent of the analytic decomposition of a hybrid *collectif* – the range and number of such connections that are unravelled – is a 'matter of taste'. But what is this 'matter of taste'? In contrast to Callon and Law's narrative, or aesthetic, *truncation* of such networks, or Strathern's empirical form of *truncation* that is grounded in property ownership, or Button's ethnomethodological empiricism, I want to explore a tactical dimension by *inventing* hybrids (or, where possible, deriving them from popular culture). That is to say, I hope to invent new characters made up of a few humans and non-humans (including mundane technologies and aspects of 'nature') by which to narrate the processes of ordering and disordering. The aim is to begin to uncover previously unseen pathways of heterogeneous interaction, mediation and relationality. If Law (1994) presses the case for a sociology concerned with verbs as opposed to nouns (hence his preference for 'ordering' over 'order'), and if Serres proposes a philosophy of prepositions, I aim to deploy *new* nouns – new hybrids, cyborgs, that is, co(a)gents. This aim is to take an initial step toward the derivation of new verbs and new prepositions, and to begin to map otherwise unapprehended doings (verbs) and relations (prepositions).

In deploying this analytic strategy, we begin to get away from 'following the (human) actors' as recommended by Latour (1987a). Rather, I want to follow the hybrids: this means that we are not dependent on humans' accounts, and we do not, however provisionally, endow these humans with heroic agency. In any case, we are not seeking out 'intention' or agency in the singularized sense – the mythic heroic scientist that once served as a narrative linchpin in ANT case studies. When we follow the hybrid, we assume its agency to be distributed, pluralized, contingent. So the components of a hybrid all contribute to its agency, as do other entities that are more or less associated with the hybrid. Thus, hybrids entail *co-agents in a melee of co-agency*. Yet I also want to narrate the singularized hybrid, to deal with its *cogency*, that is, its convincing power and its unitariness. Henceforth, I will be using the admittedly ugly term '*co(a)gency*' to capture the simultaneity and ambiguity of, on the one hand, distributed, *ex*ploded agency and, on the other, concentrated, *im*ploded, agency.

What does narration in terms of co(a)gents actually entail? Whether we find such co(a)gents in popular culture (e.g. the couch potato) or make it up ourselves (e.g. the Hudogledog – human-dog-lead-dog), to engage in such naming is to practise what social representation theorists would call 'making the unfamiliar familiar' by providing a category and name by which cognitively to 'anchor' these everyday but strange concoctions (Moscovici, 1981, 1984; Flick, 1995). This attempt at objectification could also be read as a strategic logocentrism that aims to ensure 'presence' for the signifier of the co(a)gent (Derrida, 1976, 1978, 1982). Alternatively, it could be regarded as (a generalized and hopeful) 'dynamic nominalism'. Dynamic nominalism implies 'that numerous kinds of human beings and human acts come into being hand in hand with our invention of the categories labeling them' (Hacking, 1986, p. 236). In deriving specific co(a)gents from popular or academic culture (although of course these are mutually implicated), or inventing them, I effectively paraphrase Hacking's comment that 'Making up people changes the space of possibilities for personhood' (Hacking, 1986, p. 229): 'Making up co(a)gents changes the space of possibilities for co(a)gency (that is, expands the possible array of co(a)gents and relationalities)'. An instructive popular cultural example of the possible fecundity of this naming can be found in Adams and Lloyd's (1983) *Meaning of Liff* (see Michael, 1997).

Let me put all this another way (which echoes the discussion of disciplinarity in Chapter 1). The 'making up of co(a)gents' is necessarily contradictory – it entails both distributedness and singularity, co-agency and cogency. But this need not be a problem. Smith and Turner (1986), in a review essay covering Giddens' (1984) book *The Constitution of Society*, complain that his notions of structuration and the duality of structure are circular: agency mediates structure, structure shapes agency. They suggest that his work may be of value insofar as it 'is well known within a scholarly community and [is] influential in the sense of directing students to well rehearsed issues and well established problems' (Smith and Turner, 1986, p. 132). Despite this, it fails insofar as it does not generate new paradigms, as significant theory would.

This criticism, however, neglects the 'cultural' dimension of the assessment of such theorization. What is to count as significant or influential can only, as many a sociologist of science would argue, be determined in retrospect. Structuration and the duality of structure, when viewed as cultural goods, generate and inspire scholarly activity not merely through their 'intrinsic' merits, but also by virtue of the sorts of networks to which they become attached. Thus, their usefulness depends on a whole range of 'contextual' factors – social (who knows who, who is in the process of differentiating themselves from whom), cultural (what theories are in vogue), aesthetic (how 'engagingly' does *X* write) and so on. Significance rests, therefore, in part, on processes of persuasion, enrolment and passing on of string figures. Co(a)gents are such string figures – they will shift and change over the course of the case studies – their significance will vary: sometimes, as with the couch potato, they will serve to unravel the constructedness of the body; sometimes as with the seeker of the environmental sublime, they will serve to focus attention upon the limits of the body. The point is that the tensions and 'irresolutions' within such concepts are not the problem *per se*. The always conditional value of such concepts as structuration and co(a)gency lies in the degree to which they enable the generation of new theoretical and substantive questions, the inspiration of new scholarly activity, the formulation of new political options, and so on.

What, then, might co(a)gents offer analytically, substantively, politically? Firstly, they help us connect the global to the local, or rather transcend – blur – the difference. Even the most mundane artefacts in their localized everyday use incorporate the global. As we shall see, walking boots, for example, by being a part of the co(a)gent 'expressive environmentalist' (that is, enabling a romantic seeker of the environmentally sublime), mediate a whole series of complex connections that reach to sites such as laboratories, factories, new social movements, gender and ethnic divisions, to name but a few. What is global and what is local become very difficult to disentangle. Rather, we can begin to explore how these interweave.

Secondly, and relatedly, the heterogeneity of co(a)gents can only be addressed (although always incompletely) in a movement through different sub-disciplines. These sub-disciplines (environmental sociology, sociology of consumption, etc., etc.) are not presented simply to be prospected. They have much – substantive and theoretical – to offer, as we saw when touching upon the way that the sociology of consumption can inform and 'nuance' ANT accounts of human–non-human relations. To investigate co(a)gents is thus to open up, at least potentially, foci of communication across previously distinct research areas and sub-disciplinary perspectives.

Thirdly, we begin to see that as co(a)gents, we need to think of new ways of situating ourselves in relation to our own texts. I ask: is it necessary to attempt to write explicitly as a co(a)gent? How in our writing practices might we incorporate, or exemplify, our own co(a)gency? How, following Haraway (1991a), do we perform our knowledge as situated, where our situation incorporates manifold other humans and non-humans? What advantages and disadvantages attach to such reflections and practices?

Fourthly, we need to address the regularity of co(a)gents. When do they appear in their particular specificities? What transient or chronic conditions of a network allow their materialization and signification? For example, when does the couch potato make its appearance? In what ways is this routine? Here we begin to look at co(a)gents as markers of heterogeneous ordering. To what extent does their regular appearance and non-appearance constitute such an ordering? How do we map the disruptions to co(a)gents when 'things go wrong' and, for example, they break up into their 'constituent parts'? Could it be that other co(a)gents – configurations of technologies, natures, persons, cultures – intervene? How routine or chance-like are these interruptions? And does this disruption evoke disordering or yield further orderings?

Fifthly, and finally, we should also ask what connections criss-cross co(a)gents, or rather, we should address how it is that co(a)gents transform themselves one into another. As our attention moves from co(a)gent to co(a)gent, do we see common entities? As such, how are we to imagine the human (or non-human) that is a common theme across a number of linked co(a)gents? What are the sorts of connectivity that are entailed? Perhaps, drawing on Serres, these persons or things can be envisaged as little versions of Hermes, or angels, engaged in passing on heterogeneous messages. Perhaps we can begin to think in terms of a material or physical hermeneutics to supplement traditional hermeneutics such that, like Serres' parasite, these 'intermediaries' translate the semiotic into the material and vice versa. How do such shifting message-bearers serve in the production of order or regularity? How do they mediate disorder, or change?

These, then, are some of the key questions that will be addressed in the chapters that follow.

3   Walking boots

Distributing the environment

Introduction

I am a sucker for the sublime. I love to be enthralled, fearful, overwhelmed by the mixture of aesthetic pleasure and awe that is the experience of the sublime, when one places oneself before a magnificent natural feature that is, preferably, both precipitous and panoramic.

In the summer of 1997, I paid my third visit to the Samaria Gorge in Crete. At 18 km, it is the longest gorge in Europe. It is famed for the steepness of its sides. At the start of the descent along the xiloskalon (the wooden stairway which leads from the plateau of Omalos into the gorge), one descends 1,000 m in 2 km. At the Iron Gates, one walks across a narrow, rickety wooden platform over a stream running between sheer rockfaces, barely 10 feet apart and rising to almost 1,000 feet. The Samaria Gorge is a place where one's breath is constantly taken away.

My first visit in 1988 had been a failure. We had taken the four-hour coach trip from Plakias on the south coast into the Lefka Ori mountain range to the head of the gorge. On arrival we were met with the news that it was too windy, that because the gorge acted like a wind tunnel there was a great danger of rock falls, making it too risky to allow tourists to enter the Gorge proper. We had to satisfy ourselves with walking down the xiloskalon to a viewing point. Despite the disappointment, I could still have my breath taken away by the magnificent sight of the pitted white northern face of Mount Gingilos, and by the view of the mountains interdigitating into the misty distance.

Eight years later I visited the Gorge for a second time. This time, there was no storm. This time I walked the length of the Gorge: it was wonderful. The guide book had warned of the swarms of tourists that would detract from the experience, that would undermine any possibility of communing with nature, yet I still managed to find moments where I could 'lose myself' in the spectacle. Certainly some tourists were an annoyance – runners racing against one another, or speed walkers timing themselves as they scrambled down the xiloskalon. Then again, they were also a welcome distraction from the (sometime) arduousness of the descent.

The following year, I was at the Gorge again. It is one of the supposed features of sublime nature that the strength and depth of the sublime experience grows with repeated visits (Nye, 1994). Once more I was looking forward to the walk. But this time things went badly wrong. Arriving at the pick-up point at around 5.30 am, I caught a glimpse of a coach driving off down the highway. Assuming it was my coach, I was infuriated and exasperated. Fortunately, I waited on. Half an hour later, my coach arrived. The journey took a couple of hours, with more pick ups in Chania involving a slow drive through the early morning rush hour traffic. So, while I had set out in anticipation, the misplaced frustration of missing the coach, and the actual frustration of crawling through the traffic, had darkened my mood.

But this was nothing compared to later trials. The walk into the gorge started off reasonably well. The skies were cloudless; there was a pleasant coolness to the air. Mount Gingilos looked beautiful. Halfway down the xiloskalon, however, I was in agony – specifically, the big toe of my left foot was throbbing with pain. The new boots I had bought, the new boots I thought I had broken in, were clearly too small. On the descent, with each step, my big toe crashed into the reinforced suede. I had sandals in my rucksack, but the xiloskalon (and most of the track along the gorge) is very rubbly and I did not think it would be a good idea to use old sandals that had worn, slippery soles. Anyway, I half-reasoned, perhaps the boots were actually in the process of being broken in: only a little further and some accommodation with my feet would be reached. Nearly a year later (at the time of first writing, April 1998), I still have a reminder of that bruised toe in the form of a discoloured purple-blackish-yellow toenail, although the discoloration has nearly grown out.

The boots were donated to a charity shop.

There was, therefore, no chance of the sublime. As I made my painful progress along the track, nature could not be a distraction from the discomfort: that required too much concentration – a sort of contemplative effort I could not manage. Rather, it was the other visitors who took my mind off the pain. The extended Greek families straggling along, supplies and equipment in carrier bags, shod in ordinary street shoes. Their shouted conversations (it seemed they were always shouted) hardly ever made mention of the scenery, let alone the spectacle, the sublime.

While it is possible to focus on more exotic technologies (such as those that gather and process the data used in the computer modelling of global environmental change), my purpose in this chapter is, of course, to explore the role of mundane technologies, specifically, walking boots, in mediating the manifold associations we have with the environment. In following up some of these mediations, we will cover – I should say, meander over – a lot of ground: we touch upon the body and pain; the romantic tradition in environmentalism and its scientific counterpart; social movements and local social interaction. As such, this chapter takes the form of a sort of intellectual perambulation, in the sense of walking through *for the purposes of surveying*. In the present case, I can only hope to survey a small a portion of the range of distributions and relationalities, and touch upon but a few of the possible forms of heterogeneity, that comprise our complex immersion in, and access to, the natural environment. The figure that guides me in this perambulation is that of walking boots – their role in, and their emergence from, these processes of immersion and access.

These boots aren't just made for walking

What are we to make of the three episodes narrated above? Most obviously, I had come to the Samaria Gorge fully equipped with the romantic notion of communion with nature, particularly in its wilderness guise. This was, after all, a major reason for the excursion. However, this is by no means the only possibility. Other reasons on which I can speculate include a certain macho bravado to complete a 'tough trek', and a touristic concern to 'do' the Samaria Gorge.

The experience of the sublime has been much discussed. As Nye (1994, see also White, 1994) points out, for Burke the sublime in nature evokes a sense of astonishment – the mind being so overwhelmed by the natural object that part of the experience is horror. If for Burke, it was nature that precipitated this response, for Kant, the mind was given a much greater role (see also Guyer, 1997). For romantics such as Wordsworth and Coleridge, the sublime connects to a transcendentalization of both mind and nature: 'they are attributed a spiritual dimension that is greater than the merely individual and the material' (Day, 1996, p. 45; Bate, 1991). Now, the sublime, as so formulated, serves in the mediation of gender differentiation. For example, Kant's and Burke's men could appreciate the majesty, infinity and 'formlessness' of sublime nature, whereas women were best suited to an appreciation of the formliness and delicacy of the beautiful. For Coleridge, sublime nature, though gendered feminine, is a conduit to higher thoughts of ultimate mind and imagination, and these higher thoughts are those of men. Day puts it thus: 'The sublime moment is peculiarly male. Nature and the feminine can help facilitate this moment of sublime apprehension, but that is as far as it goes. Priority and ultimacy reside with the masculine while the feminine is accorded a secondary, supportive role' (Day, 1996, p. 190).

The point of this discussion is not to provide an overview of the notion of the sublime, but rather, to note the ways in which such conceptions of the relation between human and nature are still with us. MacNaghten and Urry (1998) note that what they call 'discourses of the sublime' (along with the 'cult of the picturesque') have contributed to the spectacularization of landscape. So, along with other tourists, perhaps I am a sucker for the spectacular rather than the sublime (although, as Urry, 1990, 1995, suggests, there are a variety of apprehensions of nature). That noted, the gender division can still be said to reassert itself: my manly pursuit, in the sublime, of some deeper meaning in nature was disrupted by those 'masses' who were not constituted to lift themselves into this higher plane of authenticity, who showed no interest in grasping the deep lessons of sublime nature. In one sense, then, these 'masses' can be viewed as 'feminized' insofar as they seemed to move within the landscape of Samaria Gorge in a way that does not strive for the egocentric, idealized sublime (cf. Day, 1996).

Over and above this, in having (or at least believing myself to have) environmentalist leanings, the pursuit of the sublime/spectacular also resonates with a romantic apprehension of nature that is expressivist. As Szerszynski explains, such environmental expressivism 'refer(s) to the notion that individuals can reconnect themselves with nature through the recovery of an authentic state of being, one that has been lost due to the artificiality of social existence' (Szerszynski, 1996, p. 120). For the expressivist, then, there is an effort to recover the 'unmediated experience' of nature: environmentalist expressivism 'is not so much a narrative of us saving nature, but of nature saving us, for only if we abandon modernist notions of control and domination . . . can we know what to do (as environmentalists)' (Szerszynski, 1996, p. 121).

However, this supposedly unmediated contact was enabled by, and contingent upon, a number of very mundane arrangements. Firstly, nature had to play its part – it could not be too violent, too recalcitrant. It had to be a wilderness, but an amenable wilderness; it had to refrain from displaying its terrors to the full. Its radical otherness (e.g. Harrison, 1996) had to be kept in check, modulated. Secondly, the sociotechnical ensembles of humans and vehicles had to behave: if my car had broken down on the way to the pick-up point or if the coach had got stuck in Chania's traffic, or if my boots had been too tight, there would be no possibility for indulgence of my 'finer' aesthetic sensibilities. Thirdly, humans had to comport themselves in appropriate ways – they would have to give me the right sort of space to 'work' at experiencing the sublime. That other humans should comport themselves in 'appropriate ways' suggests a correct way of walking. As Wallace (1993) documents, the versions of walking-in-nature available to us are varied – from Wordsworth's companionable and familiar peripatetic, to Hazlitt's solitary, contemplative walking to Thoreau's 'westerized' sauntering into an (albeit delimited) unchartered wilderness. Each of these would yield some form of 'higher' contact with nature.

In sum, then, mundane technology mediates, this time, a particular, valued relation to the 'natural environment'. However, there are number of things going on here. What we are seeing is a process of translation where the material begins to switch into the semiotic and vice versa.

The semiotic relation to 'wilderness nature' into which I wanted to place myself was disrupted by my boots causing me pain. The material relation to the Gorge into which I wanted to place myself was subverted by the judgement of the wardens that it was too windy to allow visitors into the Gorge. The physical relation into which I had entered with my boots could be undermined by the chatter of other tourists. And so on and so forth. In Michel Serres' (1982b) terms, these interventions are parasites (recall that in French 'parasite' also refers to a non-signal – to noise – that interrupts the flow of information): they disrupt, abbreviate, curtail the signals, or materials, that pass between two entities. Sometimes these are welcome, sometimes they are not. The chattering tourists were physical distractions – they 'parasitised' on the process of communion with nature. They did so physically, their shouting and shrieking, their massing and straggling along the path, all these served to render almost impossible the experience of the sublime, that is, the smooth semiotic flow of grandeur from the wilderness. Furthermore, their chatter was a semiotic distraction too: my Greek (North London Greek

Cypriot dialect) is just about good enough to allow me to learn from their talk about the contents of their carrier bags and the states of their bladders. More generally, their dress and comportment signified precisely what someone 'authentically attached' to the environment should not be. They paid such little attention to their surroundings, they shouted and ran and stopped where they shouldn't, they wore clothes and shoes that did not belong in this beautiful place. Now this all reflects my own bigotry: or to put it in another, less egocentric, or rather, less confessional, way, the very commitment to a version of the sublime rendered these people disrupters of the sublime relation. Associated with such a commitment are also visions of appropriate comportment and style: what they lacked was the right sort of discipline, the right sort of self-identity, exposure to the right sort of governmentality (cf. MacNaghten and Urry, 1998; Rose, 1996).

Yet, this very 'indiscipline' was also a welcome parasite: it was a distraction from pain (of the boots), or arduousness (of the descent along the xiloskalon). However, it could only be a welcome distraction by virtue of not matching up to my expectations of the 'good visitor' to the Gorge. There are, of course, other ways of conceptualizing this lack of pretence, this noisy unselfconsciousness. Maybe what I was witnessing was another way of relating to nature, where perhaps there was not the same division between self and environment. Instead of my groping for the profound in the 'natural other', for these visitors the 'other' was much closer to hand, a familiar, a member of the family.

Let me re-frame all this more generally. The way each of us *stakes out* nature (how we conduct ourselves within it, how we demarcate it, shaping, and being shaped by, its spaces) also reflects different *stakes in* nature (the way we understand, use and invest in nature). Of course, in the end, there is no distinction between these two modes of human–nature relation, for we can only stake out (demarcate) by using the resources (including those refashioned as mundane technologies) provided by nature, and we can only have a stake in (value) nature by virtue of the sort of demarcatory resources (categories, etc.) that reflect the process of staking out. In other words, and rather unsurprisingly, I would not wish to make a simple distinction between facts (staking out) and values (staking in).

Stake out/stake in

In the foregoing, my main focus has been on the sublime relation to the environment as it is mediated by local, micro-configurations of humans (e.g. park wardens, other visitors) and technologies (e.g. coaches, boots). However, in these associations are embedded global and macro-cultural and sociotechnical relations. The ways in which we stake out/stake in nature are multiplicitous, and resourced by relations that straddle the globe.

I have already hinted at the sorts of Western cultural resources that enable me to pursue the natural sublime, most obviously the rise of romanticism and its resurgence in certain expressivist strands of environmentalism (e.g. Szerszynski, 1996). Often, however, this cultural (and political) contextualization is 'set apart', as it were, from the environment: the environment is seen as a social construction.

That is to say, nature is seen as the upshot of certain discursive formations (to use that term non-technically). Thus, we find treatments of the cultural resources, the discursive categories, that underpin valuations of nature across many different sites: in lay local settings (e.g. Harrison and Burgess, 1994; Burningham, 1995; Burningham and O'Brien, 1994; MacNaghten *et al.*, 1995), in the policy arena (e.g. Yearley, 1996; Dryzek, 1997), in various media (Myerson and Rydin, 1996; Williams, 1973); within nature conservation bodies (e.g. Lowe and Goyder, 1983; Grove-White and Michael, 1993); in the context of environmental politics or eco-politics (Soper, 1995; Pepper, 1996; Dobson, 1990; Yearley, 1991); in relation to environmental science (e.g. Hannigan, 1995; Yearley, 1996). Needless to say, these perspectives do not deny the reality of nature; nature *per se* is bracketed (in much the same way as it is in SSK) in order that the analyst might unravel the cultural dynamics that make up 'the natural'.

Now, as should be clear by now, I don't have many problems with the idea that nature is socially and culturally constituted. But I would wish to see this process as heterogeneous. Rather than adhering to a project concerned with the 'social construction' of nature, I would drop the 'social' – 'construction' connotes so much more: a process in which the non-human is instrumental. As such, social construction is not an amaterial process (cf. Kendall and Michael, 1997; Michael and Kendall, 1997): it entails, at minimum, the circulation of paper and bodies and manifold other materials. For example, the sublime might be culturally constituted, but the dissemination of the ideas of the sublime relied upon the paper on which are printed the tales of the sublime, and the silver that was used in the making of photographs of sublime nature (cf. Ong, 1982; MacNaghten and Urry, 1998). What counts as a cultural resource is that which can circulate materially, that which can be disseminated and distributed.

Clearly, that process of circulation rests on a number of non-human factors. Nature must play its part – it must allow humans to congregate, it must not disrupt the messages that pass electronically, so that the activities of social constructing can proceed unhindered; that is, it must not be too violent or too recalcitrant. Cronon (1996), in his haunting account of the Californian fires that threatened the extended colloquium that was to result in the volume *Uncommon Ground*, makes just this point, but also elaborates on it. Those fires were certainly an inconvenient manifestation of nature. But further, nature's doings were linked to the doings of humans, not least the building of a university in the Californian environment (at Irvine) that was informed by a series of cultural resources concerned with, say, a re-creation of an Edenic or Arcadian past.

So nature has to be amenable. But so too must technology – the mundane technologies, for example, which serve computer programmers and academics alike – chairs, boots, light bulbs and so on and so forth, must all behave. Let me put this another way. One can think about this process of circulation in terms of the corporeality of humans, their embodiment. As we saw in the preceding chapter, our knowledge is situated, and part of that situation entails our bodies and the natural. 'Cultural resources' necessarily 'pass' through our bodies and our situations. These bodies are distributed: most importantly in the present context, they 'work' (function-express) through mundane technology. The rest of the chapter is an exploration of this role of mundane technology – its complex mediation between the cultural, the corporeal and the environmental.

By way of a taste of things to come, let me begin with a little self-criticism. In the dim and distant past (Michael, 1996; Michael and Grove-White, 1993), I suggested that our relations with nature (or natural non-humans) could be viewed as a complex dialogue. In contrast to those theorists who would wish to 'recover' the status of nature as a subject with whom we could 'converse' (Buber, 1970; Tallmadge, 1981; however, see also Kultgen, 1982; Reed, 1989, and Merchant, 1980; Berman, 1981), I argued that the sorts of dialogues possible are fourfold. In addition to the orthodox human subject (I) objectifying the natural it, and the human subject–natural subject 'conversation' (I–Thou), we can treat the human as an 'object' as well – as a 'me'. Thus, we also have interrelations between a human object (me) and a natural object (it) and a human object (me) and a non-human subject (Thou). These different interrelations, I suggested, should be viewed as being in circulation, being transformed one into another, in much the same way as Cussins (1996) describes with her notion of ontological choreography, wherein the objectification of humans (or nature, for that matter) does not necessarily disempower. In all this, I failed properly to realize that, as with human–human relations, these human–nature relations are never unmediated. Latour has taught us (see above) that humans do not live in pure communities like those of baboons: human interrelations always take the form of chains of humans and non-humans – one never witnesses a pure social or pure technological relationship: intervening in the former are non-humans, intervening in the latter are humans. Generalizing this point, we can say that in these relations between humans and natural non-humans (the environment) there is always technology. These relations as processes of staking out/staking in are always mediated by technological artefacts, complex and mundane.

Walking, talking boots

The conditions of possibility for environmental expressivism lie in the revisioning of the wilderness: there has been, in the West, a partial transformation of wilderness-as-wasteland-and-threat to wilderness-as-magnificence-and-purity, from mountains as the embodiment of the ugliness of human corruption and sinfulness, to mountains as exemplars of natural beauty. This reflects a whole series of factors, not least the ways in which increasing industrialization was equated with the degeneration of the finer sensibilities of humans, of the need to find spiritual sustenance in an unspoilt natural haven (see, for example, Thomas, 1984; Short, 1991; Bowler, 1992).

Yet, it is this very industrialization that enabled increased access to the sublime landscape, for example through the development and entrenchment of various transport technologies which could, as Wallace (1993) notes, cut down the tedious journey from home to the desired countryside. Further, it was also this industrialization that changed the meaning of the 'sublime', by, for example, generating projects such as the railway and mega-constructions such as dams and skyscrapers that would become the objects of the technological sublime (interestingly, in contrast to the individualism of the romantic natural sublime, the technological was often experienced communally – cf. Nye, 1994). Moreover, the changing experience of time and space, mediated by, for example, the technologies of photography, of speeded-up travel and of instantaneous information, have also shaped our sensibilities as regards what might count as sublime (MacNaghten and Urry, 1998; Gifford, 1990).

On a more mundane level, there are those technologies that afford, let us say circumspectly, a more physically intimate access to the sublime landscape, technologies such as boots, for example. Now, the manufacture of boots (and other technologies of access – outdoor wear, transport technologies, etc.) is a complex matter that has, at its heart, the objectification of nature. To make the boots that transport us to places where our breath may be taken away, it is necessary that nature is objectified, quantified and standardized in the extraction, shaping and combination of materials. Again, here we enter into both material and semiotic relations that mutually implicate one another in complex ways.

So let us grant that the production of boots enables a certain access to, and affordances in, nature (see below) that allow reinforcement of the sublime relation. Boots (and the other technological tools of access) are the unlauded mediators of our movements into the 'wilderness' where we indulge our senses and uplift our sensibilities. Having noted this, and as many authors have stressed (e.g. Williams, 1973), in countries such as Britain 'wilderness' can hardly be said to exist in a pristine form. In other words, there has been continuous discursive labour to establish that certain environmental features are 'pure nature'. Moreover, those putative valued qualities of nature – such as richness or rarity of species – are not exclusive to 'wilderness'; these can be found at sites which would otherwise seem degraded or corrupted (see, for example, Weldon, 1998, for an account of the protected Great Crested Newt's fondness for polluted ponds; also see Cronon, 1996). The point is that, although boots can be said to 'transport' us, they do not determine where we go or what we find when we get there: a whole range of cultural factors have to come into play too.

The preceding point borders on the banal. However, we can still say that boots have some *partial* role to play in our relations with nature. This is because boots are many things: they enable a huge variety of relations. This multiple enablement serves in the complexifications of our relations with the natural. In what follows, I will explore in a little detail some of their many function-expressions (in addition to the sublime) and their semiotic and material convolutions.

On the feet of humans, as components in boot–human co(a)gents, walking boots have a culturally and technologically mediated 'tendency' to congregate. With almost every community of souls, there is a collective of soles. In the recreation (in both senses) of the sublime and of the beautiful, there is a process of damage (abrasion of plantlife, erosion of footpaths and surrounding soil, importation of foreign species, etc.) that endangers the possibility of that recreation (cf. Urry, 1990, 1995). This is not an uncommon concern. For example, on the

Yorskshire Dales webpage http://www.yorkshirenet.co.uk/visinfo/fales/ ribblesd.html – 9 June 1998), there is a description of the amenities available in the Settle, Ribblesdale and Three Peaks area of the Yorkshire Dales in Britain. Here we read: 'The combination of high rainfall, poor drainage and thousands of boots tramping across fragile vegetation have brought massive footpath erosion and damage to the natural ecology. As a result, the National Park has established several innovatory schemes to repair paths and safeguard the environment whilst preserving the natural wilderness feel'. This is one possible route to coping with the dangers posed by the massed boots of mass tourism. Incongruously, such solutions involve the use of boots in the process of repairing footpaths and, more generally, safeguarding the environment. Indeed, one can note that on the Countryside Commission's (the governmental organization charged with protecting England's landscape) webpage, its 'Our Work' logo comprises, in juxtaposition to these words, pictures of a butterfly and a pair of walking boots (http://www.countryside.gov.uk – 9 June 1998).

The ironies of this imagery (the boot as simultaneous medium of protection and destruction) can to some extent be waylaid by other claims about the boot itself. As an object it can be designed, materially and semiotically, to be more 'environmentally friendly'. Thus, for example, the Brasher Boots Company manufactures the Hillmaster and Lady Classic whose three-layer sole has an outsole 'Studded and cleated to provide maximum traction whilst design minimizes clogging, thus improving safety and reducing footpath erosion' (http://www. spelean.com.au/BRA/Hillmaster.html – 9 June 1998). So, here, in rather old-fashioned terms, is a technological fix of sorts (old-fashioned because, as has been repeatedly noted, nothing is 'purely' technological) to the problem of boot-induced erosion. However, this is but one 'local' environmental impact of boots. There are other more distanced effects. For example, we can ask, to what extent do these boots use sustainable materials and processes? If 'our footpaths' are maintained, what of those that lead down to the rubber trees that provide the rubber for walking boots, rubber trees that are in monocultural plantations that were made possible by the burning of indigenous forests (e.g. in Indonesia)?

Of course, there are manufacturers who attempt to be environmentally ethical, who routinely review the sustainability of, for example, their manufacturing processes and raw materials. As might be expected, this entails a further objec-tification, for example, in the form of the scientific procedures of Life Cycle Assessment (Molloy, 1997a, 1997b). This would be of a piece with other assessments of environmental damage. Thus, the authorities that oversee and protect particular areas must measure levels of erosion (e.g. deploy environmental impact assessment techniques: again this is a process of quantification, again a practical operation that involves boots as a medium of access (see below).

Additionally, there are more encompassing versions of risk assessment. Thus, over and above the local assessment of 'risk' (e.g. those that are potentially 'controllable' by individual manufacturers or authorities), there are those assessments conducted by governmental and inter-governmental bodies concerned with more general environmental impacts of industry (e.g. the Intergovernmental Panel on Climate Change). Once again, even complex computer models (e.g. general circulation models) must be partly based on data collected at local sites. Here again, boots will feature as scientists move from their laboratories into the field to collect their data (Weldon, 1998; Latour, 1995). One could say that there is a global murmur of bootfalls. A criss-crossing network of trajectories of boots as they move people, projects, harms and goods from one locale to another. There is, in this movement and interconnection, something akin to the network of satellites and information technologies that constitute the network that surrounds the globe, which Serres (1995a) talks of in *The Natural Contract*: a new electronic subject looking down on a globalized earth. However, between this grand subject and gigantic object are the mediation of boots that carry the technicians to the receivers, that shod the feet of those who lay the electricity lines that power the computers, and so on and so forth. This network is never simply above the earth, it is scurrying on and beneath its surface (as Serres himself beautifully points out).

Although boots mediate these different forms of access to an objectified nature (both as an object of scientific and aesthetic valuation, see Samuel, 1996), they cannot be taken everywhere. Boots signify a particular practical scientific comportment that would be inappropriate in other arenas. Thus, Weldon (1998) remarks that scientists involved in the environmental impact assessment for Manchester Airport's second runway underwent a transformation as they moved from field to public inquiry. When out looking for Great Crested Newts, an endangered species, they were dressed in outdoor gear, including wellington boots; when they gave evidence at the public inquiry they were dressed in suits. Moreover, when they were scientists in the field, they could talk of the newts as exercising a certain agency; when they were in the inquiry, there were facts and figures, and theories of newt ecology and mobility. In the case of erosion, boots must come off experts as they move from the field in which research is conducted to the bureau where official presentations must be made – all this in order that boots go on those who will subsequently 'maintain' the 'environment'.

So far, I have treated walking boots in terms of their mediation of, at the extremes, both the enchantment and the objectification of nature. However, we must not overly dichotomize these processes: enchantment and objectification can be intertwined in more obvious ways. 'Bagging' is the term applied by climbers and hikers to the process of completing ascents of mountains. Certainly, this practice entails objectification, for example keeping an accurate count of ascents successfully completed, or classifying what counts as a mountain in, say, the Munro range in Scotland – cf. http://www.gillean.demon.co.uk/munros/munros. html; also http://www.cmc.org/cmc/pk_bggr.html – 16 April 1999). But, as the comments of 'baggers' make all too apparent, bagging still incorporates a profound appreciation of the spectacle of nature.

Be that as it may, walking boots, insofar as they 'merely' enable access, are underdeterminative, are jokers or blank dominoes (to borrow again from Serres). They might, as it were, pass between humans and non-humans mediating the interaction between (all sorts of) walkers and environments, but they do not specify the local relations between them. Nevertheless, many of the relations would certainly be much more difficult to establish in the absence of these mundane technologies. This is their *partial* role that was mentioned above. It is a 'multiplicatory' role that increases the range of human–environment contacts – a role which, complicated and complicating as it is, I have only begun to examine. Yet, for all this multiplication and indeterminacy, there is one aspect of boots which, it might be argued, is determinative of relations between humans and nature. In an obvious, gross corporeal capacity, boots must ensure some minimal level of comfort, or a general absence of acute pain, that enables humans to do what they do in the environment. However, as we have already seen, and as shall be explored further, this is by no means the simple matter it appears to be.

Walking the talk/talking the walk

So far I have basically treated walking boots as technical artefacts that enable certain movements, for instance toward the sublime, or in pursuit of measurements. However, as the example from Weldon (1998) implies, boots also signify. In certain situations, such as public inquiries, they are matter out of place (Douglas, 1966). The point is that boots, as clothing, are also cultural artefacts. They symbolize different 'tastes' (Bourdieu, 1984) – they enable certain styles of consumption. They might seem, on the surface, less aestheticized (Featherstone, 1991) than other sorts of objects of consumption, but they are aesthetic nevertheless (advertising and users' comments certainly reflect this). For example, there is a proliferation of different styles, most obviously in relation to gender categories, but also in relation to different 'uses'. Hybrids such as boot-trainers – for example, the Adidas Backlander – or boot-sandals – such as the Adidas Black Banshee – are now being produced (*The Guardian*, 25 April 1998). The title of this section of the chapter is meant to evoke the way that, in the mundane use of boots, one displays cultural situatedness and identity (talking the walk). Conversely, in displaying such identities, one is engaged in the processes of mundane, embodied and environmentally impacting activity (walking the talk). In what follows, these will explored as two faces of the same coin.

As we might expect in light of Bourdieu's (1984) classic analysis, and the wealth of work that has followed in its wake, such 'uses' of artefacts are not purely functional or instrumental, they also come to symbolize different categories of person (e.g. serious walker versus scrambler/rambler). In other words, these boots signify differing modes of comportment in relation to the 'natural environment' (and, of course, its other – the 'urban environment'). For example, brands like Berghaus, Meindl, Salomon, Zamberlain or Scarpa signify the serious or committed walker. In contrast, a brand like CAT seems to me to be predominantly identified with urban use. Produced by the longstanding (since 1883) shoe manufacturer Wolverine World Wide, CAT boots signify the company Caterpillar, which is a major manufacturer of construction and mining equipment and industrial engines. This 'industrial' and urban connotation is further signalled in the advertising moniker that attaches to these boots: 'walking machines'. So, despite the fact that the Caterpillar range includes 'country footwear', the brand has proved particularly popular amongst young urban groups.

Now, for 'serious walkers', boots are not supposed to signify lifestyle or fashion at all. In conversation with members of the Lancaster University Hiking Club, when I asked them about the ways in which they chose their walking boots, the very evident consensus was that this was a purely functional matter. The boots should do the job, they should be durable, they should fall within their price range, they should, above all, be comfortable. The same set of criteria is to be found in a walking shoe poll of subscribers to the website 'Walklist' (http://www.Teleport.com/~walking/shoepoll.htm – 18 May 1998). For example (where 1 refers to the question: 'What kind of shoes (brand and style) do you wear walking?', and 2 refer to the question: 'What do you look for in a walking shoe?'): '1. I wear SAS Shoes; 2. I look for comfort, durability and price'; '1. New Balance 580; 2(a). Comfort; (b). heel support'; 'I wear Rockport Pro-Walkers. Although I am easy on shoes, I still want comfort and durability, and the Pro-Walkers seem to give me those qualities'; '1. Vasque hiking boots for rough trails, Etonic Trans Walkers for moderate trails and SAS shoes for easy trails. 2. I look for shoes that are very light, good flexibility and plenty of room for the front part of the foot, i.e. the toes'; '1. My preferred footwear is Merrell All Terrain walking sandals; during cold weather I wear Reebok walking shoes. 2. I look for footwear that is well cushioned, contoured to the shape of my feet, and which provides a maximum of ventilation. With most shoes, I have severe problems with athlete's foot or blistering due to heat and sweating; however, I don't have these problems with walking sandals. The sandals are extremely comfortable, and yet sturdy enough in rugged trails rated 4; they are really a cross between a hiking boot and a sandal'.

Here, the criteria for the choice of particular boots are 'practical' – based on the fundaments of 'need'. The aesthetic aspect, as a part of consuming boots, is barely mentioned in this walking shoe poll, and it was actively denied by my Lancaster respondents. But then, it is this very act of denial, the indifference to style, or the view that it is a pleasant surprise if the boots are 'good to look at', that is part of the process of signification in these acts of (non-)consumption. The 'serious walker' is not bothered by aesthetics: functionality is all that matters. Yet, this posture is still a posture: it marks difference, it signals a particular excellence.

Let me put this another way, in terms of the notion of 'need'. These people can be said to draw upon a discourse wherein function and meaning are kept separate. As Slater (1997) puts it (albeit referring to the work of Douglas and Isherwood, 1979): 'The problem lies in interpreting this to mean that one can sensibly talk about functions and meanings independently of each other. That is to say that one can talk about either functions (or basic needs or basic objects) that are defined independently of particular cultures . . .' (Slater, 1997, p. 144). 'Comfort' can be viewed as a basic need; pain, like the pain I experienced in the Samaria Gorge, is an intolerable burden. Walking shoes are about 'need'; any cultural dimension is supplementary.

At this point we can return to the issue of pain, and its construction. Williams and Bendelow (1998a, 1998b; see also, Bendelow and Williams, 1998; Bendelow,

1998) review a number of conceptualizations of pain. They themselves adopt a sophisticated phenomenological and constructionist perspective in which they suggest that pain can have a number of effects: the 'distanciation' of the 'self' from the agonized body (the self is somehow 'outside' the body); or the fragmentation of self such that there is 'a "psychic splintering" and "disintegration", devoid of content, entirely cut off from the surrounding sociocultural world' (Williams and Bendelow, 1998b, p. 139). There is, in Scarry's (1985) words, an unmaking of the world. However, Williams and Bendelow (1998a) also note that pain can be 'narrativized'; pain can thus become meaningful (say, in terms of the discourses of gender difference in 'coping' with pain), or productive (say, in that pain narratives serve in the re-evaluation of lifestyle). For Williams and Bendelow, then, 'Bodies impose themselves on social categories just as social categories shape bodies: materiality and culture are therefore dialectically intertwined' (Williams and Bendelow, 1998a, p. 141).

Here, we have the sort of indissolubility of 'need' and 'culture' that Slater recommends. Further, we can underline that 'disintegration' is not simply a negative: certain mystics actively pursue such pain-prompted disintegration as a route to a higher state of consciousness (Eliade, 1964). Of course, the insights or enlightenments that flow from this altered state are mediated through local cultural resources. The narratives that render pain productive are, in sum, specific to times and places.

The general point, then, is that in relation to our movements through the environment, whether in relation to a pursuit of the sublime and the expressive, or in the process of the objectification of nature, walking boots mediate the relation between the body and the environment in culturally distinctive ways. This concerns not only the mediation of cultural categories concerned with identities of 'consumer', or 'environmentalist', or 'tourist'. Boots are also present in corporeal relations to environments, where corporeality is conceived of as incorporating the cultural.

The different 'body-boot-environment-culture' (e.g. the 'type of walker', the 'type of consumer', the 'type of pain') stories I've touched upon here seem to me to map onto each other in complex ways. Our relations to the environment, insofar as they are partially mediated by walking boots, are multiplicitous. For example, such relations can signal 'seriousness' and 'respect' for nature (environmentalism of whatever sort), in which pain and discomfort might become possible resources in the narration of this seriousness. Alternatively, such relations might reflect 'frivolity' and 'consumption': as articles of fashion, any pain that arises from boots serves as the narrative pretext for further purchases. The main observation I want to make, however, is that these 'needs' for comfort, these meanings of pain, are already embroiled in cultural systems of meaning, and these are not necessarily distinct systems. The 'serious' walker exercises the fashion of no fashion (to adapt Sharon Traweek's (1988) phrase 'the culture of no culture'), but into the heart of her or his relation with nature, boots import social relations of distinction, consumption, individualization and so on and (and as we have seen, these social relations are mediated by other mundane technologies).

Of course, the distinction between 'seriousness' and 'frivolity' is highly problematic. Processes of consumption are themselves highly serious for consumers. The distinction, as I have framed it here, rests on the equation of 'seriousness' with some version of ecological consciousness. Yet, this ecological consciousness is itself wrapped up in the dynamics of self-identity. As Melucci (1989) notes, new social movements (and that includes environmentalist variants) are as much concerned with the generation and reproduction of new identities as they are with the politics in which they are engaged. Indeed, these two dimensions are inseparable. As such, consumption – as a prime medium for the expression of such identity – can be said to lie close to the heart of 'environmentalism'.

What this meditation on walking boots suggests is that distinctions between seriousness and frivolity, environmentalism and consumption, need and culture are breaking down, or, at the very least, are actually very complicated. This complication is exacerbated by the relations with scientific expertise that consumption and environmentalism enter into. As various commentators have documented, the relations to, and the trust invested in, the likes of scientific institutions are shot through with ambivalence (Yearley, 1991; Wynne, 1996; Bauman, 1991). So, for example, Beck (1992) and Giddens (1991) tell us that we 'late moderns' are deeply ambivalent about science. On the one hand we trust in, and depend upon, science and 'its' mediating institutions for our continued well-being (including the identification and measurement of, and the possible solution to, numerous environmental threats). On the other hand, we are deeply suspicious – after all, science has had a big hand in the production of all manner of risks, hazards, dangers, anxieties and the like. As Beck puts it: '. . . the risk consciousness of the afflicted, which is frequently expressed in the environmental movement, and in criticism of industry, experts and culture, is usually both critical and credulous of science' (Beck, 1992, p. 72).

This credulity is deeply embedded: for instance, we are chronically dependent on, and credulous of, science and the multifarious institutions in which it is embedded in the most unreflexive (as well as reflexive) of ways. We invest trust in 'abstract systems' as Giddens (1991) would have it. Thus, in relation to boots, we assume that the materials of which they are made are not toxic for us, or that they function as claimed by the manufacturers. Less dramatically, but no less an indication of this 'constitutional' credulity and trust, we assume that boots are made to particular standards, by which I mean that 'sizes', for example, are common within and across brands. Here, we take for granted the most basic units of measurement. Yet these too have to be constantly checked and 'surveilled'; that is, standardized (e.g. Bowker and Star, 1996; O'Connell, 1993). As O'Connell wittily shows, such standards (right down to the measure of a centimetre or a volt) must be constantly checked and calibrated through a circulation of what he calls 'particulars' – those bits of equipment that embody the standard for this or that unit of measurement. Yet how does one know that such an exemplar of a standard remains so? By checking and calibrating it too. But then how does one know that that which is being checked against is also 'true' or accurate? Again, by checking and calibrating. And so on and so forth in an infinite circuit of calibration, an unceasing circulation of 'particulars' whose status as instantiations of a standard is always temporary. Inevitably – and this has become a refrain now – boots are involved here too, in the mundane conveyance of these impermanent standards.

However, standards do not suit all bodies. As we have noted, the importance of good fit is stressed over and over in the popular culture concerned with walking. Indeed, this concern with, for want of a better phrase, the 'fit-function' is extended beyond the moment of purchase (cf. Dant, 1999). It is an ongoing process of fitting boots and feet together. Thus, one webpage concerned with (male) outdoor pursuits (http://www.manslife.com/oudoors/backpacker/html) devotes several pages to the means by which hikers can ensure comfort (e.g. breaking in boots, caring for them, caring for one's feet). *The Great Outdoors* magazine recently organized a 'boot camp' where experts would be on site to advise walkers on fit, feet and boots (see *The Great Outdoors*, August 1998, p. 15). Here, we see in operation the late modernist ambivalence mentioned above: there is a 'bespoking' of boots that simultaneously expresses a trust in the standardization techniques of experts, and a suspicion that such techniques are faulty (and hence recourse to 'artisanal' advice). We find similar ambivalences for the claims made for certain materials used in boots. The value of Gore-Tex has thus been an issue of some contention (see the 'Is Gore-Tex overrated?' discussion on http://www. thebackpacker.com/ques/gore/html). We might speculate that this uneasiness is a manifestation of a broader ambivalence: boots are seen as both a product of the objectification of nature (which includes both the environment and the body) and as a medium for the problematization of that objectification (expressed in re-tailoring the relations between bodies and environments).

The preceding section has been deliberately fragmentary, or, rather, peram-bulatory. The account that has been so far elaborated comprises an attempt, as it were, to follow walking boots as they heterogeneously mediate, and criss-cross, ecological consciousness or activism (or, more broadly, citizenship) and con-sumption and consumer culture, and as they embody the complexities of trust and suspicion in abstract systems. As such, I have treated walking boots as a figure that ties the human and non-human, the world and the word, the corporeal and the cultural in multiple, interlacing, folded networks. In the next sections, I approach this heterogeneity from a somewhat different direction. Instead of assuming the initial separation, or difference, of humans and the natural environment (which must be brought together in the sublime or scientific relation), I start from the presupposition that there is a 'unity' to their relation, that there is mutual immersion. Thus, the version of the local I want to focus upon now is not so much that of the sublime-seeking walker or the objectifying scientist, but that of the practical 'taskscape' (as Ingold, 1993, calls it).

From difference to unity

To embrace the natural sublime, to consume nature's spectacle, to measure nature's objects, to extract nature's bounty means, obviously enough, to bring bodies into contact with nature. This is no simple process, as I hope I have shown. It is shot through with the cultural, which is shot through with the technological, which is shot through with the natural, which is shot through with the cultural, and so on: a knot, a black hole, as Haraway calls it. Boots are the little angels, the quasi-objects, that serve in the circulation of these entities and in the ongoing (re)production of relations – that bring into alignment in complex, fragmented, splintered ways an array of disparate entities.

In referring to walking boots in terms of the ways in which they complexly and heterogeneously mediate relations between humans and nature, and humans and humans, I have aimed at avoiding representing their role as in some way causal or determinative. Rather, the purpose is to evoke the way that they serve to *enable* particular relations to the environment – and such enablement is not simply a matter of their 'function', but also a reflection of their role as cultural artefacts that signify (that is, express) 'fashion' (taste, seriousness, etc.). In other words, I have conceptualized walking boots as polysemic (where, as noted in Chapter 2, the 'semic' refers as much to the material as to the semiotic – they are polymaterial too). This plurality in their function-expressions means that, as quasi-objects, they are underdetermining. They are jokers or blank dominoes, in Serres' terminology.

Now, the multiple enablements mediated by walking boots reflect the fact that they emerge out of numerous heterogeneous networks. In walking boots are to be found the traces of many other enabling relations and associations. As enabling artefacts themselves, walking boots do not simply 'tell' relations to nature or speak openly of the relations amongst people or between people and natures: they *whisper* them. They quietly and tacitly evoke suggestions and embody indistinct possibilities for such relations. Yet, at the same time, this multiplicity of hetero-geneous significations is being *reduced*: the whisper of walking boots entails a shout whereby various actors deploy various sorts of discourses to try to represent walking boots as artefacts meant for a particular, specified sort of use (or rather function-expression). In marketing terms, this might be called something like developing and/or targeting a market niche. In Callon's (1991) terms there is an attempted convergence of manufacturers' networks and those of consumers, between the boots of producers and the desires and hopes of walkers. One need only browse through the catalogues produced by any boot (and outdoor wear) manufacturer (or retailer) to note the delimitation of walking boots' meanings. In these texts, we find photograph after photograph of boots modelled by good-looking humans in, or *en route* to, idyllic, even sublime, settings. These boots promise at once an arduous and an effortless process of access to spectacular nature. The co(a)gent walker-in-boots-in-motion is both in spectacular nature (arrived at without problems), and is in itself a spectacle (engaged in the tough process of arriving). Boots here are being used to signify particular sorts of lifestyle. To reach this idyll, this lifestyle, one must pass through the product and the producer, must adopt and adapt to the walking boot. But, as we have seen, there are other ways in which boots signify; for some subcultures (e.g. hikers), boots promise their own material and semiotic disappearance in the sense that they are so comfortable and so functional that they do not impinge on the process of walking. Any limits to access are those placed by the fitness and talents of the walker rather than by the character or branding of the boots. The key point here is that while boots are under-determining in their role of bringing humans and nature together, they are nevertheless subject to numerous discursive efforts to delimit their function-expressions, efforts that span, for example, such constituencies as manufacturers and retailers, walkers themselves, and environmental groups.

Now, the various narratives that have appeared in the preceding sections have essentially been concerned with the way that walking boots facilitate in very many ways the *encounter* between humans and the environment. In other words, I have so far treated the relation of humans to environment as the *bringing together* of two separate classes of entities, even while trying to show, through the figure of the walking boot, how these interweave in complex, multivalent ways, which straddle the intersubjective and the intermaterial.

The model of this encounter, then, can, in part at least, be regarded as a cognitivist one. By this is meant that our cognitive representations of the environment are derived from 'sense data [that] is [*sic*] highly impoverished and, in itself [*sic*], quite insufficient to specify the objects and events that subjects claim they perceive in the environments . . . All knowledge of the environment is therefore to be reconstructed from these inadequate and fragmentary data, and this is achieved through processing the "raw" sensory input according to cognitive schemata located in the head of the perceiver, not "out there" in the world . . . The only activity in perception, then, is mental activity . . .' (Ingold, 1992, p. 45). My account of the perception of the environment (mediated in part by walking boots) has been 'cognitivist' insofar as nature has been something that has been grasped by a separated human. To be sure, this grasping has not just involved 'cognitive schemata'; the tacit emphasis has been upon the process of the 'reconstruction' of our knowledge of nature through various cultural schemata – discourses of the sublime, or of science. This poses the question of what happens when we think of human–nature as a unity at the outset, rather than try and re-establish their unity through, for example, the sublime.

We can frame this presupposition of unity in terms of the notion of 'affordance'. According to Gibson's (1979) ecological theory of perception, the concept of affordance captures the fact that the surfaces and structures that make up an animal's environment specify a range of possible actions for that organism. Crucial here is the idea that such possible actions reflect the capacities and limits of the animal's body. An area of flat ground thus 'affords' a variety of actions – lying, sitting, standing, crawling, hopping, jumping – which mirror the animal's corporeal capabilities. The environment, as a set of surfaces, does not determine an animal's doings, it merely 'suggests' the array of possible doings. But this 'suggestion' is oriented not toward a passive, sedentary perceiver (as is common in cognitivist, Cartesian models, cf. Heft, 1989; Michael and Still, 1992), but toward an active organism that explores its environment, actively seeking (picking up) information. In other words, the structure and meaning that we find in the world are already there in the information that we extract in the act of perception; their source lies in the objects we perceive, they are not added on by the perceiver. Therefore, perceiving is, *ipso facto*, knowing – to have seen something is to have sought out information that enables one to know it. But the knowledge gained through such perception is essentially practical; it is knowledge about what the object affords. Depending upon the kind of activity in which we are engaged, we will be attuned to picking up a particular kind of information, leading to the perception of a particular affordance.

(Ingold, 1992, p. 46)

The upshot of this model is that cultural constructions of nature are not the precondition of our contact with the environment. Rather, there is, Ingold tells us, 'a contemplative disengagement from the world' (Ingold, 1992, p. 52) when we discursively represent nature. Here, then, Ingold is advocating a model wherein there is a mutual immersion of human and environment – the notion of affordance implies not only a perceiving, active human organism, but also a view of the environment which itself, so to speak, 'perceives' the human (cf. Merleau-Ponty's 1968, notion of the 'flesh'; see also Thrift, 1996; Crossley, 1995; and Grosz, 1993, for a more critical analysis). Or rather, just as the organism's embodiment allows certain affordances, so the environment can be said to embody the organism's actions and activities within itself. Ingold frames the following questions:

I regard embodiment as a movement of incorporation rather than inscription . . . a movement wherein forms themselves are generated . . . thus organisms may be said to incorporate, in their bodily forms, the life-cycle processes that give rise to them. Could not the same be said of the environment? Is it possible to identify a corresponding cycle, or rather a series of interlocking cycles, which build themselves into forms of the landscape, and of which the landscape may accordingly be regarded as an embodiment?

(Ingold, 1993, p. 157)

Part of those cycles is the activity of organisms, human included. Thus,

once we think of the world in this way, as a total movement of becoming which builds itself into the forms we see, and in which each form takes shape in continuous relation to those around it, the distinction between animate and inanimate seems to dissolve. The world itself takes on the character of an organism, and the movements of animals – including those of us human beings – are parts or aspects of its life-process. . . . This means that in dwelling in the world, we do not act upon it, or do things to it; rather we move along with it. Our actions do not transform the world, they are part and parcel of the world's transforming itself.

(Ingold, 1993, p. 164)

On the basis of this ontology, Ingold (1993) impresses upon us the need to think of landscape as a dwelling, which incorporates both nature and culture, mind and matter. This is because landscape is effectively connected with those who dwell there, their movements, their practices, their workings. To dwell entails a present that embodies, retains the past and projects into the future. This dwelling, Ingold tells us, is fundamentally concerned with practices – or 'taskscapes'. Taskscape is crucial to the social meaning of landscape; it persists only so long as there are people continuing to practise those activities, those practices of dwelling in the particular landscape.

MacNaghten and Urry (1998) draw out the following implications of Ingold's analysis:

> . . . that there are spatially and temporally distributed tasks; that these are organised through a variety of social practices; that relationships with what is taken to be nature are embodied, involving a variety of senses; that there are 'physical' components of walls, textures, land, plants and so on, which partly constitute such 'dwellings'; that the past is continually redefined in terms of the present and projections into the future; that such redefinitions of the past involve forms of collective memory work; and that landscapes are never completed but always subject to contestation and renegotiation, using materials, signs and activities from various pasts as they are projected into diverse futures.
>
> (MacNaghten and Urry, 1998, p. 168)

There are a number of points I wish to raise on the basis of this, all too compressed, account of Ingold's analysis. Firstly, the embodiment of humans encompasses, in obvious addition to the environment, other humans (Costall, 1995a) and, importantly in the present context, mundane technologies. Indeed, these technologies themselves are material surfaces that afford (where 'afford' is a verb of 'affordance', a technical term from Gibson referring to corporeality and temporality of animals' perceptions of their environment). In other words, affordance is not simply emergent out of the relationality, even unity, of humans and nature. Affordance, as Ingold is acutely aware, is interwoven with all manner of other relations: combinations of humans, animals, technologies that can constrain or expand possible affordances. Let me elaborate on this point with the aid of walking boots.

Walking boots are one technology that mediates this mutuality – they expand and constrain the affordances that arise between bodies and natures. Boots make certain surfaces more walkable (and hence enhance the accessibility of certain valued sites, or else enhance accessibility *per se* wherein the act of walking is transformed from means to end). Further, boots themselves are a series of surfaces that afford. They do not simply constitute 'footwear' – they are also weapons and small buckets. Their role as 'leisure footwear' is, as I have repeatedly indicated, a deeply cultural and historical matter. In other words, much work needs to be done before walking boots are 'reified' and their meanings circumscribed (and this always contingently). As we have seen, this work involves, for example, the efforts of manufacturers at marketing their boots. Again, as hinted above, the cultural endeavours of various groups such as hill walkers, ramblers, environmentalists, conservationists and so on all play their diffuse, disparate and dispersed parts in the 'definition' of the walking boot, and in delimiting its affordances.

However, there is a problem here. The foregoing account is in danger of reproducing the cognitivist model of giving meaning to nature, although now it is boots that are being 'ascribed' meaning by humans who are 'separate' from them. As Ingold notes in relation to the taskscape, the meanings of nature emerge temporally – out of the past, oriented to the future, but always realized in the present. However, what, out of the past, might inform ongoing activities? Ingold's brilliant analysis of Bruegel's *The Harvesters* in which he unravels the intertwining of humans and landscape is based on a distinctly local society. The footwear of the farm workers depicted in this painting (footwear that was a part of the mutuality of persons and nature in the taskscape) was, we might suggest, conceivably the product of local artisans. The meaning of such articles of clothing was, possibly, relatively unproblematic – afforded in relation to the indissoluble cultural/material character of their local taskscape.

These links between taskscape and mundane technology will, I suspect, be reflected as local or regional variations (not least in terms of available materials). Let me consider, in brief, some of the ways in which footwear featured in these rural settings. Cunnington and Lucas (1967) tell us that, for rural workers in the Middle Ages, it was often the case that labouring on the land meant stripping from the waist down i.e. working barefoot. For women in the Middle Ages, 'shoes of normal shape or heel-less slippers, like our mules of today, were the usual footwear' (Cunnington and Lucas, 1967, p. 42). In the fourteenth century, leather overshoes or galoshes were used, but their more familiar incarnation in rubber did not appear until around 1830, introduced from South America. In eighteenth-century Britain, there were different sorts of footwear that varied with location. For example, for men, there were shoes studded with iron around the heel, there were short boots known as 'highlows', and in some places (the north of England) wooden clogs were favoured. Rubber boots and shoes were originally footwear for the rich; they only became normal protective footwear for agricultural labourers around the turn of the twentieth century. It was only in this period that rubber wellingtons became the usual wear for those workers needing protection from the wet. On the whole, as Cunnington and Lucas note, the evolution of protective clothing was very slow, a fact they put down to such factors as 'lack of means, lack of available materials, lack of invention' (Cunnington and Lucas, 1967, p. 386). In addition, however, there were also more obviously cultural conditions: gender divisions, aesthetics, fashion, conservatism. These latter, Cunnington and Lucas (1967, p. 392) suggest, militated against developments that would have, from a 'purely practical point of view', made the task in hand much easier. However, Cunnington and Lucas also note that the preservation of occupational costume in the face of change can be linked to a 'laudable solidarity' (Cunnington and Lucas, 1967, p. 392) – that is, to reiterate a point made in Chapter 1, what makes a garment 'work' rests as much on 'cultural' as 'practical' criteria.

Now, the point of this seeming digression is to underline that, in Ingold's analysis of the taskscape, the footwear of these peasants seems to be, relatively speaking, 'unproblematic'. By this I mean that their affordances are 'simple' insofar as they are used in practical tasks that are 'local', a part of the taskscape (although this is not to deny that they are caught up in the processes of rendering 'distinction'). In other words, the lineages of tasks, and the tools through which they are conducted, and the projects which such tasks realize and open up, are circumscribed by locality and community. This world of the taskscape is an almost hermetic world.

In contrast, affordances related to communities (now full of incomers) and localities (now visited by tourists) in the modern world are mediated by tools such as walking boots that have a much more complex lineage. For example, walking boots derive from sporting and recreational activities such as mountain climbing. Interest in these activities as pastimes first emerged in Britain at the beginning of the nineteenth century, but did not gain any great popularity until the middle of that century, being largely regarded until that period as an eccentricity. On the whole, men and women's clothing for mountain climbing mirrored that used in winter walks (although, needless to say, as in relation to other items of clothing, women were considerably disadvantaged). Thus, '[b]oots were frequently ordinary hobnail boots . . .' (Cunnington and Mansfield, 1969, p. 321). It was recommended that these be well greased, be extended well above the ankle, have laces, and be nailed (preferences were expressed for the Swiss wrought iron nails over the English cast iron variety – Cunnington and Mansfield, 1969, p. 328). With regard to the less arduous pursuit of country walking, boots and shoes were used. Sometimes these were simply ordinary, everyday items, but occasionally it was recommended, for women, that clogs or galoshes be used (Cunnington and Mansfield, 1969, pp. 336–337). Moving into the twentieth century, for women there were a wide variety of fashionable boots and bootees available, although constraints were placed on the range in wartime. For the men, too, there was variety that reflected different function-expressions. For example, in the early part of the century, jackboots were used in hunting, and boots with a long pointed toe were considered correct 'dress' (Mansfield and Cunnington, 1973). In the middle of the century, boots (and also rubber galoshes, though not wellington boots) began to decline in popularity although they continued to be used by workmen and in the country. After the rationing of World War II, new styles began to appear (e.g. ankle-length boots with elastic side gussets).

Here, we seem to have lineages that cross-cut sporting use and ordinary 'everyday' use. The point is that, for 'recreational walking', there were no distinct local forms of footwear. This is hardly surprising because recreational walking (and that includes that which seeks the sublime) itself was not a local activity. Indeed, the activity was not 'practical' in the sense of contributing to the process of rural production (in the traditional sense). Furthermore, if seeking the sublime was once a 'simple' goal, a 'pure' project, that too has become more complicated. The affordances wrought through walking boots are themselves much more complex – the temporal horizons of such projects have both shrunk and extended: shrunk in the sense that, say, the consumption of natural spectacle is becoming more routinized and more easily accessible; extended because the project attached to walking might also be associated with a concern with long-term, currently invisible, damage to the environment, with the natural legacy left for future generations. The meanings of landscapes and taskscapes are, it would seem, undergoing major shifts. The imagery of *The Harvesters* cannot capture the complexity of the contemporary 'local' that is now so caught up in global processes that some have been tempted to coin the term 'glocal' (e.g. Adam, 1998).

Now, this transformation is informed by cultural changes in our apprehensions of the 'natural' environment. The rise of the risk society is tied to a burgeoning awareness, partly prompted by the work of scientists, of the invisible dangers that lurk around us. But this representation of a dangerous nature is not purely the upshot of a 'contemplative disengagement from the world' (Ingold, 1992, p. 52). We are never disengaged from the world, we do our representing in the context of quiet affordances that link us to other humans, but also to mundane technologies (armchairs and desks), and even natures (see Ulrich Beck's, 1992, account of the hillside where he composed *The Risk Society*). These mundane material contexts are, like walking boots, not determinate; they enable this disengagement, even as they entail a quiet engagement.

In talking about the quiet affordances that operate in the background, even in the process of disengagement, we can draw a parallel with the quiet agreement that Wittgenstein talks of in relation to language games and rules (Lynch, 1993). For all the conflicts that arise in social interaction, for all the objectification of the 'other' in these conflicts, these are still realized against the backdrop of quietly agreed rules. However, sometimes these rules are disrupted, most famously in Garfinkel's (1967) breaching experiments which, in undermining these quiet agreements, led to confusion, anger, disorientation (Heritage, 1984) – an unmaking of the social world, so to speak. We too have witnessed such breaching in the interactions with nature. The pain generated by ill-fitting boots breaches the relation between bodies and natures – there is an unmaking of the world. Of course, in the specific circumstances of ill-fitting boots, boots usually afford their own removal. The point, however, is that within the affordances entailed in the environment, are the mediating affordances embodied in boots. There is a *cascade* of affordances – feet-boots-environment – for the boots to function in nature, and nature to function through the boots (see Michael, in press, for more on this).

In summary, for nature to come to be accessible – to be in a position to afford – a series of other affordances need to be in operation: for a mountain to afford climbing, the affordances between boots and feet have to be realized. But such micro-technological affordances are not simply or unproblematically 'physical'. As we have seen, even at the ostensibly 'basic' level of pain derived from the mis-fitting of boots and feet (and, by implication, the environment), we find the operation of cultural resources.

Now, MacNaghten and Urry make a number of important points in relation to Ingold's analysis of paths as the taskscape made visible, where paths are conceptualized as the 'accumulated imprint of countless journeys that have been made by people as they go about their daily business' (MacNaghten and Urry, 1998, p. 168). They further speculate that paths, insofar as they are a key sedimentation of community activity, when destroyed or altered, say through the building of new roads, understandably generate anxiety and anger. Over and above this, the meaning of 'taskscape' must itself be elaborated, Macnaghten and Urry argue, in order to accommodate the recent developments of modernity. For example, they suggest that: science itself now comprises a taskscape that is globalized, that, indeed, sometimes operates as if the world itself were its laboratory; the dwelling of the moderns is highly complex, entailing resistance against the scientific taskscape; new communications media are reshaping our apprehension of nature; diverse new spatial practices (including mass travel, tourism, photography) involve somewhat different trajectories through the landscape.

However, as I have argued, taskscapes, local or 'global', fundamentally entail mundane technologies. Mundane technologies make the immersions between humans and the environment possible insofar as they enable affordances, indeed are part of the cascade of affordances that comprise taskscapes. Globalization is nothing more than a longer network of 'locals'. At each of these junctures, affordances – the relations between mundane technologies and bodies, cultures and materials – still operate. Let me put it another way. The medieval local taskscape may be thought of as a hybrid in which natures, tools, people 'exchange properties', in Latour's terms. The contemporary local taskscape is no different, it is just that the properties that are exchanged have travelled further. They are in the form of, for example, rubber, tourists, imported species. And, of course, these new taskscapes are co(a)gents too – at once cogent and distributed, only now the distribution extends further and the heterogeneity is more opulent.

Conclusion: monoculture/multiculture

It is difficult not to read Ingold's account of the mutual immersion of human, culture and landscape as a sort of pastoral idyll. What we seem to have is a monoculture wherein humans are neatly, more or less homogeneously, intertwined with nature through their taskscapes – marked by the landscape, marked in the landscape. Yet, as Croll and Parkin (1992) note, the relation between humans and their environment, even for such 'pre-modern' societies, can be highly ambiguous, shaped by, for example, the power relations (gender, age) within those communities. Moreover, when we see these communities entered into modernity, in the sense of coming into contact with the state, corporations, development agencies, non-government organizations and so on, then matters become even more complicated (e.g. Hastrup and Olwig, 1997). Whereas the co(a)gency of traditional 'unthreatened' taskscapes entails mundane technology, when those taskscapes are in need of protection, or preservation, then the range of technologies expands – or rather, different taskscapes begin to interweave. The taskscapes of modernity – those that MacNaghten and Urry call global – are entered, and their technologies are appropriated as a means to ecological and cultural protection. Thus, when Haraway (1992b) analyses a photograph in *Discover* magazine of a

Kayapo Indian, in indigenous dress, using a videocamera, she does not see this as an amusing boundary crossing, an ironic contrast between the modern and the primitive. Rather, it can be thought as a 'forging [of] a recent collective of humans and unhumans, in this case made up of the Kayapo, videocams, land, plants, animals, near and distant audiences, and other constituents' (Haraway, 1992b, p. 314). Indigenous people, in fighting to protect their ways of life and their ecosystems, seem readily to draw on these new technologies. Here is another rough and ready example of the interleaving of the modern and the traditional. Typing into the Infoseek search engine (4 November 1998) the key phrase 'indigenous people', 16,648,592 references are counted; when one refines the search with the keyword 'web', 3,071 references come up. The implication is that some fraction of this 3,071 is made up of websites by and for indigenous people. Indeed, this example of 'cyborg' activity has become subject to academic treatment. Thus, on the website for the journal *Leonardo* (http://mitpress.mit.edu/e-journals/ Leonardo/ijast/journal/journal.html – 4 November 1998), we come across the abstract of an article entitled 'Indigenous people in cyberspace' by Adam Lucas. These are indeed new collectives.

However, the audiences that are addressed through these technologies are also potentially dangerous allies. The support they offer can contain the assumptions, the tacit interests of the West. Where there is a move from a 'monoculture' to a 'multiculture', or rather (and less patronizingly) an attempted 'forging of new collectives', there might well be a monocultural response where Western scientific imperatives predominate. So, for example, in a case study of the development of policy regarding the Amboseli National Park in Kenya, Charis Cussins (1997; see also Whatmore, 1997) documents two broad strategies that emerged in a scientific meeting convened to discuss the role of elephants in the local ecosystem (in particular, their possible part in the loss of woodland habitat). On the one hand, there were the views expressed by the Amboseli elephant researchers; on the other, there were the views expressed by conservation biologists who had built up alliances with members of the local community. Whereas the former tended to advocate universalistic (i.e. Western) principles of scientific rigour, peer review, animal rights and so on, the latter argued for a policy grounded in the active involvement of the community, local people having a direct custodial input into the management of the elephant population. Thus, the elephant researchers argued for the conservation of a particular animal species (the elephants), while the conservation biologists promoted the conservation of biodiversity, which incorporated accountability, planning and management. In essence, then, we have the monoculture of Western science opposed to a situated, local, multiculture of alliances and contingencies (Cussins is careful not to reify the local community – it was certainly *not* politically homogeneous). As it turned out, the conservation biologists won this particular argument. In other cases, the importation of the standards and priorities of Western (techno-)science, even into Western local communities, such as those of the sheep-farmers of Cumbria in Britain (Wynne, 1992, 1996; for a critique, see Michael, 1998) leads to messier – that is, discriminatory – outcomes. As Croll and Parkin (1992) point out, the success of a conservation project might be more likely if local people are consulted and are instrumental in the decision-making process. Part and parcel of this is taking into account the fact that internal tensions or hierarchies within local communities can lead to different sorts of responses, where one section of a community can be happier to embrace Western intellectual and technological goods than another (see also Pfaffenberger, 1992a; Hess, 1995a). However, even where we find multiculture – or rather hybridities of scientific and local knowledges – these are still partly instituted through the monoculture of the standards that structure such mundane technologies as walking boots. In other words, what, at one level, might appear to be a relatively fluid and unhierarchical multiculture, is partially mediated by mundane technologies of the West, which embody, at another level, a monoculture that is anything but fluid and unhierarchical.

Now, the foregoing discussion has been concerned with a nature at risk – the risks posed by humans, by technoscience, by the New World Order. However, nature itself is a source of risks. Croll and Parkin (1992) touch upon the many and varied ways in which local communities deal with nature's violent, destructive otherness. But for the 'modern', this otherness is also an anthropogenic one. The 'quiet agreement' that characterizes affordance in the taskscape has become problematic. The 'flesh' (Merleau-Ponty, 1968) that perceptually binds humans and the environment has become rotten. To move within the landscape is to engage in affordances that are circumscribed. Speculatively, we might say that there is, following Paul Ricoeur, a sort of material hermeneutics of suspicion in relation to 'our' movements, our comportment in the environment. 'We' are suspect of our own comportment (e.g. how do we damage this nature through our various technologies of accessibility?), we are suspicious of nature (e.g. what chemical lingers in that wood?). But, then again, just as we have talked about the quiet mutuality of humans and nature, perhaps we should be talking about mutualities of suspicion – suspicion of danger (from humans) maybe also resides in nature. Again, walking boots play their part not only in the cascade of affordance, but in these mutualities of suspicion. To reiterate, even where walking boots may be appropriated for subcultural use, that is, even where they multiply feature in a multiculture, they can also mediate an emerging Western monoculture of risk. That is to say, by enabling (however multivalent an) access to an anthropogenically risky natural environment, walking boots serve as a conduit for these material hermeneutics of suspicion.

In this chapter, I have, through the figure of walking boots, explored, albeit in a rather perambulatory fashion, the idea of co(a)gency, of the simultaneity of distributedness and unity. I have examined, for example, how walking boots have been instrumental in numerous connections and disconnections. Thus, they mediate the immersions, the mutualities, of bodies and nature, bodies and culture; but they are also instrumental in the partial dis- and re-connections of bodies and nature, of bodies and culture. What I have attempted to do is convey some sense of the way that such mundane technologies feature in the flux of hetero-geneous ordering and disordering. In the next chapter, I will pursue this theme further, this time through a consideration of the phenomenon of 'road rage'. Here, too, we see the patterning of order and disorder, this time in relation to (un)controllable emotion (as opposed to an (un)controllable environment), and proper and improper human comportment. In exploring the car's material as well as cultural role in these dynamics, we shall see how co(a)gents – in particular, that of the 'person-in-their-car-who-does-road-rage' – can be 'policed'. Often this policing reflects Latour's (1993a) 'Modern' constitution insofar as the human and non-human are purified, so that the former can be pathologized. But, sometimes, there are indications of a move, in popular culture, toward the naming and shaming of co(a)gents *per se*.

4   Co(a)gents and control

Purifying 'road rage'

Introduction

For about five years I was working in Lancaster and leading my family life in Cambridge. During term time, I would do the 200-mile or so drive along the A14 and M6 twice a week. This was not something I was keen on. I hated driving for all sorts of reasons – environmental, economic, emotional. On the journey to Lancaster, there was always the danger of missing meetings, lectures or seminars due to delays, traffic, accidents or breakdown. On the journey to Cambridge, there was a pervasive fear of never arriving. Whichever direction I was travelling in, the journey was always tainted by the gloom and guilt that I was about to miss, or had missed, out on family life. I would have loved to travel by rail. All that work I could have done, all that sleep I could have caught up on, all that moral high ground I could have occupied. But time and timetables and cost persuaded me to use the car. Consequently, I would routinely entertain the idea of buying a bigger, more powerful, safer car. Regularly, I would have the car serviced – I could not abide the thought that it might break down.

Over those five years, I discovered a long unexercised capacity to feel and express gross anger, even fury. Whereas outside the car I was, generally speaking, pretty laid back, inside the car I was intolerant. In the car, I rediscovered my short temper; behind the wheel, I nurtured an unexpected talent for swearing and cursing; in the flow of traffic, my skills in the arts of feeling aggrieved, of taking umbrage, blossomed. When someone was driving too slowly (by my judgement), when someone hogged the middle lane, when I was tailgated by a fast car, when I was cut up – then I would, without hesitation, draw on my burgeoning repertoire of scowls, mutterings, cursings. I suppose I was 'suffering' from one of the milder forms of 'road rage'.

What are we to make of this sad, extended episode? Well, let us begin with a definition of road rage. Drawing on the unpublished policy document 'Road Rage' (undated), produced by the UK's Royal Automobile Club, road rage is 'simply a term to describe a range of anti-social, ill-tempered, foolish or violent behaviours by a minority of drivers. It can be, and has been, defined as "an altering of an individual's personality whilst driving, by a process of dehumanization" and as "a total loss of self control"' ('Road Rage', p. 2). Accordingly, 'Given the wrong conditions almost anyone can lose their control' ('Road Rage', p. 2). I was, therefore, prone to losing my control. But what are these conditions? What leads to this dangerous 'dehumanization'?

This chapter will, as might be expected, problematize this notion of dehumanization, for the aim is to show how the human is already a hybrid – a co(a)gent that is immersed in a complex, although mundane, technological artefact, the car. The 'car', however, is a sociotechnical system – it spans many actors, relations, networks, hybrid *collectifs*, which are both material and semiotic, ordering and disordering.

Over and above all this, both pro and contra Latour, I want to suggest that discourses on the phenomenon of road rage both exemplify the process of modernist purification (that is, the keeping separate of human and non-human), and begin to undermine, even transgress, this purification. In other words, I want to suggest that we can find evidence that moderns are able to articulate, identify and comment upon, human–non-human co(a)gents.

In what follows, I will firstly consider the way that road rage has been purified in the media and by driving organizations. In particular, I will explore how the driver is identified as the locus of pathology and the site of intervention. The tacit naturalistic discourses of emotions entailed in these accounts will then be contrasted with social constructionist treatments. However, via a detour through the work of Elias on civilization and the ANT analysis of technological scripting, I will attempt to show how the technology is itself involved in the structuring of emotions. In the process, I will draw upon the cultural history of the car. Finally, I will consider how certain pockets of popular culture judge not only the driver, but the combination of car-and-driver; that is, particular co(a)gents.

Driven around the bend

Lynch (1993) provides a brilliant ethnomethodological account of the nature of people-in-cars-in-traffic. He shows that traffic is situationally organized from 'within' the flow of traffic and not from some panoptic 'above'. The 'gaps' between cars are 'temporally composed and modified by a complex assemblage of drivers' actions mediated by and expressed in the traffic. Recognizable social relations are established in reference to gaps between cars, as each driver adjusts to the relative speeds, temporal relations of leading and following, and the common forward-moving directionality of the local traffic' (Lynch, 1993, p. 155). This sensitivity to the traffic is grounded in the specificity of road systems which are, Lynch tells us, 'meticulously engineered for an aggregation of standardized vehicular units' (Lynch, 1993, p. 157) which incorporate 'headlights, signals, and the simple sets of codes for using them [that] are embedded in the linear matrix of traffic' (Lynch, 1993, p. 157). As such, the driver's body and its actions are 'circumscribed by the conventional modes of perception, gesture and communication within a speeding and nomadic assemblage of vehicular units' (Lynch, 1993, p. 157). Lynch is keen to convey that, within this setting, meanings abound. Not only are there 'signs and signals, which are placed and formatted in standardized reference to the linear flow of readers situated in traffic' (Lynch, 1993, p. 156), but drivers can readily infer from minimal events, say the swerving of a car, the kind of person the driver is, composing as they do so, 'remarkably precise complaints' (Lynch, 1993, p. 157). These complaints, judgements, assessments, attributions and associated sorts of escalations 'into explicit games, races, offenses given and offenses taken' (Lynch, 1993, p. 158) have their own specificity – they do not signal the simple translocation of a more general set of power relations (e.g. gender). Put simply, there are certain 'rules of the road' that enable the particular social dynamics of the road, and these rules cannot be reduced to the rules of other social settings.

However, why should there be such an escalation of offences given and taken? In particular, what are the range of conditions that enable the extremes of road rage? How, we might ask, do such factors as the car itself, as both a material artefact with certain capacities and affordances, and a historico-cultural artefact imbued with certain meanings, contribute to the possibility of road rage? What might all this tell us about human–car co(a)gents? In the following sections, I will consider how the British press and key UK driving organizations have portrayed road rage. As we shall see, the emphasis here falls primarily upon the frailties of a human psyche such that it is the driver who becomes the object of correction. Subsequently, I will examine the complex role of technology in those events that are categorized as examples of 'road rage'.

Representing road rage

The media

Road rage has been a particularly potent term in Britain over the last 10 years or so. It signifies a number of comportments. From a brief survey of the media, the range of behaviours that are now subsumed under the term include: tailgating, headlight flashing, obscene gestures, obstruction, verbal abuse, running over offending drivers or pedestrians, smashing windscreens with various implements, poking in the eye, stabbing with screwdrivers and knives, punching, throttling, spraying with ammonia, threatening with guns, and even shooting. There are many examples of road rage reports in the press (as well as two dedicated TV documentaries) usually documenting individual incidents. A lone, none too lurid, example is:

> A driver needed hospital treatment after being sprayed with what was thought to be ammonia during a 'road rage' incident in Chiswick, west London.
> (*The Daily Telegraph*, 9 January 1996)

However, reports of individual cases of road rage vie with reports of the frequency and distribution of its incidence. Again, here is just one example:

> Almost three-quarters of drivers have been the victims of road rage, according to the 1996 annual Lex Report on Motoring. Aggressive behaviour, ranging from gestures and verbal abuse to physical attacks, is spoiling motoring for many people, says the report. During the past year, 1,800,000 have been

forced to pull over or off the road and 800,000 have been threatened. Some 500,000 people have had their cars deliberately driven into, and 250,000 have been attacked by other drivers. Another 250,000 have had their cars attacked by another driver. . . .

The things which upset drivers most were identified as cruising in the middle lane (60 per cent) and outside lane (55 per cent) on motorways, inside lane overtakers (50 per cent), and speeding in towns and cities (45 per cent) . . .

(*The Daily Telegraph*, 24 January 1996)

A great number of explanations for road rage have been put forward by commentators. Some of these are 'folk theories' or ethnopsychologies; others derive from 'expert discourse' (needless to say, the boundaries between these two forms of explanation are not impermeable). Moreover, we see here not only the way that the term 'road rage' is used to categorize certain events, but how the cumulation of such events serves in the substantiation of that category. In general, these media accounts point to a combination of explanatory factors. Often these are indiscriminately listed – there's a sort of 'morassification' of discourses in which explanations are juxtaposed arithmetically, irrespective of any formal or intellectual contradiction. A short list could include: stress, territoriality, vengeance, the provocatively animalistic quality of car headlights, the primitiveness of human nervous systems and the reflex aggression triggered by overcrowding. Almost invariably, these explanations focus upon the 'nature of the driver'. This is not to say that the car is ignored: it too plays a part – say as a cocoon that makes drivers feel 'empowered'. Further, very occasionally, road rage is placed in the context of cultural changes such at the rise of the Thatcherite ethos of assertiveness or the psychotherapeutic injunction 'not to bottle it up'.

These abstractions from a large corpus of reports are fairly representative insofar as they reflect the explanations that appear over and over again. This is, in part, because the sources of these explanations are limited. In addition to various experts (mostly psychologists), it is the driving organizations – the Automobile Association (AA) and the Royal Automobile Club (RAC) – which provide much of the copy. Given the longstanding centrality of these organizations in advising UK government policy (cf. O'Connell, 1998), I will consider a number of key documents that they have produced in order to examine the sorts of explanations they have generated for the phenomenon of road rage. More precisely, I will address how, in their different ways, they have gone about reifying road rage, and how, in the process, they have attempted to normalize offenders and potential offenders.

RAC

The RAC has targeted road rage as a policy and campaign issue. Thus, in one policy document ('Road Rage', undated), we read the following: 'A recent survey suggests that as many as 90% of motorists may at some time have been the victim of seriously anti-social behaviour on the part of other motorists . . .' ('Road Rage',

p. 1). Now, the RAC is clearly aware that in addressing the issue of road rage it might be seen as alarmist; nevertheless, it is keen to establish the reality of road rage. As we saw in the RAC's definition of road rage at the beginning of this chapter, dehumanization is a key motif. However, it is a particular form of dehumanization that the RAC is concerned with, one that tends toward the super-human. A quotation from RAC psychologist Conrad King makes this clear: 'At the root of it all . . . is the "dehumanisation" process that occurs inside a car. "This is caused by road-use frustrations and an artificial sense of insulation, protection and empowerment provided by the car," he says. In other words, when you're behind the wheel, you're God' (*The Sunday Times*, 25 June 1995).

The RAC is not averse to categorizing the sort of person who displays road rage. Two groups are identified. The first, unlikely to respond to advice, is that group comprising individuals who are 'aggressive, impatient or inconsiderate in every-thing they do' ('Road Rage', p. 2). In contrast, the second group is more common, made up of 'normally calm individuals who react badly to the frustration, exasperation or anxiety caused by their lateness, unexpected or unexplained congestion, or the aggressive behaviours of other road users' ('Road Rage', p. 2). These individuals may be amenable to advice.

The response of the RAC to this state of affairs is threefold: to conduct research so as to quantify the 'scope and scale of the problem' ('Road Rage', p. 3); to launch campaigns designed to raise public awareness of the benefits of courteous driving; and rehabilitation courses to be attended by those convicted of dangerous driving that is classed as an instance of road rage (successful attendance could earn the driver a reduced period of disqualification).

The latter response has also featured in a press release (dated 19 April 1995) 'RAC Call for Road Rage Counselling'. In this release, it was mentioned that Conservative MP Cheryl Gillan announced a rehabilitation proposal in the House of Commons: 'To counter this violent trend [of road rage] the RAC is proposing that rehabilitation programmes, similar to those for drink drive offenders, should be introduced as one of the sentencing options available to the courts'. This would take the form of 'rage counselling' as the release goes on to state.

Importantly, it is humans who are the focus of change here: the focus is resolutely upon the human who must be 'civilized', in Elias' terms (see below). For the RAC, this mostly takes the form of rehumanizing them through therapy. The road rage offender must be helped by the expert. As Conrad King was reported as saying: 'I will help motorists to understand their frustrations on the roads by encouraging them to express their emotions on the couch, not in the car' (*The Daily Telegraph*, 20 December 1995). To this end, the RAC, as well as others, has organized psychotherapy and stress management sessions for drivers at a number of motorway service stations.

AA

The Automobile Association (henceforth AA) is also keenly aware of the issue of road rage. Road rage has featured in the AA's report on *Fatigue and Stress in*

Driving (1994), as well as in other documents aimed at AA members or directed at company fleet drivers and managers. Here, I will concentrate on one particular unpublished policy document – 'Road Rage' (Matthew Joint, AA, March 1995).

For the AA, '[i]n its broadest sense (road rage) can refer to any display of aggression by a driver. However, it is a term often used to refer to the more extreme acts of aggression, such as physical assault, that occur as a direct result of disagreement between drivers' ('Road Rage', 1995, p. 1). The AA has attempted to quantify the problem by commissioning a survey (of 526 motorists – carried out in January 1995). Statistics are provided that tell us what are the most common forms of road rage behaviours (tailgating, headlight flashing, obscene gestures), what percentage have been victimized (62%), and lost their tempers behind the wheel (60%), and that gender differences in aggressive driving were not as great as expected (64% men; 54% women).

In contrast to the humanistic psychology of the RAC's 'dehumanization' thesis, the AA takes a more behaviourist perspective. Accordingly, we have the following analytic schema. Road rage is seen to draw upon the frustrations of everyday life. Thus, 'a poor manoeuvre by another driver may be enough to trigger a release of pent-up frustration which is directed towards the offending driver' (Joint, 1995, p. 2). An additional background factor, over and above congestion, is territoriality: 'Human beings are territorial. As individuals we have personal space, or territory, which evolved essentially as a defence mechanism – anyone who invades this territory is potentially an aggressor and the time it takes the aggressor to cross this territory enables the defender to prepare to fend off or avoid attack . . . The car is an extension of this territory . . . If a vehicle threatens our territory by cutting in, for example, the driver will probably carry out a defensive manoeuvre. This may be backed up by an attempt to re-establish territory . . .' (Joint, 1995, pp. 2–3).

The report also suggests ways in which to avoid succumbing to road rage or becoming a victim. As regards the former, it is important to avoid stress and fatigue, and not to assume that apparently aggressive acts are intended (one could always interpret these actions as 'stupid' or 'mistakes'). To avoid becoming a victim, one must not react to aggressors: avoid eye-contact, which is often seen as confrontational, do not manoeuvre suddenly, drive to a busy place to get help, do not be tempted to 'have a go'.

The AA's suggestions for remedying road rage are likewise behaviourist (i.e. a form of behaviour modification). People must change their behaviours and perceptions and the AA provides a series of behavioural injunctions: avoid eye-contact, be calm, be forgiving, do this, do not do that. The reward is safety and security; the punishment is physical threat and harm.

In sum, for the RAC, road rage requires help from a specialist – a process of rehumanization through the recounting of experience and expression of emotion. For the AA, road rage is the displacement of stresses and strains through the exercise of animalistic territoriality. If the RAC addresses the tendency to hubris – our willingness to play God born of the illusory omnipotence afforded by the car, the AA points to our basic animalistic nature of territoriality now associated with the car. For the RAC, the word of the Lord, and, thereby the wrath of God, must be modulated; for the AA, the behaviour of the beast must be modified. In both cases, the issue is individualized: change the person. And this change takes the form of re-establishing and reinforcing offenders' 'normal' human agency, which has been so disastrously transformed within the car. Practise your agency in order to protect your agency is the injection that both the RAC and the AA tacitly invoke here: learn to avoid eye-contact in order to stay in control; learn to relax in order to stay in control. The decision to learn these lessons reflects the practice of agency in order to keep hold of, to keep incorruptible and to sustain, the practice of agency.

Here, we seem to have a good example of the operation of the 'psy disciplines' (psychology, psychiatry, psychotherapy, psychoanalysis) as portrayed by Rose (1996). For Rose, psy disciplines are 'intellectual technologies' that serve to render 'visible and intelligible certain features of persons, their conducts, and their relations with one another' (Rose, 1996, p. 10). But psy is also intrinsically tied to a range of accredited professionals and acknowledged techniques that administer persons and rationally manage human resources. Now, while psy disciplines feature heavily in the administration, management, visibilization and so on of a variety of fields, such as the military, education and the family, Rose claims something more. Psy disciplines, by virtue of their claim to access, map and shape the 'interiority' that putatively underpins human conduct, are inextricably interwoven with all those 'more or less rationalised programs, strategies, and tactics . . . for acting upon the actions of others, in order to achieve certain ends' (Rose, 1996, p. 12) – that is, 'governmentality' in Foucault's sense. In 'resourcing' Western liberal governments, psy disciplines have been partly comprised of the invention of 'technologies for governing individuals in terms of their freedom' (Rose, 1996, p. 16). As such, psy disciplines have also contributed to the technical means by which persons are governed through, rather than in spite of, for example, their autonomy and enterprise: the forms of 'subjectification' that recent government has entailed – forms that stress freedom of choice, authenticity, enterprise and so on – are shown to be linked with psy techniques that focus on the enhancements of self-esteem, social skills, empowerment. So, on this reading, what we have here in the case of road rage is the operation of (Foucauldian) government – that is, 'governmentality'.

However, this subjectification and governmentality also operate to 'accomplish' something else – namely, the 'invisibilization' of technology: it is the human that is the site of this momentarily fragile agency. The complex role of the car is largely ignored.

In order to allot a role to the car, I need to make a brief diversion through some social constructionist accounts of emotion.

The social construction of emotions

For the AA and the RAC, it would seem that certain external factors enter into a particular context and 'trigger' those behaviours we have come to know as road rage. For the RAC, the context is one of cocooned over-empowerment, for the

AA the context is one of territoriality. A factor such as another motorist's apparently aggressive driving sets off retaliatory actions. There, then, is a pre-set, natural human condition that is contravened in one way or another, leading to reflex responses. The formal qualities of these causal explanations bear a marked resemblance to the traditional, commonsensical naturalistic accounts where an emotion is a natural response caused by an external triggering event (for variations on this motif, see Edwards, 1996).

Warner (1986) argues against this orthodox causal view of emotion, in general, and of anger, in particular. For Warner, anger is not the product or effect of an external cause: 'the angry person believes she is being caused to be angry . . . she believes herself to be responding to a threat provided wholly independently of her will' (Warner, 1986, p. 137). In contrast to this conventional view, Warner provides an agential rendering of anger in which the angry person is responsible for her anger. This is allied to the doctrine of self-deception, which 'implies that the angry individual is not simply wrong about what, beyond her control, is responsible for her anger, but about whether *anything* beyond her control is responsible for it' (Warner, 1986, p. 139, emphasis in the original). The main lesson to be drawn from Warner's complex account is that the warranted 'cause' for an emotion, in this case, road rage is, in principle, a 'choice' (i.e. agential) and this is denied (self-deception).

In some ways, this is something that motoring organizations have grasped in that they argue that typical causal triggers of road rage offered by its practitioners – namely, others' ostensibly aggressive or offensive driving on the roads – is not 'pure' in its causality. Interpretative work has to be done to render such 'aggravating' action as just that: it has to be interpreted as malicious, unjust, aggressive and so on. The AA and RAC have themselves noted that these 'provocations' could easily be dismissed as the behaviour of idiots or simple, routine driver mistakes. As we have seen, their remedies entail, in large measure, a process of reinterpreting these provocations, which, in turn, entails a recapturing of one's own agency.

However, while these remedies focus on the individual, most social constructionists would, as I see it, say that what is actually being proposed is a reworking of the *social conventions* that characterize interactions on the road. This is because constructionist accounts 'view emotions as primarily dependent upon the definitions of situations, emotions vocabularies, and emotional beliefs, which vary across time and location' (Thoits, 1989, p. 319). Thus, subjective experiences 'are influenced not only by a society's emotion vocabulary, but by cultural beliefs about emotions . . . rules regarding what one should or should not feel or express; ideologies about emotions such as romantic love; shared understandings of the typical onsets, sequences and outcomes of emotional experiences and interactions . . . and beliefs about which emotions can and cannot be successfully controlled' (Thoits, 1989, p. 322). These are 'ethnopsychologies' or 'emotion cultures'. As other authors have noted, this background of shared assumptions serves as the medium by which displays of emotion, and emotional talk and behaviour, are warranted in situated interaction. For example, Sarbin (1986), in advocating an interactional imagery for the exploration of emotions, contrasts this with the traditional psychological, physiological or phenomenological approaches that regard emotion not as occurring 'in social life or drama, but in happening inside the individual' (Sarbin, 1986, p. 85). In Sarbin's dramaturgical analysis, one needs to uncover the dramatic resources available for emotional conduct. Thus, '[T]he logic of anger . . . is reflected in its plot structure described by Solomon as Courtroom or Olympian mythology; oneself as legislator and judge; the other as defendant. Oneself as the defender of values, the other as offender . . .' (Sarbin, 1986, p. 92).

Another more ethnomethodological approach to emotions is presented in the work of Coulter (1986). For Coulter, we should treat 'self-reports like "I feel angry" as circumstantially justified or unjustified *expressions* of anger, instead of as descriptions of internal events or states, the "something" that may be present or absent is nothing hidden in the chamber of the mind or body, but is some justifying or entitling [set of] circumstance[s]' (Coulter, 1986, p. 122, emphasis in the original). Thus, '(N)ot only do emotions characteristically have meaningful objects or situations as their occasions, but such objects and situations *make emotions intelligibly present*' (Coulter, 1986, p. 123, emphasis in the original). As such, common ground is needed to make emotions intelligible: '[T]ypes of situation are paradigmatically linked to the emotions they afford by *convention*. The link is . . . sociocultural . . . in a broad sense moral; a person may be found morally deficient not to be . . . angry at a miscarriage of justice – given, that is, that he [*sic*] concurs in the relevant description of the situation' (Coulter, 1986, p. 127, emphasis in the original).

Now, these constructionist accounts of emotion are slightly too functionalist. This is because notions such as convention and warranting are implicitly functional – there are agreed sociocultural conditions, deviations from which have to be explained, legitimated and so on, thereby reproducing those very conditions. What is happening where there are emotional acts that are deviant with respect to one convention, but consonant with another?

Thoits (1990, p. 181) addresses the issue of emotional deviance, which she defines as 'experiences or displays of affect that differ in quality or degree from what is expected in given situations'. She suggests that there are four structural conditions 'under which self-perceived emotional deviance might be reported more frequently' (Thoits, 1990, p. 188). The most important for the present purposes is multiple role occupancy: here, 'when a person holds multiple roles that have mutually contradictory feeling expectations, emotional deviancy might be reported' (Thoits, 1990, p. 188). In the case of road rage, as we shall see, we find different roles or, better still, scripts, that are ambiguously, or even contradictorily, related to one another. In other words, the conventions that structure a situation are not always clear-cut; they can be multiple and disparate.

Moreover, we should not see this ambiguity as an aspect of exclusively inter-subjective situations. As has been argued in some of the more recent perspectives on emotion, the emphasis upon the social or the cultural in social constructionism is not unproblematic. What also needs to be taken into account is the embodiment of the feeling subject, an embodiment that should be theorized through an, albeit contingent, biology (Lyon, 1998), and which can accommodate inter-corporeal relations, as well as social ones (not that the two are ever distinct). As Williams puts it: 'emotions . . . are *emergent* properties, located at the intersection of physiological dispositions, material circumstances, and socio-cultural elaboration' (Williams, 1998, p. 750, emphasis in the original; see also Williams and Bendelow, 1998a).

Inevitably, my interest tends toward the material, not least because this dimension has been neglected. Specifically, I explore how emotions come to be structured by the complex but mundane technology that is the car, tracing how, as a material and semiotic object, it contributes to emotion conventions *in their ambiguity*. Phrasing this in the terminology of ANT, we might put it thus: the 'order building' around which Akrich and Latour structure their redefinition of semiotics (see Chapter 2), taken in the context of a discussion about deviant emotions and ambiguity, becomes somewhat suspect. We do not have unitary orders projected by technologies, but multiple orders that sometimes operate in unison and sometimes conflict. As we shall see, this ambiguity reflects the contradictory scripts encoded into car technology: be good, be careful, be forgiving, against be fast, be efficient, be aggressive. However, before considering this tension, it behoves us to draw upon a classic treatment of the relation between emotion and technology.

Technology and emotions

In his ground-breaking work *The Civilizing Process*, Elias (1939/1994; also see Mennell, 1989) traces the trajectory of what he calls 'civilization'. Whereas, in Medieval–Feudal society, the restriction of behaviour was seen to be grounded in the need to be noble (without so much concern for the ways in which one's behaviour upset others), in Court Society, there is a heightened awareness of the way in which one is, so to speak, under scrutiny to conform to the dictates of *civilité*. This increased process of surveillance is mediated, amongst other means, by the many volumes offering advice on the proper way to behave (e.g. for the bourgeois hopeful of gaining entry to Court). Part of the process of civilization is also the introduction of new technologies – the fork and the serviette are examples in Elias' work. The use of the fork becomes a focus of social attention. However, its use has little to do with a desire for better hygiene. Rather, revulsion at its nonuse reflects new standards of conduct. As Elias states: 'Certain forms of behaviour are placed under prohibition, not because they are unhealthy but because they lead to an offensive sight and disagreeable associations; shame at offering such a spectacle, originally absent, and fear of arousing such associations are gradually spread from the standard setting circles by numerous authorities and institutions' (Elias, 1939/1994, p. 104). For Elias, this (self-)controlled use of the fork reflects a civilizing of emotions and comportments that were once more 'instinctual' or child-like. We do not, of course, need to buy into this developmental schema – children are also *constituted* as 'instinctual' (Aries, 1962). The point is that there has been a change in a particular 'civilizing' direction and the use of the fork contributes to this.

Elias' work is particularly important because it allows us to address the way that emotions and manners are interwoven with historical change and technological innovation. However, in this account, although the fork provides a terrain in which certain comportments may be judged, it is not itself instrumental in the structuring of those comportments.

By comparison, for ANT, as we have repeatedly noted, the comportment of humans is shaped by technologies. In the case of the car, these technologies reside both within and outside the car. In examining the shaping role of technology, Latour notes that technologies vary according to, on the one hand, their figurative-ness (degree of depiction of the human form) and, on the other, their humanness (whether humans are co-present with the technology). In illustration of these dimensions, Latour (1992) provides us with the example of the ways in which drivers are made to slow down:

> The distinction between humans and nonhumans, embodied and dis-embodied skills, impersonation or 'machination', are less interesting than the complete chain along which competences and actions are distributed. For instance, on the freeway the other day I slowed down because a guy in a yellow suit and red helmet was waving a flag. . . . I recognized [him] to be a machine. . . . We . . . could move much further in the direction of figuration . . . we could have added (why not?) a furious stare or a recognizable face like a mask of Mrs Thatcher or President Mitterrand. . . . But we could also have moved the other way, to a less figurative delegation: the flag by itself could have done the job. . . . And why a sign at all? Drivers, if they are circumspect, disciplined, and watchful will see for themselves that there is work in progress and will slow down. But there is another radical, nonfigurative solution: the road bumper, or speed trap. . . . It is impossible for us not to slow down, or else we break our suspension. Depending on where we stand along the chain of delegation, we get classic moral human beings endowed with self-respect and able to speak and obey laws, or we get stubborn and efficient machines and mechanisms; halfway through we get the usual power of signs and symbols.
>
> (Latour, 1992, pp. 243–244)

However, it is worth noting that these physical/technological impediments can also be re-interpreted as excellent aids to joyriding (Simmell, personal communication). There is an important point to be made here, one to which I shall return below: the phenomenon of joyriding reflects not only the gradation of figurative–non-figurative delegation, but also the crossover between the figurative and the non-figurative, the semiotic and the material. Suddenly, the bumper, instead of being a physical barrier, becomes a signifier of authority that must be subverted, a sign upon which a subculture focuses in the pursuit of forbidden physically wrought thrills.

To return to the technological shaping of comportment – this also obviously occurs within the car. Latour focuses on the functioning of the seat belt. First, he notes the process of delegation: 'The same incorporation from written injunction to body skills is at work with car manuals. No one, I guess, casts more than a cursory glance at the manual before starting the engine of an unfamiliar car. There is a large body of skills that we have so well embodied or incorporated that the mediations of the written instructions are useless. From extrasomatic, they have become intrasomatic. Incorporation in human, or "excorporation" in non-human, bodies is also one of the choices left to the designers' (Latour, 1992, p. 246). He then goes on to unpick some of the contradictions entailed in the excorporation to non-humans:

> The beauty of artifacts is that they take on themselves the contradictory wishes or needs of humans and nonhumans. My seat belt is supposed to strap me in firmly in case of accident and thus impose on me the respect of the advice DON'T CRASH THROUGH THE WINDSHIELD, which is itself the translation of the unreachable goal DON'T DRIVE TOO FAST into another less difficult (because it is more selfish) goal: IF YOU DRIVE TOO FAST, AT LEAST DON'T KILL YOURSELF.
>
> (Latour, 1992, p. 247)

However, the seat belt is also a contradictory mechanism: it must be both constraining and elastic, and it must both buckle quickly and unbuckle quickly. 'The safety engineers have to re-inscribe in the seat belt all these contradictory usages. They pay a price, of course: the mechanism is folded again, rendering it more complicated' (Latour, 1992, p. 247).

Clearly, chief amongst Latour's interests in this context is the way technology should be studied, especially how it is designed. But he is also interested in the way that this technology shapes human comportment and yet is also 'resisted'. He is thus addressing the question of how designers try to cope with this sort of subversion. Yet this reading of the designers' responses and innovations – this analysis of technologists' second-guessing of users' foibles – is a little too simple. Latour's model here seems to assume a series of discrete 'moves' in a sort of contest between designers and users: if users are likely to do 'something bad', designers design the technology such that that 'something bad' is negated or dealt with. Of course, this might lead to another 'something bad', which is in response to the new design, and so on. However, this 'contest' is structured by broader, culturally embedded 'rules' that reflect the complex, convoluted function-expressions of cars. In other words, the scripts (in Akrich's terms) that are incorporated into such technologies reflect a long, entrenched lineage that, we might say, forms part of the 'grammar' of car design. The 'grammaticality' of such scripts (which are, of course, both semiotic and material) does not mean, as we shall see in detail below, that they are consistent with one another. Indeed, these scripts, in being contradictory, serve in the reproduction of complex, even antithetical, and from some perspectives at least, 'subversive', modes of behaviour.

So, in contrast to Elias' perspective, ANT emphasizes the impact of technology itself upon human comportment (although, to reiterate, ANT's version of technology is social through and through). As we have seen, this impact can be resisted. However, in contrast to a view of resistance that comprises, as it were, the rational operationalization of a just cause, I want to look at those 'resistances' – in particular, road rage – that are routinely judged 'pathological' (of course, 'justifiable resistance' and 'pathology' have been known historically to be inter-changeable). To put it in ANT terms, I do not want to treat road rage as a process of de-inscription, that is, the subversive re-reading of the moral script embodied in a technology, or the motivated production of a counter-script. Rather, I want to treat road rage seriously in order to theorize those moments, say, when there is an 'inappropriate' emotional response which is partly, and perhaps obscurely, enscripted in the technology itself.

In sum, for Elias, technology mediates self-control: resistance and misuse implies 'loss of self-control', a volatility of emotions, a shift toward something like rage. The ANT account of the constitutive role of technological artefacts allows us to consider how resistance and de-inscription occur. Putting these together, we can ask: how does one approach analytically a situation where a technology enables uncivil emotions and comportments, despite the civil moral injunctions embodied in that technology, and irrespective of the marshalled discourses and the media of surveillance that ordinarily ensure the smooth, civil interactions and associations between humans and technology, and amongst humans?

Let me set out these issues in preliminary relation to the case of road rage. The complex sociotechnical system of car, roads, police, law, training schools and texts, driving organizations and so on are 'suddenly' faced with the phenomenon of road rage. The 'loss of control' ordinarily associated with road rage can be viewed as a counter-moment in the civilizing process (the increasingly microscopic insinua-tion of power-knowledge or panoptical surveillance signified, in this case, by technology). It is a form of subversion (in the sense of 'misuse') of the smooth functioning of a sociotechnical system. As I argued above, however, the subversive resistance associated with road rage is a misbehaviour, a decivilization that differs in type from the principled subversive resistance instanced in Akrich's (1992) example of the French Polynesians' 're-working' of photoelectric lighting kits. All this highlights an emotional component that is partly born of the promises made by the technology. As mentioned in Chapter 2, technologies entail not only scripts, but also promises. What, then, are the promises incorporated into, and signified by, cars that facilitate road rage?

Road rage and technology

Now, according to Elias, persons of the Feudal–Medieval period were altogether more volatile, swinging from intense gaiety to extreme rage. This volatility reflected the circumstances of the age: death was everywhere and the uncertainty of life chronic; there was no centralized monopoly of violence; populations were dispersed in feudal enclaves constantly at war with one another. In essence, life entailed 'an existence without security, with only minimal thought for the future. Whoever did not love or hate to the utmost in this society, whoever could not stand his [*sic*] ground in the play of passions, could go into a monastery; in worldly life he was just as lost as was, conversely, in later society, and particularly at court, the man who could not curb his passions, could not conceal and "civilize" his affects' (Elias, 1939/1994, p. 164). But with the rise of the state and its 'expopropriation of physical vengeance' (Spierenberg, 1984), and the increasing mutual dependence of people upon one another, there was a restructuring of the emotions, and specifically, a tempering of emotional volatility.

In light of this Eliasian scheme, it is strange to read the following statement by Allison and Curry (1996, p. 1):

> In our daily consumption of media, 'rage', 'outrage', 'enraged' increasingly appear in print or are splashed at us from our televisions and radios. Rage appears to define the daily existence of some groups in the United States; further, our own experience suggests that few individuals in our media-dominated culture fail to encounter en-, out-, or just plain rage each day . . . Rage seems to have gained a currency in the past decade which it previously did not possess.

However, the rise of this signifier is not a simple matter. As these authors go on to question: 'Has the experience of individuals in our society shifted so significantly that vastly more people experience rage? Or, have we simply hyperbolized such a term as "anger" . . .?' (Allison and Curry, 1996, p. 1). Other accounts are also possible, they suggest: perhaps 'rage' discourse reflects an increased willingness to discuss previously private emotions; perhaps we are suddenly sensitized to a rage that had always been present. Thus, they ask: is rage a real cultural phenomenon or a consumable catchword? Will it fade away or continue to express something profound?

In relation to the civilizing process, we might generate the following sorts of Eliasian speculations. Perhaps the expropriation of physical vengeance has been (temporarily) halted or reversed. Relatedly, perhaps the interdependence of groups has broken down and new social enclaves have arisen. In both these cases, the expression of rage becomes a genuine phenomenon. But then again, perhaps the media representation of rage of one sort or another is part of the spectating that is part of the equilibration of the economy of emotions – that is, such hyperbolizing is another twist to the civilizing process.

In any case, when it comes to road rage, we see that a complex series of issues is raised in light of the Eliasian perspective. On a socio-centric reading of Elias, rage and violence on the road might reflect a fragmentation of social interdependence and a reduction in the monopoly of violence by the state. However, we can also provide a heterogeneous rendering of Elias' work. In all this, technology clearly has the role of a mediator and shaper of social relations. For example, the expropriation of violence by the state entailed the technical paraphernalia of execution, punishment and torture. But these are not simple tools;

they actually serve in the structuring of this expropriation insofar as they facilitate, by virtue of their design, particular sorts of spectacles and rituals of physical vengeance. The rise of road rage can be partly read in light of this emphasis upon the contributory role of technology. The car can thus be said to enable (always in under-determined and contingent ways) the reappropriation of physical vengeance that is road rage. The car, as a heterogeneous technology, therefore 'acts': it is a mediator of 'regression', that is, of 'de-civilization'.

This formulation, however, lies somewhat uneasily with Elias' own later views. In his essay 'Technization and Civilization', Elias (1995) argues, without attributing any definitive or final causal status to either 'technization' or civilization, that there does seem to be a correlation between the cumulative acquisition of self-regulation (civilization) and the exploitation of 'lifeless materials to an increasingly greater extent for the use of humankind, by treating and processing them, in war and in peace, mostly in the expectation of a better life' (Elias, 1995, p. 7). This link expresses itself in various ways. In the case of the car, Mennell, commenting on Elias' paper, remarks:

> On the roads of modern society, the dangers from other people are very different [from those faced by members of the warrior society of Medieval times]. The danger of physical attack is – in spite of popular fears – objectively relatively low. But the flow of cars and pedestrians in all directions is very dense. There are road signs, traffic lights and police to control the traffic. This external control, however, is founded on the assumption that every individual is regulating his or her own behaviours exactly in accordance with the flow of traffic. Constant vigilance, foresight and self-control are needed, whether a person is driving or on foot.
>
> (Mennell, 1995, p. 2)

However, Elias is keenly aware that this link between technization and civilization is not secure: de-civilization also occurs with increasing technization. For example, the compression of time and space, and the increased contacts with others, that motor (and aeroplane) transport affords, does not necessarily yield a simple identification with these others. There can be a process of (re-)differentiation with attendant de-civilizing pressures. This version of de-civilization rests on a view that these technologies allow the possibility of new, potentially problematic, social relations that mediate de-civilization. In contrast, I would also want to stress that a technology like the car, by virtue of its particular semiotic (in the heterogeneous sense) heritage, itself enables such de-civilization. Thus, one can reframe Mennell's argument, which reflects this focus upon social relations, that '[e]ven greater danger, though, comes from the frustrations of traffic leading someone to lose control, vent his or her aggression on another driver, or in any way "do something stupid"' (Mennell, 1995, p. 2). Instead, it is possible to say that, in this loss of self-control, the car itself is instrumental. It is an actor that, embodying multiple scripts as it does, facilitates rage. In other words, what is missing in the Eliasian account is the role of the vehicle – its physical design and the latent scripts it incorporates – in de-civilization. That is to say, the car not only 'demands' self-regulation for its proper functioning, it also enables (materially and semiotically) certain 'deviant' emotions, certain 'mis-uses'. Thus, in its broad context, the car affords multiple comportments in both civilizing and de-civilizing directions.

What then are these scripts? We have already hinted above that these are multiple and contradictory, material and semiotic. In the next section, I will explore some of these.

Heterogeneous and distributed scripts

So far, I have not expended much effort in demonstrating the distributedness of the car. It is, of course, a part of a much wider sociotechnical system (cf. Urry, 1999). The rise of the motor vehicle is fundamental to changes in our social fabric and personal comportment, changes that were foreseen at the very birth of the car. Sachs (1984) notes that, even in the 1900s, commentators were beginning to articulate what he calls a 'traffic education discourse': 'Drivers have to be "qualified"; pedestrians should behave "correctly" and not "wrongly"; . . . one and all, in view of the new requirement for discipline are to be seen in need of training. Only in this way could an "order" be created on the public streets that would minimize the dangers of motorcars" (Sachs, 1984, p. 28). If there are changes to the behavioural environment, there are also changes to the physical and the domestic. Houses changed to accommodate cars – garages become a key architectural theme (Marsh and Collett, 1986). As Flink (1988) documents, with the 'automobilization' of America, there was, in the 1920s, a suburban housing boom (and a subsequent loss of tax revenue for city councils who still had to provide the services for non-driving commuters). Public transport systems degenerated and planning became shaped by the 'needs of the automobile' (Flink, 1988, p. 371). One could even point to seemingly more trivial physical changes such as the erection of speed signs. Thus, in pre-1970s Norway, traffic flow occupied regulators' minds and to this end the speeding driver was conceptualized as 'uneducated' in the rules of the road, but essentially rational. Therefore, as part of the education of the driver, '[w]e needed more traffic signs to show what was right, and we needed more education to learn about the rules' (Stenien, 1994, p. 277). After the 1970s, the emphasis shifted to a danger regime, and the speeding driver was criminalized – a container of bad attitudes – becoming the object of normalization and surveillance through automatic traffic control (speed cameras). These physical environments entail extended or distributed scripts that are intimately associated with the car. They structure forms of movement: for example, the lack of public transport in certain areas necessitates car ownership; the location of speed cameras is the subject of local knowledge that governs motorists' speeds. But there are also counter-knowledges, or 'de-scriptions', that arise. For example, people draw upon general knowledge about the economic constraints faced by police forces in the UK such as that they cannot afford to develop speed camera film; or they share folk knowledge that certain car number plate scripts are less prone to being legibly photographed by speed cameras.

These last examples hint at the complexity with which the car is folded into the cultural. Clearly, it is central in the signification of some forms of subcultural identity (Marsh and Collett, 1986; Rosengren, 1994; Lamvik, 1996). Furthermore, to state the obvious, the car has served simultaneously to shape, mediate and reflect broader cultural changes. For instance, it has featured as a motif in all manner of popular cultural idioms (cf. Bayley, 1986), functioning as a medium of prevailing gender differences (e.g. Hubak, 1996; O'Connell, 1998) and 'national character' (e.g. Hagman, 1994). Interestingly, road rage itself has served as a ground for interrogating national character in the UK. For example, there are a number of examples of comparisons with the conditions – conditions that reflect supposed national character – under which road rage styles of behaviour are manifested in other European countries (e.g. *The Sunday Times*, 25 June 1995). Even more broadly, the car has been intimately connected with the modernist commitment to technological progress and speed (Sachs, 1984, 1998; Virilio, 1977/1986, 1995; Millar and Schwarz, 1998). This general modernist desire for speed, when frustrated, finds expression in rages other than that of the road. Thus, for example, the following have been documented:

> Trolley rage: Often sparked by small children, slow unpackers and change-fumblers. Queue jumpers have felt the force of a fist. . . . Pavement rage: A US import, typified by aggressive comments and shoving. Phone rage: Brought on by answering machines, voice mail and inefficient receptionists. Golf rage: The latest rage has hit the sport of gentlemen. Caused by slow players who do not allow faster and more experienced ones to go on ahead.
>
> (*The Observer*, 15 October 1995)

The latest, at the time of writing (November 1999), is air rage, where travellers become enraged on aeroplanes.

The questions we must now ask include: how are these broader cultural dimensions expressed within the motor car? How do they interact with other semiotic and material characteristics of the car? Social psychologists Marsh and Collett (1986, p. 5) argue that '. . . the automobile satisfies not our practical needs but [also] the need to declare ourselves socially and individually'. However, they also go on to describe a corporeal dimension: 'The car provides us with a shield and a feeling of invulnerability, a shelter for all manner of activities' (Marsh and Collett, 1986, p. 11). Sachs (1984) can speak of corporeal verities too: 'The theme of gratification – "the protective shell against wrongs from without" – is by no means bound exclusively to confrontation with the forces of nature: in the car one can seal oneself from all kinds of stress. . . . My car is my castle' (Sachs, 1984, p. 131). But he also embeds this in a nuanced historical and cultural trajectory. This feeling of security within a car is an outcome of the bourgeois requirement for comfort transmogrified through the design of the car: 'the technical development of the automobile was also oriented on the tacit assumption that human beings are defined by their need to be sheltered and relieved of burdens. . . . Vehicles become the repository of their drivers' desires for comfort.

. . .' (Sachs, 1984, p. 131). But this need is contingent: '. . . when the supply of comfort has exceeded a certain limit, the probability rises that what once was welcomed as shelter comes to be experienced as a disabling prison . . . of understimulation' (Sachs, 1984, p. 135).

For Sachs (1984), the car serves as another medium in the modernist process of individualization. In contrast to public transport, constrained by its timetables, fixed routes, and its communality, the automobile gave free rein to the individual: 'As the "forwarding of people like bundles of goods" became a virtually inescapable fact of daily life, the automobile . . . came to be the focus of desires for individualization' (Sachs, 1984, p. 98). This was because '. . . the automobile is fit for marriage with an unfettered lifestyle, a desire that can be undermined only by the experience of one person's craving for freedom colliding with that of another, resulting in traffic jams everywhere' (Sachs, 1984, p. 99; see also Urry, 1999).

This freedom and individualization are connected with another key motif of the automobile – that of speed. In the earliest periods in automotive history, racing and speed were key signifiers: '. . . the drawing of pleasure and superiority in the role of the driver, by teasing the limits of both the automobile and one's fate, so that the world . . . flew by and an admiring glance looked after . . . the thrill of high-speed driving (became) established in the public's fantasies through the spectacle of car racing' (Sachs, 1984, p. 111; O'Connell, 1998). Speed has been designed into the car – levels of engine capacity, responsivity, safety and so on reflect this genealogy. However, speed, and competition, are also an integral part of the driving mentality:

> . . . the driver is truly in need of dynamism and strength, for only then can he [*sic*] win the manifold competitions of the street. . . . Because, by the nature of the thing all drivers want to proceed quickly for reasons of their own, traffic is oriented from the beginning toward conflict; the intentions of any one individual stand opposed to those of all the others, threatening constantly to collide. Drivers therefore see themselves, whether they want to or not, as pressed into rivalry, a competition. . . .
>
> (Sachs, 1984, p. 116)

The world of the driver is thus characterized by chronic competition, 'experienced as a series of small rebuffs and triumphs' (Sachs, 1984, p. 116). In the process, 'every hindrance becomes a personal attack and begs for retribution' (Sachs, 1984, p. 117).

In Sachs' account, then, aggressiveness is tied to a historically impressed desire for speed – it is when this 'promise' of the car is frustrated, hindered, that aggression takes hold. This desire for speed is something quintessentially modern: the race, the competition, as a modern form is all about the transcendence of limits, the achievement of records, the gaining of 'the highest marks in a struggle against centimetres, grams and seconds' (Sachs, 1984, p. 119). Prior to this mode of sporting accomplishment, which arose in the latter half of the nineteenth century, 'in early modern times [athletic activity] was a matter of perfectly executing required movements at a predetermined tempo . . . whereas in traditional disciplines of movement spatio-temporal harmonies were paramount and exercises were to be judged according to the "gracefulness of form" or "proper proportion"' (Sachs, 1984, pp. 119–120). Nowadays, it is a question of 'top perfomances viewed quantitatively' (Sachs, 1984, p. 120). This transformation reflected another modernist ideal: the belief in the future, in progress: 'The transformation drew its meaning from the faith that the future will always be superior to the past and that history strides forward in a straight line to ever greater accomplishments' (Sachs, 1984, p. 120).

In essence, Sachs' account holds that driver aggression is the upshot of a series of historically contingent factors that, at their most abstract, concern the modernist investment in a vision of the future, progress and speed. These are mediated through competitive sport and capture the popular imagination, coming to characterize the entrenched 'desires' of the driver and the 'nature' of his or her machine. Aggression flows from this structural necessity to compete, for the desire for unimpeded speed. These desires – manifested in both drivers and designers – are, we might say, 'entrenched'. This is a rather clumsy way of getting at the traces that actors carry over time. Perhaps a better way would be to talk, drawing on Muhlhausler and Harre's (1990) analysis of pronouns, of 'grammatization'. Networks entail the modes of comportment that they 'recommend', forms of translation that they incorporate, heterogeneous norms that they distribute: these can be said to comprise deeply embedded material-semiotic resources grammatized in language, behaviour (what Bourdieu would call 'habitus') and technology (Wise, 1997). As such, they structure the ways in which we routinely bring to bear a set of assumptions, proclivities and skills.

Rediscoursing road rage

I have tried to argue that the car is polysemic (in Akrich and Latour's (1992) heterogeneous sense of semiotic): in its historical and physical, its discursive and corporeal, its subjectifying and objectifying constitution, it furnishes conflicting scripts or orderings for the driver. In its multiple, heterogeneous and dispersed significations it encourages us to be careful, safe, considerate, but also to compete, to love speed, to exercise aggression. In its physical design – its cocooning effect – it relaxes us, it removes us from the stresses of everyday life, but it also makes us feel godlike, powerful, all too ready to exercise our territorial imperatives. In its responsiveness, the car enables us to comport ourselves with normative grace, but also to attain great speeds, to compete. It demands the most routine of emotions, and enables the most 'deviant', the most animalistic, the most hubristic of emotions. If such multiple scription can be represented as ambiguous, this ambiguity is not uniform or constant. Multiple scription or ordering can operate in different ways. In making these points, I echo the discourses on road rage of the driving organizations referred to above, but rather than place the emphasis on the driver, I stress the role of the technology in its material and semiotic historical specificity.

That these scripts are embodied in the car is apparent when we approach it counterfactually. John Adams (1995) suggests that if we were serious about reducing the possibility of road rage, or, more generally, dangerous driving, car design might render the car less safe, less big, less responsive, less fast, less accurate. Indeed, as Adams (1995) remarks, 'if all vehicles were to be fitted with long sharp spikes emerging from the centre of their steering wheels (or, if you prefer, high explosives set to detonate on impact), the disparities of vulnerability and lethality between cyclists and lorry drivers would be greatly reduced' (Adams, 1995, p. 155). In the light of the dramatic counter-script of the spike, the existing scripts embodied in the car come into sharper focus.

Now, let us consider two scripts that are furnished by the semiotic-material car. One script demands a careful, civilized comportment on the roads; it prescribes a careful deployment of embodied skills in order to control the machine. However, in the case of road rage, the reappropriation of physical vengeance, in the form of using the car to intimidate and punish offending drivers, suggests a de-civilization, and a reaction against the dispersed significations that proscribe 'misbehaviour'. There is a drawing upon another script that encodes aggression, competition and speed. One might say that there is a 'dys-scription' here: there is a contradiction between these scripts. At this point, I can tentatively formulate the following rule of method: ask not only how this or that technology furnishes an order (or, rather, enables an ordering), but also how it resources the abuse of that order (or, rather, disrupts that ordering).

The central point is that these scripts are part and parcel of the conventions that make road rage 'do-able'. As we have seen, the key to the doing of anger is the idea that one has been wronged. However, the action that is doing the 'wronging' has to be interpreted as such. It is always possible, in principle at least, to see such apparently aggressive or unreasonable driving actions as mistakes or foolishness. The perception of such actions as 'wronging' rests, I am suggesting, partly on these scripts, in particular those that mediate competition and speed.

However, things are more complicated. The driver is bound to contradictory scripts, which for convenience we can dub the 'safety' script and the 'speed' script. (A nice example of this ambiguity is a recent Volvo slogan: 'The Response of a Sports Car. The Responsibility of a Volvo', where Volvo connotes a safety-conscious, family-oriented marque (see also, Urry, 1999)). The driver-in-their-car is normally engaged in smooth, heterogeneous and ambivalent interactions with their car: there are complex communications between driver and car that follow the dual scripts we have just identified. This smoothness, this flow is disrupted by the intrusive actions of another driver: the cycles of communication within the car are, to draw on Serres again, 'parasitised'. In response to this interruption, there is a shift, a redress – and *sometimes* this takes the form of road rage. I say 'sometimes' because, as we might expect, the expression of road rage will reflect the specificities of *local* circumstances, as well as broader conditions (such as a tendency toward de-civilization or the re-appropriation of the means of vengeance, and the modernist predilection of speed and competition). These local specificities concern not only proximal traffic conditions, for example, but also the 'nature' of the cars that might be involved in the road rage incident. Different cars entail different scripts, or rather, differing balances of scripts. The relative potency of scripts thus varies from model to model. Some cars will be scripted for relatively more speed, some for relatively more safety. And this balance might well be reflected in the likelihood of road rage being expressed. Yet, of course, there is also the driver to take into account. Beyond the modern 'desire' for speed and lack of impediment, there are other predispositions to the performance of road rage that are present, ones that reflect, and mediate, professional, subcultural, gender, etc., positioning. (Although I cannot examine this issue here, I suspect that such predispositions to road rage are also expressed in the way that the very category of 'road rage' is used reflexively in the distribution of culpability, excuses and warrants.)

Now, all I have done in the foregoing is merely hint at the complexity of the relations between cars and drivers. In particular, through Akrich's notion of the script, I have nudged into greater alignment – 'hybridized' – the human and the technological, the semiotic and the material/corporeal. In fact, at the very most, I have begun to establish some grounds for thinking about the ways in which road rage might be seen as an instance of such hybridity (or, in my terms, of co(a)gency). That is to say, there is a hint in the foregoing that different co(a)gential combinations of particular humans and particular cars, within the broader (say, modernist, decivilizing) network of heterogeneous relations, are more prone to road rage than others. Here, we are beginning to address the question of how it might be possible to go about judging different co(a)gents. It is to this issue that I now turn.

Ranking road ragers

Let me begin by making a seemingly rather different point. In order to conduct the 'misbehaviour' (which is road rage) effectively, one actually needs to be more skilful, to push both body and machine into quantitatively greater alignment, than in the case where one is a responsible, civilized driver. That is to say, the control of the self-within-the-car is enhanced. In order to exercise 'loss of social control', one needs to practise greater technological control. We might put it like this: as one moves away from the local cultural conditions of good social conduct, one moves closer to the 'machinic' conditions of skilful technological conduct that enable such things as accuracy of tailgating, precision of obstruction, exactness of sudden braking, and so on.

One could say that there appear to be different levels of hybridity, that the degree of coupling of human and non-human varies quantitatively. As such, one might argue that, in the practice of road rage, there is a 'hyper-hybridization': the human is more lost or obscured or immersed in the technological and vice versa. The typical 'driver-in-their-car' is a 'normal' hybrid that goes unremarked upon insofar as it reproduces the sociotechnical order (from within which one renders judgement). In contrast, hyper-hybrids threaten this order. In relation to Latour's (1993a) 'modern constitution', these are virulent hybrids that, in their undesirability, must be purified. Or rather, they are purified before we even have the chance to interrogate their hybridity. In other words, the term 'hyper-hybrid' serves to point to the sorts of 'latent representations' that become the *virtual foci* for the process of purification, a process that is particularly aggravated, panicky even. (To reiterate, I do not want to reify the hyper-hybrid as a distinct species; hyper-hybrids are moments where the discursive separation of the human and non-human is noticeably more agitated.)

Thus, the normalizing discourses of the RAC and the AA, as we have seen, are all about recovering the human from this dangerous technological embroilment in order to make it responsible, to render it the figure of pathology and the locus of remedial intervention. The problematic human suffers from excess – too much hybridity is translated into too much rage (that is, too great a loss of agency). Another example is joyriding. Here, there is the de-civilization of joy, of too much pleasure. Once again, too much hybridity is translated into an excess of 'joy' (or criminal pleasure-seeking, more accurately) and the humans are the subject of correction, whether through punishment or through the more 'humane' schemes, such as car offender groups or motor projects (cf. Whitehouse, 1993). In contrast, an uncriminalized hyper-hybridization is racing-in-its-proper-context. In this case, the human figure is recovered not through the negative normalization strategies of 'pathologization' and so on, but through praise and 'heroization'. This last example illustrates that there are many ways in which the virtual hyper-hybrid serves as a moment of recovering the traditional dichotomies of the modernist constitution.

Therefore, in attempting to bring the naughty hybrid under control, it is the human that is to be corrected. If I were to formulate a second tentative rule of method, it would go something like this. Wherever there is discursive normalization always ask: 'what is the technology that enables "deviance" but which is rarely itself the object of "correction"?' Wherever there is a moral panic, pose this question: 'what is the hyper-hybrid that is the virtual focus of this moral agitation and whose "human aspect" is, in the process of this agitation, pathologized?'

Having made this suggestion, it is necessary to qualify it. It is not inevitable that it is the humans who are the objects of modification in these cases. There are technological adjustments that can be instituted. As Adams (1995) suggests, one could correct the technology, remove the scripts that enable such hyper-hybridity: make the car less safe, less big, less responsive, less fast, less accurate. In contrast to this 'simplification' of the technology, there are more complicated innovations that can be advanced. One example of this complicating technological fix is the potential installation in cars of computer-controlled sensors that calculate the appropriate speed for a given distance from the car ahead. Such sensors can automatically warn the driver, or, in more advanced systems, actually temper the speed of the car. The apotheosis of this is a technological systemic fix where the speeds of all the cars on a given stretch of roadway are remotely controlled.

In sum, I am not saying that the RAC and AA accounts are 'wrong': what they do is reflect and mediate the identification of a particular point of intervention, namely, the human. I have, by and large, simply stressed a contending point of intervention, namely, the technology. But turning the dichotomy on its head is not enough. For, as Latour (1993b, 1999b) has recommended, we need to see how a particularly distressing activity (in this present case, the exercise of road rage) is the outcome of the interaction between a human and a technology, that is, their exchange of properties which yields a new hybrid entity – a co(a)gent. We can now begin to consider such co(a)gents as a new point of intervention.

Once I raise this, however, I also have to ask 'What are the sorts of "conventions" under which co(a)gents operate in practising, warranting, understanding and explaining "road rage"?' In other words, can we talk of co(a)gential norms – rules that apply to co(a)gents – which enable or constrain the expression of road rage? This leads inexorably to the issue of how we re-invent the notion of 'rage' so that it applies not to humans but to co(a)gents. And this, in turn, directs us to a supplementary question concerning the ways we go about judging good and bad co(a)gents (although this also raises the issue of who or what is doing the judging – see the next chapter). Such judgements are not simple and, unsurprisingly, reflect underpinning (political) presuppositions about the basis upon which judgement is rendered. For example, witness John Whitelegg's (1997) criticisms of Latour's (1996a) *Aramis* on the grounds that it did not engage with the 'real issues' at the heart of the transport technology, namely (for Whitelegg), its role within an ethic of 'environmental sustainability'. The judicious sorting of good and bad co(a)gents in relation to road rage does not simply concern 'safety' or pathology or breaking the law, it can also reflect such parameters as 'contribution to sustainability'. On this sort of environmentalist moral and political terrain, 'road rage' and its expression in peculiar co(a)gents is, at best, tangential.

With this proviso in place, how might we go about differentiating good from bad co(a)gents in the case of road rage? Or, to put it another way, how might we engage in the normalization of co(a)gents? In raising such a project, I place myself firmly within what Callon and Law (1995) call the 'normal discourse', in which agency is not attributed to networks, interactions or fields, but to singularities. In contrast to Callon and Law's effort at working out what it means for both, when 'agency' and 'distributedness' are brought together, I am, from within 'normal discourse', trying to explore what it means to narrate and judge a deliberately constructed singularity – the car–person co(a)gent.

One way of getting a handle on these co(a)gents, of giving them some narrative substance so that we can better attend to them, is by 'objectifying' them. Naming is, as argued in Chapter 2, one way of 'making the unfamiliar familiar', of objectifying the car–human co(a)gent so that it moves from the realm of conception to that of perception. Two possible (and tentative) ways of deriving names are: conflation (collapsing the names of the separate actors, for example 'cason' out of 'car' and 'person'); and the production of anagrams ('car' and 'person' yield 'proscenar', for example). Let us, for the moment, stick with 'casons'.

We can set about the task of sorting casons by generating typologies of those predisposed to do 'good' or 'bad'. But we do not have to go about this sorting *de novo*. In some corners of popular culture there exist what we might call proto-typologies of such co(a)gents. For example, an Austin 1100 home page editorial (http://www.users.dircon.co.uk/~canstey/1100_ed5.htm – 18 August 1996) begins to do this. While stressing the role of marketing and design in road rage, the writer also assumes a particular sort of associated driver. So, in a contrary analysis, the modern car (e.g. 'Vauxhall Vomitra' (Vectra), 'Ford Mundano' (Mondeo) and 'Renault Mogadon' (Megane)) is a 'deeply unpleasant place to be' – full of cheap plastic and synthetic seating materials that 'assault every sensibility'. Moreover, the marketing, which emphasizes the open road, belies the reality of '12 mile motorway tailbacks', something with which modern cars are not designed to cope. It is different for classic cars such as the Austin 1100, of course. Their wooden and leather interiors allow the driver to luxuriate in comfort and style, to be always calm.

However, throughout this piece, the aforementioned modern cars are linked to a particular human character, 'Rupert Rep' – an archetypical sales*man* figure. While he is not fully fleshed out, he does carry certain connotations, best signalled in the view that when he is frustrated 'his total plonker index' rockets off the scale (where 'plonker' is British vernacular for a foolish, idiotic person). That he has a 'total plonker index' at all says something about this character and his relation to the car: he is always in a hurry, has a tendency toward aggression, and is superficial in that he is exercised deeply by the status that attaches to his car. Here, there is a hybrid waiting to be named: an auto*mo*bile and sales *rep*resentative that is an explosive mixture of inappropriate design and fantasy, and total plonker – the 'repmo'.

Implicit in the editorial's tacit characterization of what I have dubbed the 'repmo' is a nexus of relations between the repmo and the other casons that populate the highway. It is as if casons are being compared and ranked. At the top are those casons composed of civilized drivers and Austin 1100s (or similar vehicles). At the bottom is the repmo. However, I would hesitate to see this process of construction and judgement as a purely intellectual (or cultural) exercise. I would want to stress that these construals are practical matters. Recall Lynch's account of the ease with which motorists can summon insults (that is, perform milder forms of road rage) at another's 'inconsiderate' driving behaviour. We might suggest that these judgements address not simply the driver, but in the practical, culturally embedded process of driving, also involve assessments of the significations of the offending car. In other words, perhaps there are, in the context of the complex, heterogeneous scripts afforded by the car, judgements of co(a)gents that entail fine, nuanced distinctions between hot hatches, sports cars, family cars, classic cars and so on. Importantly, these distinctions are not set in stone: in the ongoing practical context of driving, such distinctions are also emergent, particular to the immediate circumstances. In sum, the implicit typologies I have imputed to the Austin 1100 home page editorial draw upon already existing stereotypes about cars and drivers that are combined to produce stereotypes (and thus judgements) about casons.

Concluding remarks: the judgement of co(a)gents

In this chapter, I have considered the link between emotions and technology. This has been a multifarious, heterogeneous link. Within it we find the embodiment of the driver-in-their-car, the complex and distributed cultural and material resources that structure car–driver and driver–driver relations. More generally, the argument has been put forward that when we think about the conventions that make emotions 'do-able' and warrantable, we also need to consider the contribution technology makes, especially insofar as it embodies cultural and material conditions, that is, meanings, in the heterogeneous sense of Akrich and Latour.

However, we have also gone on to consider how these relations are judged and reacted to. In the foregoing section, I suggested that we routinely engage in judgements of co(a)gents, specifically casons such as the repmo. Yet, who is this 'we'? It might seem, at first view, that this 'we' is comprised of pure humans who are once more the arbiters of good and bad.

But is this really the case, for are we who render judgement not co(a)gents too? Some of us are casons, others are bisons (bicycle-persons), others still putrasons (public transport-persons), and some are shifting combinations of any number of these (cf. Simmell, 1999). We humans can, instead, be conceptualized as the spokespersons of these co(a)gents. Here, the 'spoke-' dimension of representation is pivotal: it is in the domain of language that these judgements are enacted and warranted amongst casons, bisons and putrasons, and so on.

We need to sound a note of caution here. As Callon and Law (1995) note, 'To imagine that we can assimilate the Other [in this case, complex technologies, but the Other also includes the 'natural'] in any of its forms is hubris. Instead, . . . these Others will ignore us most of the time. Instead, they will continue, as they always have, to perform their specific forms of agency to one another' (Callon and Law, 1995, p. 504).

However, this ontological modesty seems to revert to an 'us' that is purely human, in which assimilation means something like 'expression in language'. However, perhaps it can be assumed that the 'us' that counterposes the 'Other' already incorporates it in the sense that 'we' are already heterogeneously constituted. This is a rather awkward way of saying that these others – these technologies – can, on occasion, use us as their intermediaries, their angels. More radically, as we shall see, it becomes possible that this 'we' emerges in the process by which co(a)gents interact with one another, or rather, transform themselves from one sort of co(a)gent into another. Suffice it to note at this point that it might be possible to think of 'judgement' as something that is not simply enacted by persons, but performed heterogeneously. In other words, I want to try to imagine a form of judgement conducted by co(a)gents upon co(a)gents, that is, a form of judgement practised by, and through, arrangements of heterogeneous entities. This is one of the issues that is taken up in the next chapter.

5 Disciplined and disciplining co(a)gents
The remote control and the couch potato

Introduction

It is not unknown for me to be completely engrossed in whatever programme is on the television, often irrespective of quality. I sit or lie on the sofa, remote control to hand and watch. I can watch for a long time. I can watch when I am clearly exhausted and should be asleep in my bed. I can watch when there are many far more pressing things to attend to. I can watch when the sun is beating down and there's a gentle cooling breeze blowing. Occasionally, by my side, or in my lap, there'll be a snack; more often, there'll be a drink. I sit and I watch and flip through the channels. Every so often I feel little pangs of guilt – I should be doing something productive, constructive. In sum, I suppose I am being a couch potato.

Sometimes, after I've been away for a time – anything from a few days to the briefest moment – I discover that the remote control is missing. It is easy enough to switch on the TV; to change channels is a matter of raising myself from the sofa and walking about two metres, pressing the button and returning. Yet frantically I search for the remote . . . I am usually too angry and frustrated to see that this is 'ridiculous'.

What are we to make of these episodes? As usual, many interlocking issues can be attached to these activities. Why do I do 'couch potato-ness'? Why do I feel guilt? What are the discourses that resource these negative feelings? But further, what is the relationship between body, agency and technology that the remote control mediates? What does this interaction with the remote control presuppose about my body and that of others? How is this mundane technological artefact implicated in the heterogeneous ordering that comprises 'television watching' and how are we to understand its routine disappearance? More precisely, if in the preceding chapter we have shown how co(a)gents can be discursively assessed in terms of their propinquity to road rage, can we think of the absenting of the remote control as a form of *heterogeneous* disciplining of the couch potato?

This chapter is thus concerned with exploring, through the figures of the remote control and the couch potato, the way that co(a)gents are scrutinized in discourse. But, over and above this, I aim to examine how this process of scrutiny, assessment and judgement might not simply be the prerogative of humans, but is conducted heterogeneously – by co(a)gents themselves.

The chapter begins with a consideration of the relations between bodies and technologies. In particular, I address the idea that there might be a general trend to disembody humans, to circumvent the body, to attach directly the wills of humans to what technologies have to offer. However, despite these attempts to bypass the body, I will suggest that the body returns in various guises. I elaborate on this with reference to the remote control – an artefact to which are delegated the functions of various body parts, or rather, a body part complex. I also show how this association is thoroughly constituted – pilloried and valorized – in discourse. Thus, the couch potato – made up minimally of human body and remote control – is discursively surveilled (put under surveillance in a Foucauldian sense) in a number of ways, which try to recover the body, that is, that strive to purify this co(a)gent. In contrast to these 'critical' discourses, there are others that celebrate this association and extol the virtues of being a couch potato. Finally, I will suggest that this 'policing' of the couch potato is not exclusive to humans. In exploring how the couch potato is 'policed' by other co(a)gents, I show how co(a)gents themselves 'disassemble' one another in unexpected ways.

Embodiment and disembodiment

No longer do sociologists complain about the lack of attention paid to the role of the body in social processes. There is a thriving intellectual industry examining the role of the body in a number of ways. Brian Turner (1994, 1996) identifies three areas where the body has been attended to in some detail: the body's symbolic significance as a metaphor for social relationships; as a necessary component in the analysis of gender, sex and sexuality; and in the context of the study of medical issues. However, as Turner notes, within these various enterprises, the body and embodiment remain 'illusive and ill-defined' (Turner, 1994, p. x). Turner provides the broad outlines of what a general sociological theory of the body would require: a complex account of the idea of embodiment which can incorporate the 'systematic ambiguity of the body as corporeality, sensibility and objectivity' (Turner, 1994, p. xi); a conceptualization of the social actor as embodied attached to an analysis of how the 'body image functions in social space' (Turner, 1994, p. xi); an understanding of embodiment as communal; a sense of the body as a thoroughly historical and cultural entity.

In the present context, this outline, highly suggestive as it is, strangely misses out on the relation between bodies, embodiment and technology. Or, rather, Turner does not explicitly mention the role of technology within the commonality of embodiment. This lack is thrown into relief when we recall Latour's (1992; also see Falk, 1995) account of the delegation of bodily movements to the door groom, and the door groom's part in the ordering of comportment. More importantly, if we accept Latour's broader point, namely that technology is fundamental in the mediation of human relations, the absence of technology seems odder still.

Latour's door groom example is primarily concerned with how an X (say, a hotel manager) delegates the bodily functions of a Y (say, a porter) to a technology. In this story, the will of the user of the door, which previously had to pass through the unreliable body of the porter, now bypasses that human body altogether and hinges instead upon the door groom. Here we see an instance of the interlocking of human bodies and technology. It would seem that this is a process of dis-embodiment: certain functions are lifted out of a particular body and invested in a particular technology. Furthermore, however, we might suggest that there is, within the Western tradition, a more general ethos of disembodiment. By this I mean to connote the ways in which various activities are concerned with removing the body, making it redundant, delegating its functions, wholesale or in parts, to other entities. There is a sort of bypassing of the body, attaching human wills to the world without the interventions, the mediations, of the suspect body. Virilio puts it thus: 'To expand, to dissolve, become weightless, burst, leave one's heavy body behind: our whole destiny could now be read in terms of escape, evasion' (Virilio, 1995, p. 80; see also George, 1998, whose equation of speed, ubiquity and power readily evokes the ethos of disembodiment). This can be supported anecdotally: in the Star Trek series, the move onto an advanced evolutionary plane seems always to entail the transcendence of materiality, let alone corporeality. Pure energy is a higher state of being. The idea of disembodiment is thus attached to a notion of progress. As such, it stands in contrast to Turner's (1992) treatment of 'disembodiment' in relation to anorexia nervosa. He writes: 'the anorexic avoids the shameful world of eating, while simultaneously achieving personal power and a sense of moral superiority through the emaciated body. Their attempt at disembodiment through negation becomes the symbol of their moral empower-ment. It is on this basis that we can connect the age-old practices of Western asceticism and saintship with the moral dilemma of Western affluence in a world of starving millions' (Turner, 1992, p. 221). In contrast to this view of dis-embodiment with its version of asceticism that buys into gendered consumerism (the slim body), I am interested in disembodiment as a mode of luxuriance, where will is attached to the world without the unruly mediations of the body. Of course, as I note, this process is gendered too.

However, this ethos of disembodiment seems always to be undermined by what we might call the 'return of the body'. In Latour's example, the body returns in the form of discriminated-against bodies (and the bodies of allies) that must negotiate the door groom (see Chapter 2). Morse (1994) notes that (masculinist) dreams of disembodiment that take the form of becoming a cyborg in the sense of downloading consciousness onto the net are suspect repudiations of the body insofar as these dreams never escape the body. Slater (1998) provides an account of the limits of disembodiment and need for authenticity, including the display of the body, in relation to Internet Relay Chat. The point is that this ethos of disembodiment always seems to come to depend upon the body in some guise or other.

Here are some additional examples. In contrast to Latour's door groom example where the will of one type of human actor is taken out of the body of another to be objectified in a particular technology, the following cases exemplify how one's own will is taken out of one's own body to be embodied in, and mediated by, a technology.

Recently it was announced that a remote control had been developed that could be activated by brain waves. In other words, the brain could act directly as a remote control. Brain waves are picked up, amplified and sent to 'a second box [that] picks up the remote signal or message, kicks in and turns on the device (that is, the device to be switched on "by" the brainwaves)' (see http://www.abc.net.au/btn/storyhtm/96061808.htm – 28 January 1998). Here, what we have is a direct bypassing of the body, even of the fingers that are still necessary for the standard TV remote control. But, of course, this is not quite the case, for the remote control device has to be configured to the body and vice versa. Contacts have to be technologically maintained, and the user's body must also be reconfigured in various ways – for example, how does hair gel or dandruff affect the flow of information between brain and receiver? In other words, at this stage of the innovation process, we are still able to invoke the body and its vagaries which will eventually need to be 'put right' if the technology is to 'work'. Eventually, the disciplining of the body, where we learn new regimes of scalp maintenance, will lead to its seeming 'disappearance'.

In another case of technological replacement of the whole body, we find that the body is 'discoursed away', allowing for the exercise of pure and brilliant will. Here we turn to the iconic figure of Stephen Hawking. Helene Mialet (1999) notes that he is totally dependent on a range of technologies and people to get through the day-to-day process of living. His body has, in large part, been replaced by a network which allows Stephen Hawking to function as the Lucasian Professor of Mathematics at Cambridge University. And yet, this network – body-regime as Rose (1996) calls it – disappears, according to Mialet. What we are encouraged to see by admirers and, on occasion, by Hawking himself, is not a body – whether that be the disabled or the distributed one – but a pure mind that is in unmediated contact with the cosmos. Here, his medically undisciplined, heterogeneously hyperdisciplined body is discoursed out of view. But, of course, it returns – it is present in the labour of Hawking's helpers, mediated in their obscured bodies that feed, clothe and clean Hawking. It is present in the form of those who put together and maintain the technologies without which there could not be the version of Hawking with which we are so familiar.

We can also consider how one's will, embodied in particular body parts, comes to be mediated by technology. The functions of body parts are most obviously delegated to technology. For example, the zip is a convenience because it saves on the complex and repetitive manipulation of fingers and thumbs that was once necessary to use hook and eye fastenings. These body-part routines could be removed with the invention, and eventual 'perfection', of a mechanism that fastened two separate pieces of material together as the zip does. That is, these movements are delegated to the zip. Of course, there are a number of conditions that need to hold for the zip to operate in this way. First, the zip must hold the material sections together until the need arises to separate them. As Friedel (1994) documents, the early versions of the zip certainly did not fulfil this criterion. But a zip can be seen to 'work' according to other criteria, say, those of 'convenience'. So, by 'lowering', or rather by changing, the expectations of users – trading 'convenience' (speed of fastening) for 'function' (security of fastening), the zip can be 'made to work'. Such a trade-off might entail new bodily practices where more caution is exercised in movement in order to ensure that the zip does not come undone. In the case of the modern, more or less secure, zipper, the shaping of our comportment is concerned with, for example, ensuring that surrounding material or proximal flesh does not get caught up in its teeth: we have developed new corporeal routines that serve the zip's function. In sum, if certain body parts and their movements were removed, consigned to the workings of a technology, other body parts and their movements have developed to ensure the workings of that technology.

Another, more risible, example. What joy no longer to have to switch lights on manually. What a load off the houseworker carrying washing into a room. This was one rather unconvincing reason given by a Honeywell engineer for a particular design feature incoporated into the Honeywell smart house prototype. For Berg (1995), a 'smart house' denotes 'the extensive application of information technology (IT) to the dwelling of the future' (Berg, 1995, p. 86). Honeywell's main reason for the installation of motion-detectors, which could switch lights on and off in accordance with people's movement through the house, concerned the attempt to increase energy efficiency.

> To try out the system in a natural situation [Honeywell] invited several people to the test (smart) house for dinner. As guests entered the dining room, the lights obligingly went on. But when everyone had settled around the table and all was still the room was suddenly plunged into darkness. The Honeywell engineers had to ask their guests to flap their arms to activate the lights again. On consideration, Honeywell now feel voice activation may have more potential, in combination with infrared remote control.
>
> (Berg, 1995, p. 78)

So, fine movements (instanced in the usual process of switching on a light), which were going to be rendered redundant with the new technology (which was operated by gross whole body motion), returned as the more or less skilled manipulations of vocal chords and arms, hands and fingers.

To reiterate, the purpose of this limited parade of examples is to illustrate the notions of 'dreams of disembodiment' and the 'return of the body'. But what I have done here is simply exemplify, yet again, one of Latour's (1993a) theses. What we see in this ethos of disembodiment is the proliferation of hybrids: humans and technologies are mixed together in new, more convoluted and extensive, configurations. The 'return of the body' merely evokes the way that these hybrids 'work' – to function as designed – a whole range of other factors have to be in place, including the re-configuration of one's own or others' bodies or body parts. Their 'inventors' have announced the arrival of such co(a)gents as the 'smart-houseworker' or the 'brainwavechannelchanger' a little prematurely: we can still detect those compliances that bodies and body parts will need to follow in order for these co(a)gents to become operational.

As we have seen in the preceding chapter, people do, on occasion, judge these co(a)gents: certain casons are regarded as more predisposed to road rage than others. In the following section, I will consider in some detail disembodiment in relation to the TV remote control, in the process documenting the various ways in which the body returns. Furthermore, I will show how one co(a)gent that is produced by the association between human and remote control can be, as mentioned in Chapter 2, named, objectified, rendered present and evaluated. Sometimes there are complaints that it is a dangerous entity; sometimes that its full potential has yet to be realized. The point is that there are numerous discourses and practices out of which this co(a)gent emerges, sometimes stabilized, sometimes destabilized. However, as we shall also go on to consider, this 'judgement' might also be reconceptualized as a heterogeneous and distributed process where one co(a)gent constructs, or deconstructs, another.

The television remote control

'Remote control' is a very broad term that essentially describes the control of a device at a distance, where cause and effect are separated. Important here is the medium of communication between the control device and the reactive device (or receiver). There are numerous types of media. Sometimes these are physical connections – wires or cables – through which tones, for example, can be trans- mitted (as through telephone wires). Other times electromagnetic waves are used – infrared, for example. Infrared signals only work over relatively short (about 10 m) line-of-sight distances, especially as these signals are highly sensitive to atmospheric conditions that increase absorption and/or scattering of the signals. In contrast, radio signals have the advantage of working through walls and radio frequency remotes typically have a range of 38 to 61 m (see http://hometeam. com/lighting/remotes.htm – 21 January 1998).

The remotes with which most of us are familiar usually control the television and/or the video, and the hi-fi. In June 1996, the TV remote control was 40 years old. First introduced by Zenith as the Space Command Remote TV Control, it was marketed under the slogan: 'Nothing between you and the set but space!' The Space Command was a replacement for an earlier version that was connected to the television by a wire (the Lazy Bones model – *The Daily Telegraph*, 25 June 1996). According to Zenith itself, the first remote was the 1955 Flashmatic which shone highly focused light beams at four receivers situated around the screen. Unfortunately, viewers often could not remember which receiver did what, and, moreover, sunlight could change channels. In 1956, Zenith started production on a remote control that used high frequency sound – this, the Space Command, was the first practical wireless remote. The most common TV remote controls now use infrared light. The remote control device flashes a rapid series of signals (like Morse code), each signal code designed for a particular function. The signals are determined by a microprocessor in the remote control, and are translated into infrared flashes produced by a diode located at the front of the remote. These different signals, repeated five times a second to ensure the receiver in the TV has read them, serve numerous functions, such as changing channel, colour, volume, operating the VCR and so on (http://www.zenith.com/main/about/howremot. html – 28 January 1998).

Of course, the development of the remote control has not stood still. So, for instance, combined controls are coming onto the market. For example, US Electronics (self-proclaimed as the world's largest independent manufacturer and distributor of cable television remote controls) has marketed a four-function remote that offers 'complete control over your cable box, TV, VCR and either a Digital Music terminal, or a second cable box, TV or VCR' (http://www. shopnetmal.com/use/use – 28 January 1998). More radically, Zenith has noted that many controls have become overcomplicated and have developed a Z-Trak, a PC mouse-like device that uses a track-ball controlled cursor to bring up various function menus on the TV screen (http://www.zenith.com/main/about/ howremot.html – 28 January 1998).

Now, in terms of the Latourian model of the relation between human and technology, the standard remote control can be regarded as the technology to which the functions of certain body parts are delegated. The body parts are the legs, the back, the arms – all those that together operate in moving the fingers from the sofa to the television. The remote control is, in such an account, the functional equivalent of this body-part complex. The potentially unreliable body parts, which would otherwise have to be disciplined, surveilled, are replaced by a machine that does their work for them more reliably, more efficiently. Of course, as noted in Chapter 2, and further exemplified below, the notions of reliability and efficiency are themselves contextual, resting, at the very least, on a conception of the viewer as someone 'interested' in minimizing the energy expended on switching channels, controlling volume, and so on, in the process of television watching.

However, as argued in Chapters 1 and 2, we must be wary of conceptualizing technology as a medium that fulfils (and shapes) practical ends alone. To reiterate, the remote control, and indeed all technologies, serve expressive as well as functional ends – function-expressions. We should talk of the 'function-expressions' of technology. As Morley (1995) discusses, the television-as-furniture is not only the medium that practically delivers programmes, it also serves symbolic functions (including memorial ones – Radley, 1990): the sort of television it is or where it is placed in the home, how, indeed, it affects the architecture of the home – these signify the sort of person one is, the type of family one belongs to.

The function-expression of the remote control is intimately associated with the domestic context of its use. An American telephone survey completed in August 1994 by Opinion Research Corporation of Princeton New Jersey (of 1,013 adults comprising 508 men and 505 women aged 18 and over) found that personal control of the remote control was a major issue in American households: 62% of men said they were most likely to handle the remote control in their households, while only 37% of women said they were. Moreover, there was an etiquette associated with the use of the remote control: 62% found it rude when the person controlling the remote constantly channel surfed; 52% found it rude when the wielder of the remote control refused to take requests (http://www.empire.net/~psl/Fun_People/1994AWM.html – 27 October 1997).

A more detailed account can be found in Morley (1992) who, rather than seeing such dynamics as a matter of etiquette, analyses them in terms of relations of power. He documents the role of the remote control in the conflict over television viewing choices. Amongst his participants, it was the 'man of the house' who, when present, had monopoly of the remote control. Moreover, some of the women complained that the husband used the device 'obsessively, channel flicking across programmes when their wives were trying to watch something else' (Morley, 1992, p. 147). The remote tended to sit on the arm of the father's chair, and was used almost exclusively by him. As Morley puts it, the remote control 'is a highly visible symbol of condensed power relations' (Morley, 1992, p. 147). Of course, there are exceptions to this model of use. But, importantly, this view of the remote control is in danger of missing out on the functionality of the remote control. It is not just a symbol, but because of the sorts of actions it enables, it serves as a mediator and shaper of such family relations of power.

With the mention of channel surfing (or hopping), we can also address how the ease of access to multiple, fractured, fragmented images structures (post)modern consciousness. Consequently, the remote control serves as one technological tool (out of very many) through which we are exposed to a disorderly parade of signs. Our selves might become 'saturated': as Gergen has phrased it, 'a multiphrenic condition . . . in which one swims in ever-shifting concatenating and contentious currents of being' (Gergen, 1991, pp. 79–80). However, this can also be viewed as a consumption of signs that refer only one to another, with no especial connection to referents – reals – beyond (e.g. Baudrillard, 1983). Our attention span diminishes, what we become used to, what we desire, is the flow of signs – the surface, the spectacle of their rapid procession is what pleasures us. A note of caution needs to be sounded here. This postmodern viewer is by no means a given: it is a disputed entity, especially when one takes into account Abercrombie's (1996) analysis of the contrast between postmodern 'inattentive regimes of watching and [the] tendency to "zipping and zapping"' and the continuing audience preferences for 'traditional genres [of] soap opera and action-adventure, for example' (Abercrombie, 1996, p. 206).

Be that as it may, we can still suggest that the 'man of the house', through the very monopoly of the remote control's channel hopping facility, comes to reproduce the relations of power within the family. That is to say, in order to enjoy this luxuriant consumption of fragmented signs, there needs to be in place a set of social, political, economic and cultural circumstances that enable such consumption. Thus, if there is something like a saturated self, this coexists with another social self that is endowed with 'capacity' to become saturated: the identity of the postmodern is couched within the practices and privileges of an indulgent consumer (e.g. Lury, 1996) sustained in a network of relations of power.

These complex function-expressions, bound up as they are in the relations of power that are exercised within the household, are facilitated (though certainly not determined) by the physical possibilities enabled by the remote control. Its ability to translate the inconvenient, complex manoeuvres necessitated by old-fashioned channel switching into the simple movements of a few fingers is a partial condition of possibility for the function-expressions outlined above. However, it should also be noted that these uses of the remote control are only possible if an array of supplementary circumstances hold good. Most basically, we might say, is the requirement that fingers are dextrous, not too large or shaky or immobile. Further, the remote control must assume and ensure that it is used in an appropriate way in relation to the television – it must give certain clues that enable functional use (by whatever sort of user). Overspecification on remote controls has led to the design of a new generation with a much simplified button layout (e.g. large, colour-coded buttons). However, there is also, occasionally, under-specification. For example, Donald Norman (1988), from a cognitive science design perspective, has picked out some of the things that can go wrong with these technologies by virtue of bad design. A colleague of Norman's had a new CD player with a remote control, the latter having a little metal loop protruding from one end. The friend assumed this loop was an antenna for the remote and always aimed it at the CD player. The remote didn't seem to work well, and he could only operate the player by standing within a few feet. Later, the colleague discovered that the hook was just that, a hook, for hanging up the device. He had been pointing the remote control at his own body; when turned around, the control worked as expected. Norman's point is that the hook acted in terms of 'natural mapping' for function, but it was the wrong function. This particular remote had no other clues about which end the transmitter mechanism was situated, so he assumed it was the hook end. Now, we don't have to resort to notions of 'natural mapping' to make the simple point that, in certain contexts, particular design features militate against the proper, or enable the improper, use of the mechanism. (After all, presumably others could equate a loop with a hooking mechanism, or have extensive enough experience with remote controls to know that the lack of external, visible signs of the transmitter mechanism is the norm).

In sum, for proper functioning of the remote control, there needs to be in place a certain bodily comportment which, ideally (though not always successfully, as we have seen), is invoked by the remote control (design). However, the body is also socially distributed, and for the remote to 'function' it also requires a certain social configuration. Consquently, the domestic relations of power mentioned above need to be in place for the remote to 'work'. This simple statement implies that there is a multiplicity of cultural resources through which the 'working remote control' is constituted. If the members of a family physically fight over the control of the remote control, can it be said to 'work'? Conversely, if the 'man of the house' monopolizes the remote control, it might 'work' for him, but does it 'work' for the other members of the family? In other words, the 'workingness' of this technology rests on relations of power between a number of (potential) users-in-interaction. This point can be recast in the terms of the social construction of technology. We might thus regard the different constructions of the remote control as reflections of the differing 'interests' and 'resources' of different relevant social groups (see Chapter 1). Yet the remote control is not an innocent in this struggle, it also mediates – symbolizes, crystallizes and materially affects – these relations.

Above, I have, once again superficially, traced some of the complexities entailed in the delegation of body functions to a mundane technology – the remote control. Not unexpectedly, we find, instead of delegation, complex distributions of function-expressions, mediating, and mediated by, relations of power that operate on a terrain of contestation. The body-part functions that were disembodied, that is, delegated to, and re-embodied in, the remote control return in the form of others' more or less docile bodies, and one's own, more or less, re-disciplined, re-configured body. No longer do we see the separated body and technology, no longer purification, but the co(a)gent as a distribution. One can put this another way, this co(a)gent of human–remote control–television is maintained by the exclusion of parasites (in Serres' terms), and amongst these parasites are the other family members who would generate noise and disrupt the smooth communications between these three entities.

In this section I have attempted to show how the remote control operates within a network of heterogeneous relations – relations that concern the body, furniture, relatives, technological design, to list but the most obvious components. This network is what allows the remote control to mediate the relation between the viewer and the television set. This 'heterogeneous threesome' can, as we have noted, be thought of as a singularized entity (Callon and Law, 1995), that is, a co(a)gent in its own right. Unlike the cason and the repmo, this co(a)gent already has a name: the couch potato. The discussion in this section can now be seen as a tacit account of the way that the couch potato is emergent from the networks we have described. I have been looking at what parasites need to be excluded, and what quasi-objects need to be put into circulation, for the couch potato to be constituted, to perform (in Callon and Law's terms).

However, the couch potato is constantly being exposed to other parasites – those discourses that, circulating in professional and popular culture, formulate and/or problematize it. In the following section, I examine a range of these discourses, in order, partly, to show how, contrary to Latour's (1993a) view, these everyday hybrids are subject to scrutiny by moderns.

The couch potato

What is the couch potato? Here are two definitions:

> Couch potato *n*. American: a lazy, greedy person. This expression from the late 1980s describes a person whose only activity is to lie in front of the television and eat and drink . . .
>
> (Thorne, 1990, p. 110)

> Couch potato *n*.: one who is addicted to watching television and does this while lying on the couch, as inert and braindead as a potato.
>
> (Green, 1995, p. 78)

Now, the link between the couch potato and the remote control is not hard to exemplify as the following examples show: 'The TV remote control is 40 years old this month. The couch potato's friend made its first appearance in June 1956 . . . ' (*The Daily Telegraph*, 25 June 1996). An article entitled 'Fun with Mummy' has the by-line: 'Nicci Gerrard takes pleasure in her children's visits to today's new youth-friendly concerts and museums that are helping to kill off the culture of the couch potato'. It goes on to provide the following description: 'He sits back on the sofa, his face vacuous and dumb, and stares at the television screen, and shovels popcorn, crisps, chocolates into his agape mouth while programmes reel by. Occasionally he aims the remote control at the screen, randomly selecting another channel' (*The Observer*, 30 March 1997). The webpage for the Couch Potato Olympics (a page that directs readers to other television-related homepages such as those of the Discovery Channel, MTV, Dr Who, Star Trek Voyager and so on) has the title: Where is my Remote? (http://hubcap. clemson.edu/ ~scotc/television.html – 21 January 1998).

In light of these, and many other, examples, it can be accepted that there is some evidence for a common-sensical connection between the remote control and the couch potato. However, what are the *particular* discourses that construct the couch potato? Are there different versions of the couch potato? To what extent do such discourses attempt to separate human and remote control, and to what extent do they attempt to reinforce their association, bind them closer together?

As an initial response to these questions, one can identify two broad discursive complexes that constitute the couch potato. On the one hand, the emphasis is very much placed on the 'badness' of the couch potato. It is bad for health, for culture, for politics. An ironic statement of this status of couch potatoes can be found in the adult comic *Viz*: 'TV viewers. Avoid laziness by screwing your TV remote control to a wall or piece of furniture at least ten feet away from your chair' (Donald, 1994, p. 67).

On the other hand, the couch potato is accepted as a 'matter of fact' and celebrated in a number of ways. It is a common moniker for committed television viewers (and especially, perhaps, sports fans); it is a way of being to which various markets respond (e.g. the fast food, investment, PC industries). Here is another illustrative quote from *Viz*: 'Attach a "bayonet" to your TV remote control by taping a fork to it. This way you can keep control of the television whilst eating TV snacks' (Donald, 1995, p. 60).

Let me now more fully exemplify each of the positive and negative discursive complexes.

The couch potato is bad

The discourses that construct the couch potato as a bad entity are primarily concerned with its wastefulness – its lack of productivity. This productivity can take several forms.

Health (the unhealthy body)

There are numerous accounts that document the terrible price in terms of health that must be paid for the indulgence of the couch potato. Individuals will personally suffer because they have not engaged in what is deemed to be the appropriate levels of physical activity. Further, there will be consequent strains placed upon the public purse – the couch potato, and couch potato culture, works directly against national good housekeeping. Here are just two examples of this concern, where couch potato culture has resulted in the exclusion of more active 'lifestyles'.

> A three year, £9 million government health education campaign was launched yesterday aimed at changing 'couch potato' Britain by encouraging everyone to take at least 30 minutes' moderate exercise five times a week. . . . The average person watches 26 hours of television a week, compared with 13 hours in the 1960s. 'Excessive TV viewing by some individuals may encourage both sloth and gluttony, the couch potato effect,' the doctors say, while videos and computer games further contribute to inactivity in children.
>
> (*The Guardian*, 20 March 1996)

On the PSL medical news website, there appeared a feature reporting on a study by James Binkley of Purdue University, entitled 'Couch potatoes, not french fries, may be to blame for obesity'. The main claim is that obesity cannot be explained by the increasing consumption of fast-food alone. Changing 'exercise habits could be more to blame than diet' (http://www.pslgroup. com/dg/328ae.htm – 15 January 1998).

The lack of productivity (the unproductive body)

To be a couch potato means that one is not simply a drain upon one's own body and the body politic. It also means that one cannot actively 'contribute': to be a couch potato is to compromise one's capacity to be economically productive:

> John Ferguson – 'I was turning into a couch potato' – who left school at 16 with no qualifications, is with a team working on an environmental improve-ment scheme, the bulk of Newham Wise's work through a contract with Newham council. He earns £10 a week above benefits, and after an eight-week induction he will be paid a wage of £116 a week, taking him out of the benefit system.
>
> (*The Guardian*, 19 March 1997)

The destruction of culture (the uncultured body)

Further, to be a couch potato is to slip into a sort of animality where false bodily pleasures are preferred over true cultural self-development. There is, in other words, a surfeit of animality and a deficit of culture. In the following extract there is an all too apparent sigh of relief that the frontiers of couch potato culture are being rolled back so that 'real' culture can have the chance to flourish. Children and adults who might have fallen prey to the lure of the couch potato are once more beginning to engage in 'proper' cultural activities. In the article entitled 'Fun with Mummy' mentioned above, the author goes on to celebrate the 'fact', derived from a Cultural Trends study by the Policy Studies Institute, that 'maybe our endless pessimism about young people is incorrect and our assumption that we all, adults and children alike, live increasingly in a passive tele-age, is just wrong . . . there are signs that the British are becoming more active and more cultured. We are reading more books, going to more museums and art galleries . . .' (*The Observer*, 30 March 1997).

The decline of citizenship (the uncivic body)

Finally, we also find discourses that lament the couch potato as an uncivic body, or a politically sequestrated body. In this account, to be a couch potato is to be politically passive – sybaritically lost in the pleasures of television, as opposed to exercising political will, for example, over the contents of television, or, more generally, in the public sphere. Thus, the author of an article entitled 'Couch-potato democracy?' is responding to the view that 'Americans have become a nation of couch-potatoes, turning to television for solitary entertainment . . .' (Richard M. Vallely, 'Couch-potato democracy?', the American prospect, no. 25 (March–April 1996): 25–26 at http://epn..org/prospect/25/25-cnt3.html – 15 January 1998).

At the beginning of this chapter I remarked that, during my bouts of being a couch potato, I was occasionally assailed by diffuse pangs of guilt. The discourses that I've documented above are, I suspect, part of the reason for these feelings – parasites that introduce noise into the otherwise comfortable circuit of communication between body, remote control and TV. Strangely, these negative emotions, slight though they were, were never counteracted by (or never cohabited with) more positive ones. I consider some of these in the next section.

Good couch potatoes

The preceding 'bad couch potato' discourses are concerned with disciplining the couch potato; or rather, they have been essentially oriented toward a disaggregation of the couch potato into its constituents parts. There is a critical scrutiny of the couch potato that purifies it so that the human body is recovered, re-endowed with such 'proper' qualities as health, and a range of productivities that can be economic, cultural or political.

Now, there are certainly ways in which such discourses can be disrupted. For example, the medical discourses that equate the couch potato with ill health can be contradicted by recourse to lay epidemiologies. The correlations and risk factors that are presented by the health promotion professionals confront a lay epidemiology that has available to it various counter-instances. In caricature, these popular discourses contrast such figures as, say, Uncle Charlie, who smoked, drank, ate unwisely, and whose chosen lot in life was that of the couch potato and who lived till 108, with, say, Cousin Charlie, who exercised and ate healthily and did not own a television and died at the age of 30. Such counter-examples serve to throw into doubt the apparent certainties of medical science that supposedly underpin health promotion and advice (see Davison *et al.*, 1991). The discourses of 'slacking' are another example that counter the purifying discourses noted above.

However, in the present instance, I want to consider a number of discourses that presuppose the couch potato, indeed that seem to celebrate it, that expand its range of (non-)activity, that extol its virtues.

Expanding the domain of the couch potato

In this first example, we see that the couch potato is represented as limited – doing 'couch potato-ness' is constrained by the available technology. In other words, the couch potato is seen as a potential niche to which appeals can be made in the marketing of new technological consumables.

A webpage reviewing Windows sources and products describes a 'PC even couch potatoes will love' and goes on to comment: 'Okay, couch potatoes, Gateway's got a surprise for you. Actually, a Destination. No, it's not a notebook. It'll stay put in the family room and take over entertainment detail from that tired old TV' (http://www4.zdnet.com/wsources/context/960212/hp960212.html – 21 October 1997). Likewise, on the New Desk Potato Home Page, there is a claim that 'modern computer technology has created a new improved version' of the couch potato: The "Desk Potato!"' The page then provides a questionnaire by which to measure the reader's rating as a Desk Potato, listing ironic criteria against which one can evaluate oneself. For example: if your Nerdity has been tested at over 50%, if you can remember the most obscure commands but not family birthdays, and if you honour a different set of food groups (the reader can click for information from Desk Potato's Food Guide which provides 'details on how to maintain that spud-like body . . .'), then you count as a desk potato (http://trance.helix.net/~lekei/deskpota.html – 21 October 1997).

This marketing also extends to the selling of services. Thus, for example, we find investment services directed at couch potatoes: 'In case you aren't familiar with the Couch Potato Portfolio (you should know that it isn't difficult) . . . Running a Couch Potato Portfolio is one of the few remaining things you CAN do in the privacy and safety of your own home. And doing it perfectly requires less instruction than sex' (http://www.scottburns.com/960204su.htm – 15 January 1998).

A key point here is that irony is used to formulate and address a particular species of consumer with characteristics that remain underdeveloped and appetites that remain unsatiated. New avenues for practising couch potato activities are being ironically offered. But this irony is possible only by virtue of assuming a real set of meanings behind those on the 'surface' – the reference to the couch potato is ironic because of its of implied ludicrousness (see Muecke, 1969; Boothe, 1974).

At the same time, these advertisements are tapping into a more positive version of the couch potato – one concerned with, for example, a delight in gadgetry, or a commitment to a life of leisure. The joke that is played out in these texts concerns the disparity between these good and bad versions of the couch potato (see Mulkay, 1988; Michael, 1997). The enjoyment of the joke reflects a simultaneous distancing from, and identification with, the couch potato.

Servicing the couch potato

If the foregoing quotes serve ironically to expand the range of possibilities for doing 'couch potato-ness', the next examples suggest ways in which the couch potato can be nurtured, sustained and serviced. Again, the appeal is to a market identity, but it is a less adventurous version of the couch potato that we encounter here: its core activities remain, they are simply supported in one way or another.

For example, there is now a new armchair designed to cater for the inactivity of the couch potato.

> Your grandparents may very well have a Parker Knoll recliner – the comfy chair with a footrest that swings upwards when you lean back. Now, if you have any couch potato tendencies at all, it could be your turn. Parker Knoll's . . . most exciting new project on the blocks for the furniture and fabric company is a new reclining chair for TV watchers, with a holder for drinks on one arm and for the video remote on the other. Customers will be able to slump stupefied in front of the box for even longer periods.
>
> (*The Independent*, 24 July 1996)

If the new Parker Knoll chair attends to the corporeal indolence of the couch potato, so does a website for a delivery service called Couch Potato Deliveries – "Don't get up, we'll get it for you" (http://www.onlineguide.com/couchpotato.html – 21 January 1998). In contrast, Basketree's website services the self-identity of the couch potato. On this site, which advertises gifts ("We make gift giving easy!"), under the section entitled 'For Him' there is a Couch Potato sub-section: 'Snacks are overflowing in this container that looks like a TV set. Popcorn, nuts, cookies, and candies are included. Weather permitting we can include a chocolate remote control for further enjoyment' (http://www.baskettree.com/him.html – 21 January 1998).

Subcultural celebration of the couch potato

The preceding examples are all variations on the construction of the couch potato as a consumer. These discourses take as read the continuing existence and momentum of couch potato culture and target their products at this niche. We might sum up this form of address as follows: 'This is what you are like [a couch potato] – this is your essential nature. Here are other products or services that accommodate this nature'.

By comparison, there are less instrumental accounts of the couch potato – ones that more obviously celebrate it, that use it as a commonplace in the articulation of subcultural identity. Here we have couch potatoes talking to one another, expressing their common couch potato-ness.

Sometimes, a couch potato is the sedentary sports watcher. A webpage entitled 'Proud to be a Couch Potato' lists the homepages of various US sports teams (http://biochemweb.slu.edu/~cruz2/sports1.html – 15 January 1998). More often, the celebration of the couch potato hinges on the enjoyment of television watching *per se*. For example, one webpage entitled 'Why we like bad TV' devotes a story to TV Land, a channel 'dedicated entirely to reruns' which is recommended 'to the delight of Couch Potatoes everywhere' (http://www.bostonphoenix. com/alt 1/archive/tv/badtv/NICK_TV_LAND.html – 21 October 1997). Another webpage calls itself 'Couch Potato Heaven' and contains pages on numerous UK and US programmes and TV listings (http://www.wizgee.com/ Zany1/couchpot.htm – 21 October 1997). Yet another page, also calling itself 'Couch Potato Heaven', starts with the heading 'Good ways to kill brain cells' before listing a number of the author's favourite programmes (http://www.kis. net/toxicpig/tv.html – 21 October 1997). We might say, then, that to identify oneself as a couch potato and to address an audience, or rather, a more or less imagined community of couch potatoes (if that is not an oxymoron) is expressive of a subculture that, tacitly at least, sets itself in opposition to the negative discourses outlined above.

However, we should not romanticize this positive version of the couch potato. As a subcultural motif it can be 'recuperated' through its reconstruction as a market niche. What we begin to see here is the typical ambiguity – the oscillation – between a quasi-oppositional subcultural identity and a commercial icon (cf. Lury, 1996). In regard of the latter, we also find that the 'couch potato' can be deployed in the process of 'warranting' institutions' and corporations' activities. Thus, audience behaviour research (using a viewing laboratory in which people are electronically and visually monitored) into 'How people really watch television' is reported on a webpage (run by the WGBH Educational Foundation) entitled 'Couch Potato Chronicles' (http://www.boston.com/ wgbh/pages/ audience-research/cpc/cpc.1.2.html – 15 January 1998). In addition, the *Philadelphia Daily News* (12 August 1997) features the headline: 'Dr Couch Potato or how ABC taught us to stop worrying and love the TV'. According to the article, ABC 'not only admits TV is mind-numbing, it's bragging about it . . . to all who say watching sit-coms causes brain cells to keel over, ABC has this rejoinder: "Don't worry, you've got billions of brain cells . . ."' ABC's view is that wasting time can be relaxing. Or, as [ABC's $40 million tongue-in-cheek ad campaign] puts it, "The couch is your friend"' (http://www.phillynews.com/daily_news/ 97/Aug/12/features/GENX12.htm – 22 January 1998). Both these examples demonstrate the ease with which the couch potato moves from the margins into the mainstream.

The loss of the remote control

In the preceding examples we have seen ways in which the couch potato is variously pilloried and valorized. Those discourses that constitute the couch potato as 'bad' are concerned to extricate the body and the person: to make it less wasteful of self and state, to make it more productive – economically, culturally, politically. Contra Latour, what we have here, I think, is not a modernist uninterest in the hybrid. Rather, through characteristic modernist discourses of rationalization and government, there is a scrutiny of this hybrid (and I say *this* hybrid, because I do not want to claim that there is such a concern with hybrids-in-general, or co(a)gency in itself). This scrutiny basically advocates the dismemberment of the couch potato, a removal of the remote control from its grasp, a recovery of the technologically corrupted body that can once again be put to work. Conversely, we have discourses, more or less subversive (with all the provisos that such a term nowadays entails), that assume and celebrate the couch potato. Again, the hybrid is addressed, though this time mainly through the (post)modernist discourses of consumption.

Now, the surveillance manifested through those discourses that constitute the couch potato as 'bad' – as in need of a remedy that disaggregates the co(a)gent – operates within and through the relations of power within the household. The stereotypically surly youth who monopolizes the remote control will be subject to various sorts of discipline, not least in the form of a litany of the disastrous effects of being a couch potato.

However, these discursive forms of scrutiny barely exhaust the types of 'normalization' that are possible. If one seriously wants to be symmetrical in considering the couch potato, then one also needs to consider those modes of 'surveillance', of 'policing', of disruption that are not simply cultural, but also material. In other words, when thinking about the heterogeneous network in which the couch potato is embedded, and which includes the discursive complexes outlined above, can we also point to certain material contingencies that serve in the uncoupling of human and technology, person and remote control? Here, we would want to show that the body that is distributed through a network can occasionally be 'recovered' not only through discursive means, but *also* through material ones.

As we have seen, Callon and Law's (1995) notion of hybrid *collectifs* is an attempt to theorize distributed agency, an undertaking that stands in marked contrast to the Western tradition's equation of agency and singularity. Further, Callon and Law suggest that we cannot 'know' all these hybridities and their agencies. Nevertheless, what I want to consider here is a sort of contingent agency, where certain events are enabled (but not determined) by the conjunction of certain heterogeneous arrangements and designs. That is to say, I want to consider a sort of distributed agency that emerges in the configuration – that is, a patterned distribution – of relations and entities in which the couch potato is embedded.

The event in which I am interested is the 'loss of the remote control' – a traumatic event to be sure that, albeit momentarily, disrupts the ostensibly smooth agency of the couch potato. Or rather, in temporarily disaggregating the couch potato, this event reflects how the heterogeneous network out of which the couch potato emerges can be 'subverted', or even, one might venture, 'policed' (see below).

So, how might we think of the 'loss of the remote control'? That it is a commonplace event is not in much doubt, as advice from *Viz*'s Top Tips columns suggests: 'Avoid the frustration of repeatedly losing your TV remote control by keeping it in a "cowboy" holster fashioned out of a child's sock and an old belt' (Donald, 1994, p. 65). Further, the 'loss of the remote control' clearly stirs up great emotions. The Opinion Research Corporation's survey of Americans' relationship with the remote control found that:

> Over half (55%) of the respondents said they lose the remote control up to five times a week. And 11% of those surveyed said they lose the remote between six and ten times a week.
>
> After they've lost their remote controls, 63% of Americans say that they spend up to five minutes a day looking for it. Sixteen percent say that they spend 10 minutes a day looking for it.
>
> The most frequent places that Americans find their remotes include in and under the furniture (38%), in the kitchen or bathroom (20%), and in the refrigerator (6%).
>
> (http://www.empire.net/~psl/Fun_People/1994 AWM. html)

This piece goes on to document the reproaches and recriminations that arise with the loss of the remote control. It should, however, be noted that the survey was sponsored by Philips Consumer Electronics Company, producer of the Magnavox Remote Locator (TM) colour televisions that help TV viewers swiftly locate their lost remote controls by pressing the TV's 'power-on' button. To state the obvious, these findings do not exactly harm the promotion of this new feature.

Both *Viz* and Philips offer solutions that are, in their respective low and high ways, 'technological'. In contrast, the Megadodo homepage suggests a human solution. In an article on 'Zapping' – the use of the remote control to avoid commercials – instructions are provided for the optimal use of the remote control. Amongst the problems that arise in the process of zapping is that of the missing remote control. '4) The remote control can suddenly be missing. If this happens, try to be calm and do a rational search of the surroundings. Most often the remote is tired of your continuously zapping and can be found hiding on the floor' (http://megadodo.com/articles/6R18.html – 2 October 1997).

So, here are two contrasting solutions for the reunification of remote control and human – solutions that map directly onto the human–non-human dichotomy. However, and this is the important point here, we need to ask how it is that this local, practical dissolution of the couch potato came about. Well, clearly there are social dynamics that predispose the loss of the remote control – young children playing is one possible factor, the behaviour of companion animals another. But the 'lose-ability' of the remote is something that can be said to reflect a number of 'material ironies'. For example, there is the removal of the wire that attached Lazy Bones to the television set: while this would make the problem of tripping over the wire disappear, it made more possible the loss of the remote control – there would be no trailing wire to give a clue as to its whereabouts.

There are also other conditions. I have in mind what we might call the accidental coalition of technological designs, or *technological co-incidentalization*. For example, how are we to understand the remote control's affinity for the back of the sofa? The couch potato is at the mercy of the fact that many sofas are designed with removable seat cushions (which enable seat covers to be taken off for cleaning). One structuring assumption here is the nature of the hand: the remote control nestles neatly in the palm; the pliable gap between seat cushion and sofa back is perfect for fingers aiming to remove the former. The size of the remote control matches, more or less ideally, the space between sofa cushion and back. In his reflections on the epistemology of the hand, Turner sees the hand as foundational insofar as it grounds the 'potentialities upon which endless cultural practices can be erected' (Turner, 1992, p. 118). The partial disembodiment of the television viewer, the delegation of the functions of certain body parts to the remote control are shaped by the nature of the hand – or rather, as we have seen, its idealization (the hand must have certain properties). But the hand also plays its part in wholly different spheres of design. When these butt up against one another, then, sometimes, new potential relationalities are constituted, new pathways for the movement of entities become possible. These new relationalities, these new pathways can then serve as the basis for further cultural practices – forms of searching and technological fixes, as well as the commentaries that accompany these (the present text included).

In the foregoing sections, I have argued that, and illustrated some of the ways in which, the body is distributed across a sociotechnical network comprised of couch, remote control, television, other family members, and various discourses about the nature of television watching and the status of the couch potato. However, as the loss of the remote control suggests, such distributions must be constantly performed – they are orderings rather than orders, as Law (1994) puts it. As we have seen, these performances – in particular, that of the couch potato – can be undermined by the enablements generated by the coincidence or coalition of technological design features. Perhaps here we are witnessing some of the strange distributed agencies that are performed by hybrid *collectifs*.

Conclusion: discipline and disorder

I would now like to offer another, this time more speculative, account of these strange distributed agencies. Specifically, I want to pursue and explore the idea that the routine event of 'losing the remote control' can be thought of as a process whereby a co(a)gent (the couch potato) is 'policed' or 'judged' by another (which is constituted in part through the relationalities born of the technological centrality of the hand). Now, it might seem odd to call the process of 'losing the remote control' that issues from the conjunction of technologies and the coincidentalization of design, a form of surveillance. Firstly, however, let us recall that for Foucault's (1979) Bentham's panopticon, surveillance is conducted by an unseen agent. The continuous possibility that one is being watched by a hidden, conceivably present, agent shapes the comportment of the body: body techniques, as Mauss (1985) would call them, are adapted. Here, then, there is a potential human agent that, through an architectural configuration, scrutinizes the comportment of the prisoner: these arrangements are, of course, moral. Secondly, let us also recall Latour's door groom. It too discriminates against certain bodies, demands certain capacities from the body. It is another moral agent that disciplines the door user. As Latour would have it, the door groom is morality objectified.

In both cases the body is distributed across arrangements of technologies and humans – it is emergent in these heterogeneous networks. What the loss of the remote control suggests is an arrangement, a configuration, an assemblage that is coincidental; such chance-like, unintended associations generate new potential pathways. The body that should be indolent, unexercised when embedded within that figuration known as the 'couch potato' is, ironically, unexpectedly manoeuvred and manipulated in the regular search for the remote control. Those body parts whose functions were delegated to the remote control must now be exercised in a game of hide and seek with the remote control: in sum, (partial) disembodiment entails the return of the body (parts).

Furthermore, however, these new pathways comprise an ongoing possibility for the loss of the remote control in the way that the panopticon comprises an ongoing possibility of surveillance. To deal with this potential catastrophe, new routines, new comportments are developed. Technological fixes aside, new arrangements can be instituted by the couch potato such that the remote control is 'guarded', and the probability of the remote control's walkabout minimized. Most obviously, such arrangements might take the form of the habitual placement of the remote control at a particular specified site.

Consequently, here we see an example of the way agencies are distributed across more or less accidental heterogeneous coalitions and collusions. We see how these distributions comprise forms of 'surveillance' of a co(a)gent. We see that the moral agent that conducts this 'surveillance' is distributed, unintended, contingent, stochastic. Part of the aim of this chapter has been to establish that moderns can indeed assess and police some co(a)gents (as evidenced in the discourses of the good and bad couch potato). Another purpose has been to show that it is not just modern *humans* who 'police'. Co(a)gents themselves – in this case those accidental conjunctions and distributions, what I have called *coincidentalizations*, of technologies (and, of course, humans) – also contribute to these processes of making and unmaking orders.

Now, there is another twist to the tale here. The couch potato, as we have seen, is constituted through forms of governmentality that are mediated through various discourses of the 'good' *consuming* couch potato. These are normalizing discourses and practices concerned with the couch potato as the site of consumption. To break up the couch potato that emerges from these sorts of networks can be viewed as a matter of 'resistance'. The loss of the remote control – its 'walkabout' – is, in a manner of speaking, the idle walking of a technological flaneur (see De Certeau, 1984), which, by following the strange unexpected pathways constituted through heterogeneous coincidentalization, interrupts this governmentality.

All this talk of normalization, discipline, governmentality, surveillance and resistance, however, underlines the paucity of the language available to us for getting a handle on these mundane events. Perhaps, rather, we should recast our observations in terms of the universalizing thesis that any technological solution always yields problems by virtue of having to organize a partly intransigent world in which those technological solutions can indeed be 'solutions' (see, for example, Tenner, 1996; Thorngate, 1984). This intransigence can be re-framed as the unintended consequences of such solutions (as the remote control), as technical artefacts become embroiled in a world that can never be wholly predicted for them. Or it can be seen as reflecting the manifold parasites that come between technology and body and disrupt their communion (in, say, the form of the couch potato). Or it can be seen as generating disorder where order was intended.

Yet, the figure of the couch potato suggests another avenue of theorizing. Its occasional dissolution is followed by its reconstitution. Is it possible, instead of thinking of this as an oscillation between cogency and fragmentation, to *presuppose* a co(a)gent such as the couch potato? In other words, can we feasibly theorize this dissolution as an inherent aspect of the co(a)gent as it goes about its everyday business? After all, elements of the couch potato must attend to matters other than those relayed by the television: sometimes all its components are co-present, sometimes they are 'purposefully' separated, at yet other moments they are accidentally disaggregated. Is it possible to regard the movements back and forth across these different arrangements not so much as the couch potato coming together and falling apart, but as part of the 'nature' of the couch potato? Put generally, can the *sequence of changes* in the degree to which the components of a co(a)gent are integrated be regarded as *patterned*? Can a co(a)gent be defined, in part, by the *routinized trajectory* along which it predictably, 'habitually', coalesces and disintegrates? Indeed, can we imagine these patterns mapping onto – criss-crossing – the patterns of other co(a)gents such that, at certain routine points, a component of one co(a)gent becomes a part of another? This complex of questions will be explored in the next chapter through a particular 'manufactured' co(a)gent – the Hudogledog.

6 Narrating co(a)gents

The case of the Hudogledog

Introduction

When my son was a toddler, the buggy (or pushchair) was his main means of transport. Together – that is, the three of us (two humans and a mundane technology) – we would routinely set off for the shops or the park. On occasion, we would come across an inquisitive dog who, dragging its 'owner' behind it, would come up to us and sniff us, or perhaps sniff the wheels of the buggy. A few words might be exchanged between me and the dog's person. My son might, if he was feeling particularly brave, try to stroke the dog. When the time came to go our separate ways, the dog might have to be pulled away. Or, if the dog lost interest – or got more interested in something else – it might pull its human away.

A regular feature of these trips, especially to the park, would be that my son would fall asleep. While he slept, I would every so often sit on a park bench, and, if for some reason I couldn't read, I'd make some effort at having deep thoughts. Or rather, I determined in some vague way to use the time productively. What could I observe in these parks? Well, amongst other things, I could see combinations of dogs, persons and dog-leads. Some leads were of fixed length – whenever the dog, or the human, wanted to move off, they would have to pull, at least in the initial instance, their companions with them. Some leads were extendable: the human would stand still, perhaps chatting to another human part of a like combination, while their dogs ran and chased and sniffed and nuzzled. More often, the dogs would be let off the leash and allowed to run freely. Less often, the lead would slip from the human's grasp and the dog would run off. Sometimes the human would give chase.

What are we to make of these fragmentary episodes? In the previous chapter, I ended with the prospect of contriving a co(a)gent as a singularity in order to see where it would lead. More particularly, I want to construct such a co(a)gent out of a few entities, a few relations, as a way of tracing out circuits of communication (in the broadest, heterogeneous sense) that would otherwise remain invisible. In other words, can we see processes, relays, relationalities that we would otherwise miss in our accountings of heterogeneous ordering? The episodes related above suggest one such co(a)gent, the Hudogledog – made up of human, dog-lead and dog and derived thus: Hu(man) + Dogle(ad) + Dog = Hudogledog. The choice of this co(a)gent is, of course, not accidental. Partly, its value lies as a corrective to the relatively impoverished treatment of the role of animals in social processes. This co(a)gent allows us to contribute to the process of adding animals, which have long been neglected (Noske, 1992; Arluke and Sanders, 1996; Franklin, 1999), onto the sociological agenda (to the extent that one can say that there is such a thing). However, the Hudogledog also serves more exploratory aims. By virtue of being mundane, invisible almost, by virtue of its evident ephemerality, it is good to think with. Specifically, the Hudogledog enables us to confront the broader problems of constituting and narrating a co(a)gent, of tracing a co(a)gent's cycles of appearance and disappearance, of treating these cycles as, at once, reflective and constitutive of heterogeneous ordering. In other words, the Hudogledog is a figure through which to contemplate what sort of theoretical skeleton we would need to build in order to establish such a 'trivial' co(a)gent as an efficacious actor. To reiterate, the main point of such an exercise is to see how such a co(a)gent might illuminate otherwise hidden pathways that serve in the process of heterogeneous ordering and disordering.

However, over and above this theorizing, the Hudogledog, like the more 'distributed' co(a)gents of humans–technologies–environments hinted at in Chapter 3, is a figure which raises important issues about the 'valuation' of animals. As we shall see, such valuations have been articulated in a number of ways. The Hudogledog comprises a co(a)gent that might be a better candidate for carrying the weight of something like rights. In other words, the Hudogledog can aid us in thinking about values in relation to distributed entities, rather than singularized ones – that is, it might help us in re-casting the notion of 'rights'.

In what follows, then, I will begin with a brief discussion of the difficulties faced when attempting to contrive a co(a)gent made up of small numbers of entities and relations. That there are difficulties reflects the fact that a leap of imagination is needed to regard such a little array of entities and relations (e.g. dog, human, dog-lead) as a singularity. This is paradoxical, especially when we are routinely able to attribute singularity to co(a)gents made of very many entities and relations. Out of this paradox emerges the issue of what sort of vocabulary could serve in the narration of such 'little' co(a)gents, thus allowing us to begin to trace their role in the process of heterogeneous ordering (and disordering). I will exemplify all this through the figure of the Hudogledog. After a brief consideration of some of the ways in which animals have been apprehended in Western societies, I will draw out some of the uses of the Hudogledog, first by pre-emptively decon-structing it, then by tracing its comings and goings, that is, its ephemerality. In the process, I attempt to expose those normally undetected pathways, those routes along which pass the signs and materials that mediate the heterogeneous (dis)orderings of the Hudogledog, but also of co(a)gents in general. Finally, I address some of the implications that co(a)gency holds for the valuation of animal non-humans.

The size of co(a)gents

In the previous two chapters we dealt with two smallish co(a)gents – casons (car persons) and couch potatoes. These were relatively easy to derive, and yet, on the whole, as Latour (1993a) tells us, there seems to be some difficulty in our capacity to identify co(a)gents. The Hudogledog can be subjected to an actor–network treatment that demonstrates its multiple constitution in and through various socio-biotechnical networks. Such an analysis (and I will be providing one below) can, for example, point to the processes of domestication, the mediation of communication and joint action through the dog-lead, the associations to a number of organizational actors including pet food manufacturers, dog trainers, veterinary services and (local and national) government. This would be a rather 'trivial' exercise in actor–network analysis. However, what makes such an analysis 'trivial' is exactly what is interesting. Why should it be so patently easy to reveal the distributedness of the Hudogledog but be such an intellectual challenge when it is, say, actors such as Pasteur (Latour, 1988b), the three biologists of St Brieuc Bay (Callon, 1986b), the physicists of Daresbury (Law, 1994), or the dreamers of Aramis (Latour, 1996a) who are to be 'deconstructed'?

The accomplishment of actor–network theory is to demonstrate how these humans can be thought of as micro-entities that are emergent from, and constituted in, heterogeneous networks in which they are ascribed singularity and agency. However, there are also macro-entities that are attributed such characteristics – institutions (for a critical review, see Douglas, 1987), and society as a whole. Indeed, to talk of society as a whole as an agent is relatively straightforward in Western culture. Thus, Bowers and Iwi (1993) in their study of discourses of society, derive eight models of society. Here is one example: society is represented as opposing the speaker – society 'is attributed with alien values, beliefs and dispositions to action' (Bowers and Iwi, 1993, p. 383) that contradict the speaker's own. Such discourses have certain functions: in the above case, society comes to be seen as deficient in relation to the speaker's positions (it is immoral or domineering or oppressive). The point is that, in this instance, society as a whole comes to be endowed with something akin to agency: it has been effectively black boxed – no longer a network of entities and associations, but a singular actor. That this is possible reflects relatively recent changes in Western ways of thinking about continuity and change. As Strathern (1992) notes, in the anthropology of the mid-twentieth century, especially that of the influential Radcliffe-Brown, one pervasive metaphor of collectivities rendered them as systems. Society was 'personified' with needs (for reproduction) and demands (on individuals to engage in this reproduction through things like kinship duty). This metaphor was countered later when a new motif arose – one that is concerned with the way that human individuals, while socialized into society, were also something more than this socialization. Nevertheless, this metaphor of 'society as agent', as Bower and Iwi's research documents, is still prevalent and ready-to-hand, that is, a commonplace.

Consequently, it would seem that it is relatively easy to talk, under the appropriate circumstances, about the way that co(a)gents such as borough councils, dog food manufacturers, an animal-loving society and so on behave as more or less unitary or singular agential entities. And yet, these too are co(a)gents. They are simply more complicated, that is, comprised of recognizably more components, than the Hudogledog. One might even say, after Donald MacKenzie's (1990) model of the 'trough of certainty', that there is a 'trough of dis-integration'. Micro-co(a)gents (humans, machines, animals, cf. Lynch and Collins, 1998) and meso-co(a)gents (institutions, organizations) and macro-co(a)gents (societies) rest on peaks of relatively unproblematic 'actorly singularity'. In the trough between are the intermediate sized mini-co(a)gents composed of what we would commonly take to be a few 'constituents' – a human, a dog-lead and a dog, for example. It is this class of co(a)gents that seem to escape the perception of actorliness most readily.

In light of this patterning of actorliness, my question, to phrase it another way, is: what does it take to narrate such an entity as a singular actor? More specifically, what candidate concepts might there be to help us in narrating the Hudogledog as a unitary actor, and thus portray it as an (always contingently) effectual character in a socio-biotechnical story? Let me begin by considering Western concepts of the animal.

Animal stories

Inevitably, when we come to recount a history of Western conceptions of animals we find that the historians differ amongst themselves. As usual, all I can do is sketch only a few of the stories that can be told about such understandings.

For some writers (e.g. Merchant, 1980; Berman, 1981), nature, which includes non-human animals, was prior to the rise of science in the Enlightenment, an enchanted domain. Nature was seen to have qualities that were part-human: the divide between human subjects (that is, conscious, agential, and so on) and non-human objects (mechanical, thing-like and so on) was by no means as transparent as it appeared to become subsequently: pigs could be hanged for murder, and mining could be viewed as a desecration of Mother Earth (see, for example, Tester, 1991; Ritvo, 1987; Serpell, 1986). Clearly, then, even where the animal has something of the subject about it, this does not necessarily mean that it is valued *per se*. The symbolism of the dog, for example, spans the extremes from a model of fidelity and courage, to the embodiment of evil and lasciviousness (Rowland, 1973); the dog has been combined with the human in the hybridic form of cenocephalics (human bodies, canine heads) serving sometimes to signify the other (the descendants of Cain), and sometimes to signify the 'good' as in the cenocephalic St Christopher of the Eastern Christian tradition (White 1991). Moreover, the beast is within the human, as well as without, and must be guarded against (Midgley, 1978).

Of course, animals were (and are) seen as different – certainly below humans in the hierarchy of beings (although we should note that the difference between species has never been wholly clear-cut – Midgley, 1983). Central to the entrenchment of this view was the rise of science, although its bases can be found in Aristotle and the Judaeo-Christian tradition (see Noske, 1989; Collingwood,

1960; Passmore, 1974). Two key figures in this development are Francis Bacon and René Descartes. While both were instrumental in the reconceptualization of nature in mechanistic terms, they were also intent on mounting a defence of Christianity. A quote from Barbara Noske neatly captures the respective roles of these thinkers:

> Descartes' philosophy . . . rested on the sharp distinction between matter (nature without intrinsic value), and the non-material soul of humankind (and God) as the seat of all that was valuable . . . Descartes safeguarded the Christian religion by creating an almost total qualitative difference between humans and animals, between mind and body, between value and fact, and between religion and nature.
>
> (Noske, 1989, p. 60)

However, it was Bacon who 'definitively succeeded in wedding the doctrine of human mastery over nature (the subject–object relationship which has always been implicit in the Christian faith anyway) to the practising of experimental science' (Noske, 1989, p. 60). Accordingly, nature was, through the toils of 'man', to be forced to reveal her secrets – she was to be exposed, pierced, made to yield.

The upshot was that animals came to be perceived as objects. For Descartes, 'animals were mere machines or automata, like clocks, capable of complex behaviour, but wholly incapable of speech, reasoning, or, on some interpretations, even sensation' (Thomas, 1984, p. 33). Now, as Thomas notes, this view met with hostility amongst certain British commentators, and was partly renounced by Descartes in later years. Further, one can point to an alternative tradition, such as that of the Paracelsans for whom a science that objectified and atomized nature could produce only defective knowledge; true knowledge could only be found amongst artisans (farmers, breeders) with practical experience of particular phenomena (Shapin, 1991). However, the 'scientistic' model of animals was the predominant one and was not seriously challenged until the nineteenth century.

It was in this period, as Thomas (1984) points out, that there arose the sentimentalization or romanticization of animals (and of nature, more generally). Accordingly, with the decline of routine contact between human and non-human animals wrought by increasing urbanization in the eighteenth century

> . . . an increasingly sentimental view of animals as pets and objects of contemplation would jostle uneasily alongside the harsh facts of a world on which the elimination of 'pests' and the breeding of animals for slaughter grew everyday more efficient.
>
> (Thomas, 1984, p. 301)

In contrast to this explanation for the rise of alternative versions of animals, Tester (1991) emphasizes the rise of the modern episteme that incorporated what he calls a *Demand for Similitude* – the idea that humans are part of nature, that their finest qualities are to be found in this 'naturalness'. This was, of course, a key dimension of the romantic movement, and contributed to what Franklin (1999) characterizes as the 'romantic gaze' that captured the nobility and beauty of the natural. However, as Ritvo (1987) documents, this and similar valuations of nature also played a social role, mediating cultural categories. Brutality towards animals came to be seen as a form of working class-deviance; at the same time, big game hunting served to evoke the might of empire. Further, as Birke (1994) notes, social distinctions wrought through the treatment of animals also included gender divisions.

Despite these contrary trends, it was the objectifying conceptualization of animals that predominated. Franklin (1999) provides a very useful account of the way that the treatment of animals evolved with Fordist developments in Western modernity. He draws attention to, amongst others, the following changes: innovations in livestock and butchery industries and in freezing technologies facilitated mass meat consumption; increased wages, leisure time and mass transport contributed to a demand for more wildlife-related activities and a massification (the production of mass movements across society) and diversification of pet keeping; allied to these were increased media representations of animals and the rise of organizations devoted to the protection of animal species; science augmented its hegemony in the characterization of animals.

However, the recent changes that comprise late or postmodernity have complicated matters even further. Franklin points to three interrelated features of postmodernity – misanthropy, ontological insecurity and risk reflexivity – as instrumental in emergent apprehensions of animals. Misanthropy, defined as the feeling that humans have generally lost their moral bearings, means that a concern for animals can serve as a solid, relatively unproblematic moral counterbalance. Ontological insecurity, wrought by the fragmentation of community and family relations, means that companion animals can now take on the emotionally supportive role once filled by friends and family. Risk reflexivity – the awareness that the 'natural', from the environment to meat, is compromised by various forms of human encroachment – makes the natural 'a permanent political fixture' (Franklin, 1999, p. 59) and makes people increasingly sensitive to their responsibilities for its (and that includes animals') protection. In light of these changes, we can but take seriously Baker's comment that 'the contemporary mentalité of animal representation has in some respects taken shape over less than the last twenty years, let alone the last two hundred' (Baker, 1993, p. 21).

Contemporary animals

The following survey of contemporary representations of animals is, once again, necessarily partial. Discourses and images of animals pervade Western culture. Representations of animals inhabit the most scholarly exchanges and the most sentimental reportage, the most unremarkable conversations and the most remarked-upon artistic productions. This section cannot do justice to such ubiquity. However, we can at the very least trace some of the key Western representations of animals.

As mentioned above, representations of animals inhabit very many dimensions of contemporary Western culture. They cut across popular cultural genres; they 'appeal' to all age groups and class factions; they are put to work in texts, in images, in still-life and as animations. In the news, they are both symbols for humans, and the subjects of news stories in which they might feature as lovable, extraordinary pets, victims of outrage, or wild, savage beasts. In elections they are used to signify the identification of parties with particular national characteristics, or else can serve as symbols for political parties. In single-issue campaigns they are the victims of humanity's inhumanity, or they are metaphors for criminals preying upon needlessly defenceless victims. In advertising they are used to sell toilet paper, toys, cereals, petrol, tea-bags and construction companies. In the 'high' arts they can be (ironically) objectified as transected corpses in the works of Damien Hirst, or (ironically) sentimentalized as cute giant floral puppies as in the work of Jeff Koons. As toys, they can be anything from realistic plastic miniatures through fighting mutant grotesques to soft cuddly playthings. They occupy children's and adults' literary and visual media: as objects of what Franklin (1999) calls the zoological gaze; as naturalistic depictions of past and present species; as hybrid monsters or anthropomorphized or neotenized cartoons; as metaphors for particular human conditions and characteristics, and metonyms for nations and states. The list goes on.

So, as Baker notes, the animal is typically seen to play 'a potent and vital role in the symbolic construction of human identity . . .' (Baker, 1993, p. x). Yet, as Baker also points out, these identities are not coherent or homogeneous. If some representations epitomize the 'superiority of humans', others can present animals in a positive light. Sometimes, 'these supposedly positive animal images have been drained of much of their animality' (Baker, 1993, p. 71), but it is well to remember that 'animality' is itself mediated through representation – a social construction as Arluke and Saunders (1996) have argued. The point is that such contrasting and contradictory representations mediate our relations with animals, even though those animals (as individuals, collectives and species) materially, as well as semiotically, impact upon us on many levels and in many different ways.

From the above list, it is possible to derive many dichotomies regarding the nature of animals and their representations. Here are just a few: anthropomorphized versus naturalistic; wild versus tame; subject versus object; sentimental versus unsentimental (or objective); victim versus aggressor; hybrid (or abominable – cf. Douglas, 1966) versus pure; exemplary versus idiosyncratic. These distinctions map onto one another, and so, in what follows I will trace the complexity of these representations as they weave in and out of a number of cultural artefacts.

Popular representations of animals in natural history programmes often portray them as subjects with their full complement of agential faculties – volition, consciousness, singularity and so on. Sometimes this ascribed subjectivity is nothing more than a convenient anthropomorphism through which plot or narrative can be carried (the Disney live action nature films of the 1950s are one notorious example). However, in other cases – say in the serious documentaries of chimpanzees by Jane Goodall – it does appear as if genuine subjects are operating before us. While these individual animals are valued for their idiosyncrasies, they are also, in the context of group and species, seen as roles in a social structure and an evolutionary chain. A middling female chimp, for all her charming characteristics, nevertheless occupies a specific place in a hierarchy that 'must' exist given the 'nature' of chimpanzee society (cf. Haraway, 1989, who has ably argued that primatology – including its popularized manifestations – is shot through with assumptions about society, nature, animals: it is a terrain on which are played out many Western concerns over male–female, human–non-human, black–white distinctions). But chimpanzees occupy an odd position – they are 'officially' wild, but they are also 'tame' insofar as they connote chimps trained to entertain. Less charismatic fauna such as spiders, ants, slugs, fish are more easily seen as both wild and objects – but even these can be ascribed the characteristics of humans – courage, stamina, cunning and so on. However, insofar as the camera follows one or two individuals, these serve not as *bona fide* individuals, but as exemplars of the species as a whole (or, less kindly, as exemplars of the operation of a complex of hard-wired reflexes). Yet, we might also suggest that the innovations in close-up photography, as well as the narrative conventions of natural history programmes, do 'individualize' those animals in focus. While this individuality may last as long as these animals are on view, for that fleeting moment they can emerge as subjects. However, this will be momentary, for the ecological message that often tops and tails such documentaries will reassert the rights of species: the individual disappears, as what is to be valued and preserved – the moral of many such programmes – are 'collectives' such as communities, populations or species. This evokes another dichotomy, that between individuals and species: individuals have been used to illustrate the worth of species, yet individuals *per se* are expendable – subjected to culling, for example – for the greater good of communities or populations or habitats (for an ethical analysis of the differences between animals and environmental rights, see Hargrove, 1992).

The above account may seem like an illegitimate exercise insofar as it has entailed the conflation of a number of different documentaries (and, arguably, genres) into one another. However, it does have the benefit of enabling us to trace the complexity and ambiguity of meanings of animals that traverse a viewer's routine intake of natural history. The same applies to children's experience of representations of animals.

For children, animals are routinely presented as subjects, occasionally superior to their human 'owners' (for example, Gromit of Wallace and Gromit fame), but also often displaying the least valued of human characteristics (the indolence of the camel in Kipling's Just So story; Mickey Mouse initially portrayed as a couch potato in Disney's recent short film 'Runaway Brain'). But they are also sentimentalized – neotenized as Bambi or Dumbo, or 'heroized' in the form of Lassie or Flipper. They are presented as the 'other' – the big bad wolf, the unremitting shark of *Jaws*. They are the objects of a proto-scientific gaze in schoolbooks and encyclopedias – body parts, bodies, instances of species, members of a community or population. All this multiplicity and all this slippage can be condensed in the figure of a chicken burger (or nugget) shaped as a dinosaur – object, myth, natural history, foodstuff, plaything, character and so on and so forth (and I have not even begun to address the symbolism of meat-eating – cf. Fiddes, 1992; Adams, 1990).

What is interesting about this disparate variety of representations is that, normally, it is not a matter for comment or reflection. This morass of contrasting representations is simply a 'fact of life' serving as a sort of well-stocked repository of signifiers for the ongoing construction of animals. Sometimes, of course, such plurality is transformed into contradiction; that is, there is a need to manage contradiction in circumstances where consistency is 'called for'. For example, self-identity may be thoroughly tied to the narratives of 'animal lover', yet one may be obliged to be involved in the routine killing of animals (see Arluke and Sanders, 1996, and Sanders, 1995, for some poignant examples; also Lynch, 1988; Arluke, 1988, 1990).

In many cases, though, these *prima facie* contrasting or disparate conceptions of (and practices towards) animals are not 'managed' as contradictions. Rather, they peacefully 'cohabit' in the same individual or group. That is to say, no tension or dissonance attaches to combinations of these representations (and associated practices). Some subcultures thus seem to manifest a sort of 'cohabitative culture' in which there is a 'balance' that accommodates the contrasting statuses of animals. However, we must be wary of not sentimentalizing these human groups. As Baker (1993), points out in his commentary on John Berger's (1980) analysis of the representational use of animals, for Berger there is 'the authentic reality of the good meat-eating peasant . . . set against capitalism's claustrophobic interior where overt exploitation of animals goes hand in hand with the narcissistic fictions of the pet-owning animal-lover' (Baker, 1993, p. 13). The danger is, of course, that groups such as the 'peasantry' (or 'dogbreeders' – see below) can come to serve as romanticized models of a more 'authentic', 'real' or 'pure' relation between human and non-human animals.

Yet, these disputes over the representations of human–animal relations are not immune from these very relations themselves. These disputes do not simply arise amongst the bickering heads of some cultural hydra. This is because culture, in its concrete mediation of, and *in*, the everyday, is itself partly affected by the presence of animals. As noted in previous chapters, we construct (culturally and materially) technologies that then feed back and contribute to the construction of us humans (as well as to natures and other technologies). The same goes for animals, although there are, of course, differences, not least in the sorts of contacts we have with animals as opposed to technologies. Having noted this, let me now consider how relations with animals – specifically with dogs (a particularly amenable example) – might serve in the production of these representations, and vice versa.

Dogs–human relations

Numerous authors have noted how humans who have dogs are often in intimate communication with them. This intimacy entails a complex mix of discourse, practical engagement and emotional mutuality. The sort of ambivalence outlined above – where animals are represented as both subjects and objects – pervades the relationship that humans have with dogs. Dogs are spoken about as subjects, as agents. They are, like severely mentally or physically disabled persons, like very young humans, attributed mind, individuality, emotionality and reciprocity, and they are afforded a social place (Sanders and Arluke, 1993; Sanders, 1993). Furthermore, people are willing to articulate for their 'inarticulate' canine companions their internal states. As Sanders (1992, pp. 6–7) notes, 'Dog owners commonly give voice to what they perceive to be their animals' mental, emotional, and physical experiences'. In addition, in the process of excusing their dogs' social misbehaviour, people have recourse to subjectifying discourses, representing their dogs as, for example, responding to the oddness of the situation (Sanders, 1990). However, at the same time, also available are objectifying discourses, say those concerned with the developmental stage of their dogs. Indeed, as was the case for some of Sanders' (1993) respondents, to admit to attributing subjectivity or 'mindedness' to their dogs is discomfiting. It is to leave oneself open to the charge of sentimentality, of anthropomorphism.

Now, this charge can certainly be aimed at those cultural artefacts produced by 'dog-owners' that portray dogs as speaking subjects. For example, in magazines and on websites for dog enthusiasts, there are sections devoted to letters sent in 'by' dogs that describe their lives, interesting happenings, new births and so on (Smart, 1993; also see Chat Book, http://www.talkingdogs.com./chatbook/ – 24 June 1998). But this must be placed in the context of objectifying discourses. Kath Smart's (1993) study of dogbreeders is a particularly sensitive account of this interweaving. These dogbreeders believed themselves to be engaged in proper conversation – in authentic forms of sociality – with their animals. Moreover, they occasionally considered themselves to be under the scrutiny, even under the surveillance, of their dogs, adapting their actions in response to these 'inspections'. For members of this British subculture, that dogs are subjects is not in doubt. And yet the breeders themselves are quite capable of representing the dogs as objective bodies – as part of a breed, or lineage, or as more or less adequately functioning bodies (e.g. conformation; levels of hip dysplasia). More importantly, these differing discourses are mobilized in the same setting. In conversations with Smart in the presence of their dogs (or, rather, in conversations with Smart *and* the dogs), the breeders could talk, and respond, to Smart and the dogs while also objectifying the dogs as bodies with varying degrees of hip dysplasia (varying depending upon whether they drew upon X-ray records or the day-to-day functioning of the dogs as examples of breeds developed to perform certain tasks). For these 'dog people', as they often call themselves, this is perfectly sensible; it is not a problem because, in Sanders' (1993) terms, it 'works' for that relationship.

However, all these complexities and 'ambivalences' must not be, so to speak, confined to the human actor in the relationship. The relationship is complex in itself. The dogs intervene in their humans' lives in highly variegated ways – they contribute to their well-being, they support them, they offer uncontingent love (cf. Serpell, 1986). Yet, just as the owners are changed, so too, as Costall (1995b) underlines, are the dogs. Sometimes, for example, within the relationship they become 'too domesticated', expanding their repertoire of actions to the point of mimicking human expressions. Yet these animals also follow trajectories wholly other – for example, in their interactions with other dogs, in their sometime indifference to human concerns (cf. Thomas, 1993).

Here we come up against the irreducible difference between humans and dogs. The complex interactions that make up the human–dog relation span the material and semiotic, dogs and humans signify and they touch, they 'talk' and they pull. The stories that humans tell about their animal companions – whether objectifying or subjectifying or 'messy' mixtures of these – are resources by which they attempt to get a 'grip' on their dogs, and thus, as it were, to gain them entry into, and present them as competent members of, the social world (cf. Sanders, 1990, 1993). Nevertheless, the dogs remain, following Noske (1989, 1992), an 'Other World'. This point is underlined by Haraway (1992b). In addition to not being objectified, Haraway suggests that:

> The last thing 'they' [animals] need is human subject status, in whatever cultural-historical form. . . . We need other terms of conversations with animals, a much less respectable undertaking. The point is not new representations, but new practices, other forms of life rejoining humans and not-humans.
>
> (Haraway, 1992b, pp. 86–87)

Out of this emerges, Haraway hopes, a new form of human being:

> Once the world of subjects and objects is put into question, that paradox concerns the congeries, or curious confederacy, that is the self, as well as selves' relations with others. A promising form of life, conversation defies the autonomization of the self, as well as the objectification of the other.
>
> (Haraway, 1992b, p. 90)

If the human self is 'diffused' (cf. Michael, 1996) in this interaction – or rather, in this conversation – it is not because the animal is some sort of human subject. Rather, there is distribution across, and through, human and animal – a curious confederacy that encompasses and escapes such dichotomies as subject/object, semiotic/material. What we see here, perhaps, is a different sort of entity, a hybrid or a cyborg. As Sanders puts it:

> When performing together, the caretaker and his/her animal constitute an acting unit engaged in the ongoing fostering of cooperative social action both within the dyad and with those outside of the associational boundaries that enclose the animal–human with [*sic*]. The members of the animal–human acting unit are (ideally) involved in the mutual performance of a definition of the situation directed at the social audience of others.
>
> (Sanders, 1990, p. 86)

Reading Sanders through Haraway, we come to see this dyad, this unit, not only as a socially efficacious actor, but also comprised of strange heterogeneous congeries – the product of heterogeneous networks, and a contributor to these heterogeneities. We have already observed how certain cultural resources enable this dyadic unit, for example discourses of mindedness, objectifying discourses, responsibilizing discourses (Hearne, 1986; Cox and Ashford, 1998), social expectations of the right-acting dog (Sanders, 1990) and so on. These expectations not only manifest themselves in local interactions, they are also constituted across various settings, such as, for example, the media commentaries on the 'Devil Dog' (Smart, 1990; cf. Ritvo, 1987, for an account of similar 'moral panics' in the Victorian age) and in legislation. Regarding the latter, in Britain, there are several strands to the legislation that covers the dog (e.g. dogbreeding; rabies; dog abandonment). When it comes to the use of the dog-lead (or the muzzle), this is covered under a number of Acts. Under the Dog Act 1906, Animal Health Act 1981 and the Environmental Protection Act 1990, there is provision for government officers to seize dogs believed to be stray – this sets up a general context in which dogs should be kept under control. More specific provision is present in the Road Traffic Act 1988. Thus, section 27 (Control of dogs on roads) (1) states: 'A person who causes or permits a dog to be on a designated road without the dog being held on a lead is guilty of an offence'. After the 'Devil Dog' scares of the late 1980s (in which various breeds of dogs were condemned for their violence toward people), there was an extension of Crown Court powers, as laid out in the Dogs Act 1871, in relation to the destruction of dangerous dogs and the punishment of owners in the Dangerous Dogs Act 1989. This Act was clarified in the Dangerous Dogs Act 1991 in which, over and above prohibitions regarding the ownership of 'fighting' breeds and other especially dangerous dogs, there were provisions made for ensuring that dogs are kept under proper control. Thus, section 3 (1) states: 'if a dog is dangerously out of control in a public place – (a) the owner: and (b) if different, the person for the time being in charge of the dog, is guilty of an offence, or, if the dog while so out of control injures any person, an aggravated offence, under this subsection'. In sum, there are a variety of cultural and legislative 'strictures' that contribute to the fashioning of the dyad.

Now, if these are some of the social and cultural circumstances that serve in the constitution of the human–dog dyad, let us not forget that a range of other non-humans also play their part. For example, dogs distant in time and space can be said to impact upon the dyad. Thus, a dog in a dyad is also engaged with other dogs or with other dogs' smells: the ongoing performance of the dyad is oftentimes affected by other dogs' scents. Further, let us recall that it has been argued (Budiansky, 1994) that (pre)historically, dogs (and other animals) were not simply 'domesticated'; rather, they 'chose' us for all manner of reasons, as well as being chosen by us. The dog–human dyad reflects, then, a mutual domestication, an intertwining of species; as Hearne (1986, p. 28) puts it: 'dogs are domesticated to, and into us, and we are domesticated to, and into, them'.

Be that as it may, what I want to focus upon here is the involvement of another non-human in the dog–human dyad. As the brief accounts of legislation and cultural expectation concerning dogs suggest, a key facet of the dyad is the dog-lead. The dog-lead is important in that it can signify both within and beyond the dyad. Thus, for both human and dog, it can signal 'walkies', and for outside observers it can connote 'dog under control'. More importantly for the present discussion is that the dog-lead serves as yet another medium of communication within the dyad. It affords a subtle mixture of intersubjective and interobjective exchanges between the companions. Further, it blurs the site of agency: who is the user – human or dog? Who is configured (Woolgar, 1991) and who does the configuring – dog or human? Where is morality embodied – animal, technological artefact or human?

These questions are complicated by the fact that the dog-lead is not of a singular type: there are varieties of dog-lead and collar (or muzzle). The dog-lead nowadays comes in two general forms – fixed length and variable length. The latter extending lead is interesting in that it begins to shift things like human motivation and the balance of modalities or senses used in the interaction with the dog. For a start, one's commitment to walking the dog can be varied: one need not walk as far in order to exercise the dog. The balance of the senses moves from the kinaesthetic (feeling the pressure of the dog's or human's tugging in the case of the fixed length lead) to the visual (judging the distances the dog has run by eye in the case of the variable length lead). Similarly, we would expect that parallel changes are experienced by the dogs too. Further, we might add that the extendable dog-lead to some extent dissipates certain aspects (the kinaesthetic) of the co(a)gency of dog and human. Like the stirrup by which the kinaesthetic was enhanced, so that 'horse and rider [were effectively] welded into a single fighting unit capable of violence without precedent' (White, 1962, p. 2), the extendable lead reconfigures the forms of communication possible between dog and human, but this time in the opposite direction, so that human and dog become a less contiguous unit (although, of course, this can be extremely useful for certain jobs such as tracking).

Needless to say, the lead (along with the collar and muzzle, and of course, the breed of dog) are also objects of consumption. The 'mongrel on a string' adopted by some UK subcultures signifies something that is very different from the sort of heavy-duty leather leads (with, say, studded collars) attached to a pitbull terrier. Between these extremes are a seemingly infinite variety of lead types in terms of materials and design (leather, single or double ply nylon, military webbing, braided or unbraided, with ergonomic cushioned handle, with built-in traffic handle, etc.). Despite this variation, the general point remains: namely, the process of communication is partly conducted through the medium of the dog-lead. It serves as a channel or conduit of communication in several senses: tactile, kinaesthetic, aural and visual. What is important here is that it allows for a mutuality between dog and human – that is, a process of *joint action* as John Shotter (1984) would call it. Via the medium of the dog-lead, the human, for example, reads on behalf of the dog (e.g. warning signs, traffic lights) and the dog, for example, smells on behalf of the human (e.g. danger, dog mess, quarry, evidence). And as we have seen at length, this co(a)gency is enabled by the wider nexus of associations – representational, institutional, legal, commercial, veterinary and so on.

In this section, I have tried to trace the interiority of the Hudogledog in the context of its heterogeneous enabling associations. I have aimed at representing the Hudogledog as a unitary entity. The three entities that make the Hudogledog are so 'interwoven', the agency so distributed across them, the action is so joint that it is senseless to think of the Hudogledog as anything other than unitary. But I suspect that this has not been altogether convincing – the Hudogledog still seems intent on falling apart into its constituent parts. So let me try another tack. Let us assume the Hudogledog is unitary and singular *at the outset*. Let us begin by taking for granted the agency, coherence and identity of the Hudogledog. And let us be puzzled by the strange fact that we keep apprehending, keep narrating, only in terms of 'separate' components.

Continuity and chronography

As I have remarked, a particular Hudogledog does not have a continuing 'existence' in the sense that a human actor appears to have. Rather, it seems to fall apart and come together at certain times – these times are, often, routine and regular. In other words, there is a rhythm to the physical aggregation (and disaggregation) of the three component entities – the human, dog-lead and dog – through which we can come to see and acknowledge this co(a)gent. To put it another way, the appearance of the Hudogledog takes the form of a sort of *pulse*. That is to say, the Hudogledog resembles a pulse in the way that it appears for a certain time period, then is absent, then appears, and so on, to produce a rhythm. Notice that what we have here is a continuity based on physical proximity, although, of course, the boundary drawn around such a co(a)gent can reflect not only physical proximity, but, as actor-network theory teaches us, also semiotic proximity.

However, when it comes to humans and/or organizations, these too can be said to make their appearances in a pulse-like way, for they too undergo routine breakdowns in continuity. While for the human this is not usually physical, the human actor can be said to be characterized by periods of non-identity, say, through discontinuous action – various routine and discrete moments of sequestration or difference – activities that necessitate some form of seclusion or some 'other' or 'not strictly relevant' behaviours. In the case of the human actor, we have a battery of discursive and practical techniques by which to re-assert unity, coherence and identity (and of course, Foucault and Derrida, amongst many others, have been pivotal in arguing this point).

In science studies it has become somewhat of a methodological truism to 'follow the scientist' – to trace what he or she does in detail, to become sensitive to their multiple talents that are not simply scientific, but also social, political and economic, all of which are deployed in the construction of a fact (e.g. Latour, 1987a). Yet the scientist who is followed is not followed *everywhere*. For example, there are commitments that make up the scientist's personal life – duties to children and lovers and friends. These too must be juggled, these too are part of the process of heterogeneous engineering (Law, 1987) which makes up scientific work, even if they become, in the process, 'marginal' or 'tangential' to that scientific work. But these aspects do not often feature in our empirical accounts.

The notion of the pulse suggests that when we are advised to follow the scientific actor, we are being tacitly urged to presuppose a 'particular relevant set of activities' and 'a particular sort of actor'.

In other words, what we seem to be doing when we 'follow the actor' is produce – indeed, presuppose – a *chronography*, by which I mean to suggest a mapping of the moments at which the actor (broadly predefined as the scientist *qua* heterogeneous engineer) makes its appearance. We focus upon those instances where the 'actor-of-interest' presents itself and goes about its business. Those moments of difference, of non-identity, to this actor-of-interest are not taken up analytically. To be sure, there are practical and ethical issues at stake here – but, importantly, these 'informal' or 'private' facets of the actor are barely acknowledged (although sometimes these are noted when they appear in scientists' accounts of discovery and the 'Aha!' experience – see Brannigan, 1981).

Now, the point to this apparent digression is that these moments of difference and 'non-identity' can aid us in narrating the Hudogledog. In the context of the foregoing treatment of the co(a)gent, we would expect a co(a)gent like the Hudogledog to be discontinuous. When it is not explicitly 'present' (in the sense that its components are 'demonstrably' separated), this does not signify its 'break-up' as such (in the same way that a 'scientist' does not break up when on holiday or bouncing her daughter on her knee). Rather, this periodic dissolution, this rhythm or chronography of appearance and disappearance, of coming together and falling apart, merely reflects the different aspects of the co(a)gent that come into, and go out of, view. If we assume, as I am proposing, the cogency of the Hudogledog, then it is the 'falling apart' that becomes the 'problem', not the coming together of the constituent parts. Thus, when we see a human physically alone, that is, without dog and dog-lead attached, then what I suggest we should now see is not the disaggregated Hudogledog, but an *aspect* of the Hudogledog.

Let me elaborate by drawing out some of the properties of the co(a)gent. We can liken it to a black blob, as distinct from a black box. The latter, a conceptual mainstay in science studies, refers to some phenomenon – a fact, a technology, a technique – the internal workings (contingencies, heterogeneities, politics, etc.) of which are obscured: all that we see are what goes in and what comes out. Latour, elaborates on this: '[When] the assembly of disorderly and unreliable allies is thus slowly turned into something that closely resembles an organised whole[,] when such a cohesion is obtained we at last have a black box' (Latour, 1987a, pp. 130–131). We find a black box, then, 'when many elements are made to act as one' (Latour, 1987a, p. 131). The solidity of the black box suggests the same output – e.g. a camera always works thus (of course, what the notion of black box signifies is all the hard work of coralling disparate elements to ensure that a camera 'always works thus'). The black blob, by comparison, is a softer entity with more fluid boundaries. The elements that comprise it work together – cohere – but what it produces, what it does, shifts and varies. Moreover, those components sometimes do things seemingly on their own, yet always within the borders – the skin – of the black blob.

Let me try again, even at the risk of a profligacy of metaphors. The amoeba is a protozoan, a single-celled organism that moves by pushing out foot-like extensions of itself that remain bounded by the cell membrane. These are pseudopodia. As such, the amoeba is a bounded mass whose interior contorts to produce all sorts of boundary shifts but whose surface remains intact. What we see, then, are forms of external 'morphing' while the internal workings remain a mystery. The extensions of the amoeba – the pseudopodia, prominences, protrusions, protuberances – are sent out to do the business of the amoeba. Yet, when we look at the amoeba through the microscope, we often see, from a certain perspective – or rather, within a certain focal plane – only those extensions, those psuedopodia, etc. They seem to have a unity, a discreteness of their own for their connection to the rest of the amoeba is not apparent to us. Only 'experience' tells us that there is such a connection – that they are part rather than whole.

The amoeba is, of course, an analogy for a co(a)gent such as the Hudogledog. The Hudogledog's 'components' – say, the 'human' – might seem to wander off, to separate itself from the main body of Hudogledog and appear to engage in associations with other heterogeneous actors. But this is a trick of the light. This component is but a pseudopodium – we have failed to see the strands that connect it back to the co(a)gent. Or rather, we could say that the Hudogledog has moved itself into such a position that only the pseudopodium-that-is-the-human enters our focal plane. When these movements are rhythmic – when we sometimes see this pseudopodium, sometimes the amoeba-that-is-the-Hudogledog as a whole, then we witness the 'pulses' of the Hudogledog, as I've called them above.

'Characterology': facetting the Hudogledog

In trying to set out some resources for narrating the Hudogledog, I have, of course, been stressing its unity and its singularity. In this respect, to reiterate, the narratives I am pursuing are traditional ones, parts of what Callon and Law (1995) have called 'normal discourse' where agency is not attributed to networks, interactions or fields, but to singularities. I am trying to explore what it means to construct and narrate, from within 'normal discourse' (a discourse that I am no doubt abusing with my proliferation of metaphors), the peculiar singularity I have called the Hudogledog.

I now want to take yet another perspective on this co(a)gent. The Hudogledog, as we have seen, is subject to discrete, punctuated appearances. Even when we encounter the Hudogledog at those moments when its components are in close proximity (e.g. 'taking the dog for a walk'), there is still a tendency for the Hudogledog to fall apart before our eyes. What we are always tempted to see are the separate components. Yet, these different components can be treated as nothing more than the different facets of the same entity. The different strands, pseudopodia, protrusions, prominences, can be rethought as something like different sides of the Hudogledog's character. In the same way that we can decompose a human into different characteristics – emotionality, personality, skills, intelligence (and variations and subdivisions thereof), so too can we de-construct the Hudogledog. However, we do not need to draw upon individual (psychological) traits to draw the parallel between person and co(a)gent. Sociological categories (e.g. roles) can also serve in allowing us to see how the different facets (components) of the Hudogledog have their analogy in the human (role player). Of course, there are different implications between these psychological and sociological models, not least in that the latter has the advantage of evoking different networks, trails and connections, as do the components of the Hudogledog.

If, however, we follow the psychological parallel for the moment, we inevitably encounter the issue of individual differences. Just as there are common-sensical differences between individual humans, so there are between Hudogledogs – although rather than recounting these in simple psychological terms, we can now additionally point to differences in technology (the dog-lead) and breed of dog. Again, this can be reworked in sociological terms, say, of interests or goals, which, as before, afford the advantage of enabling us to see co(a)gents' distributedness (especially where such interests are conceived as relational or emergent – see, Callon and Law, 1982). In sum, and to return to our amoebic model for a moment, these different facets can be viewed as the different topological features of the co(a)gent – the different 'pointy' bits.

Fragments of agency and identity

The human is, therefore, but an extension of the Hudogledog. Let us follow this pseudopodium, this protrusion. And let us give it a little more character – it is a scientist, for example (I draw on this identity again because I know a little about the sociological treatments of scientists). It 'goes off' and does scientific things – it has the agency and identity of a scientist which, as we know, is distributed, relational, and the upshot of a network. But this agency and identity – this pursuit of certain scientific goals – are also parts of the Hudogledog. Or rather, the human-as-scientist contains within it a fragment of the Hudogledog's agency and identity (which, as we know, is distributed, relational, and the upshot of a network). It might only be a tiny fragment that rarely gets articulated, but it still nevertheless partly characterizes the human-as-scientist.

The human-as-scientist I am describing here is a messy entity – it incorporates heterogeneous bits and pieces that seem to belong elsewhere. As such, this figure stands in contrast to the scientist who is the object of study for some sociologies of science (e.g. actor-network theory). Certainly, ANT's scientist is a heterogeneous engineer, but all this figure's immense effort and all its sophisticated, eclectic activity seems to be oriented purely to the eventual production of scientific facts – that is, the putting together of allies so that that the scientist's account is taken as fact. This heterogeneity, this hybridity, does receive expression on occasion, as when Latour's scientist says: 'Hi, I'm the coordinator of the chromosome 11 of yeast' (Latour, 1994, p. 797). But it is a heterogeneity, a hybridity, appropriate to the networks of science. It would not have been 'politic' to say something like 'Hi, I'm a dogperson' – a term of self-reference that 'dog owners' can use (Smart, 1993).

But let us reflect for a moment here. Perhaps it would have been 'politic' – in the broadest sense – to call oneself a 'dogperson'. After all, we can assume that scientists are not simply scientists – they are multiple too. They span, as we all do – they are the products of, as we all are – multiple networks, associations and string figures (see Chapter 2; Star, 1991; Singleton and Michael, 1993). The process of 'making a scientific fact' reflects a multiplicity that lies beyond the 'standard' heterogeneity that constitutes scientific activity. For example, scientists are not simply concerned with the enrolment of allies, the persuasion of peers and so on. They also engage in friendships and enmities, undergo interpersonal attraction and repulsion – and these processes too contribute their little bit to the construction of scientific facts. These relationalities – let us call them *sub-relationalities* (and they are, again, both material and semiotic) – are a small part of doing science then. To clarify, I call them sub-relationalities because they function beneath the usual analytic surface, that is, they do not often comprise our objects of study being altogether too partial, too 'distant' from the narrative at hand. Further, I use the term relationality, rather than relation, because I would like to echo the Foucauldian contrast between government and governmentality (see, for example, Rose, 1999), and particularly the latter's evocation of fluidity, distributedness, process and partiality.

Sometimes, however, these sub-relationalities are analytically foregrounded, as when, in for example Star's (1991) account of her allergy to onions, they operate to exclude or marginalize one from dominant networks (also see Mort and Michael, 1998). But to return to our example of the scientific actor, sub-relationalities can be thought of as contributing little fragments of agency and identity that combine with other fragments to make up the 'scientist'. And these sub-relationalities pertain not just between scientists, not just between humans (for example, scientist and spouse), but between humans and non-humans as well.

It should by now be clear that the notion of 'fragments of agency and identity' is hardly a satisfactory metaphor, not least because there is the danger of seeing these fragments as little reified nuggets of agency and identity. However, what intrigues me is the movement of these, their trajectories: the mention of sub-relationalities should indicate that my concern is still with relationality and the possible patterns that it can take up. I am thus concerned with what Marilyn Strathern (1991), in another context, calls 'partial connections'. Strathern's purpose is to theorize how one can write and converse as both an anthropologist and a feminist. Feminism, she suggests, can be thought of as 'an aid or tool; it introduces thoughts I would not otherwise entertain. Hence an anthropologist can make feminist discourse exist as a distinct exterior presence – "outside" the body, as it were, because it is an extension of it, an instrument made out of different materials, and able to do things the original body alone cannot' (Strathern, 1991, p. 39). Part of what it can do is enable conversation. Thus:

> '[f]eminist discourse creates connections between the participants – but they remain partial insofar as they create no single entity between them. What each creates is an extension of a position, which could not have been done without

the instrument of the conversation but in the end is done from the position each occupies for herself or himself. 'Partial' captures the nature of the interlocution well, for not only is there no totality, each part also defines a partisan position.

(Strathern, 1991, p. 39)

My terms of reference are somewhat different to Strathern's: where she talks of conversation, I talk of heterogeneous communications and flows; where she refers to human participants, I refer to co(a)gents. However, the general form of her analysis of partial connections applies to what I'm trying to get at with the idea of sub-relationalities. The 'fragments of agency and identity' that flow between co(a)gents do not necessarily form a totality between the co(a)gents; rather, they enable a heterogeneous communication or connection. And that connection does not escape the position of each co(a)gent – it is partial insofar as it implicates the respective networks of the interacting co(a)gents. I elaborate on all this in the next chapter.

The Hudogledog is, as I have stressed throughout, a minor, trivial co(a)gent. From one perspective on the human-as-scientist, say that of science studies, the sub-relationalities with the Hudogledog are trivial. Even worse, they are a distraction. They are parasites – disruptors of the real circuits of (heterogeneous) communication that make up the human-as-scientist as it goes about its 'real' business of 'doing science'. I am not picking on science studies especially; the same point applies to any human actor (and of course, these can be collective actors) – the politician, the sociologist, the parent, the racist, the environmentalist. We do not normally regard these in terms of co(a)gential sub-relationalities. To raise the spectre of a co(a)gent like the Hudogledog in relation to racism or sexism seems almost crass, but the point is that these sub-relationalities can partially contribute to the most reprehensible practices. For example, Hitler and Goebbels were, as Arluke and Sanders (1996) detail, partly sustained by their relations (sub-relationalities) to their dogs.

From the perspective of the Hudogledog, the scientist is more than a 'scientist' – even the profoundly heterogeneous version of the scientist we find in science studies. The human-as-scientist 'returns' to the Hudogledog – takes up its place in that co(a)gent, is once again part of the mass of cytoplasm rather than a pseudopodium (as, conversely, the human-as-a-part-of-the-Hudogledog returns to science, to the laboratory). It perhaps 'parasitises' on the internal relationalities that make up the Hudogledog. However, perhaps, it also contributes something as well – maybe a keener sense of, and deeper respect for, the dog (as animal experimentalists have claimed in relation to their companion animals – cf. Michael and Birke, 1994). The point is that these 'cross-overs' (or sub-relationalities), these movements of a pseudopodium into a different domain – which I discuss in more detail in the next chapter – might be trivial, might be inconsequential, but they might also be deeply important, profoundly consequential whether because they generate disorder or disruption, or because they contribute to the ordering processes that make up that different domain (or network). Clearly, in the end, this is, at least in part, an empirical issue – the point of this discussion has been to identify it as an issue *per se*. In other words, what I have been trying to get at is those usually unnoticed pathways – or what I have called sub-relationalities – that might contribute, trivially or profoundly, to the 'domain' (e.g. the 'nature' of the scientific enterprise) or 'objects' (e.g. the 'nature' of the scientist) of intellectual interest.

Conclusion: relationality and rights

In the initial sections of this chapter, I sketched some of the historical, material, cultural, social complexities of Western apprehensions of the animal. The point of this account was to stress that (despite later 'bracketing' this complexity in constructing it), the Hudogledog is the bearer of this rich heterogeneity and distributedness. As a co(a)gent, it has cogency, and is partly constituted through the co-agency exercised amongst its components, components that are themselves heterogeneously distributed.

In the context of this distributedness, my task has been to think through some conditions by which a co(a)gent such as the Hudogledog can be narrated. What I have attempted to show is that these co(a)gents – even one as seemingly trivial as the Hudogledog – can be narrated in terms of having consquences, effects. Through what I have called sub-relationalities, these co(a)gents impact upon figures, characters, actors that we normally take for granted (e.g. the scientist), and that routinely serve as our, more or less unproblematized, units of analysis. As such, in reifying a co(a)gent such as the Hudogledog, I have attempted to redeem, at least in part, the promissory note entered at the end of Chapter 2 – to show how co(a)gents might yield new insights into the operation of processes that we take as typical (e.g. those concerned with the figure of the 'scientist'). What has been lost in this process of reification is a sense of the mundane technology – the dog-lead. This is to be expected because it is the co(a)gent in which I have been interested. The internal relations of the Hudogledog have become backgrounded. In focusing upon the Hudogledog, I have attempted to 'step past' its components and the dualities they ordinarily entail (e.g. subject/object, human/non-human). I say 'step past' because I have not attempted to resolve or transcend these dichotomies, but to develop a vocabulary that accommodates while simultaneously 'bracketing' these divisions. That is to say, I am not concerned with conceptual advances *per se* (most of this advance has been accomplished by others), but with the production of cultural artefacts (which are, of course, never simply 'cultural'). At the risk of grandiloquence, the 'paradigm' shift to which I attach myself does not, in any simple sense, entail progress, resolution or transcendence. The aim has been to develop, partly through a new vocabulary, the conduits of a new (academic) network through which circulate new string figures (for example, co(a)gents) that, from the perspective of the old 'paradigm', are internally contradictory, paradoxical and oxymoronic.

One of my other aims in this chapter has been concerned with how we might value animals. In recent times, certainly since Singer's (1970) *Animal Liberation*, the valuation of animals has tended to be couched in terms of 'rights'. Animals should, according to this argument, be ascribed the same rights as those enjoyed by humans. This view has certainly been taken seriously; it has been debated in academic journals and has formed the basis for growing activism (cf. Jasper and Nelkin, 1991). However, this animal advocacy view has also met with hostile responses. Some have argued that rights can only be awarded if the carriers of such rights also fulfil relevant duties (Leahy, 1994; Carruthers, 1993). Tester's (1991) purist social constructionist critique dismisses the animal rights argument as reflecting animal rights activists' cultural concern with their own identities (what it means to be human – see Franklin, 1999, for a partial critique).

More sympathetic commentators have suggested that the rights argument is problematic because the very notion of rights relies on a profound process of 'separation' and is grounded in individualism. Thus, Benton (1993) argues that rights can only be understood in the context of the idealization of certain rights in the eighteenth century, a period of history when our modern separation of nature from culture was consolidated. The sphere of the 'natural' was omitted from these idealized rights. Moreover, Benton suggests that notions of rights tend to obscure 'the social-relational preconditions' (Benton, 1993, p. 172) which enabled the emergence of the 'human individual' who came to be the carrier of rights. Other authors suggest that animals (and other natural non-humans) should be viewed not only as subjects (and therefore candidates for rights), but also as objects. Indeed, Soper (1995) has argued that, in the process of political activism, it is inevitable that activists alternate between discourses that represent natural non-humans as objects and those in which they are portrayed as subjects. This is because, in order to establish the subjectivity of, say, animals, there is often recourse to their 'objective' constitution as beings with particular physiological capacities and psychological faculties.

Now, this range of accounts begins to move towards a concern with the relationality of animals and humans. That is to say, rather than assuming separation between humans and animals in the conferral of rights by the former upon the latter, there is an emerging analytic that attempts to see these as already 'in relation'. The status of this 'in relation' can vary. It can be grounded in pre-history as Budiansky (1994) explains: humans did not 'domesticate' animals, rather animals 'chose' human communities. As such, there was a 'co-shaping', a mutuality, that is deeply ingrained in us. Alternatively, it can be contextualized within postmodernity: Franklin (1999) remarks that in post- or late modernity, while human–animal relations are likely to be highly diverse, there is detectable in the decentred sensibilities of postmoderns a de-differentiation between humans and animals. Instead of rights, and the separation on which these are premised, there is a mood of 'reconciliation, community building and empathy' (Franklin, 1999, p. 199).

In contrast to these grand narratives, one can attempt to situate relationality contingently at the level of micro-relationalities. For Birke and Michael (1997), we need to think of these through co(a)gency, which might provide an alternative way to address – or at least suggests the grounds for addressing anew – the valuation of humans, animals and environments. These all become relational entities, whether they entail just a few components as with the Hudogledog, or something more complex like an ecosystem, conceived as an assemblage of natures, humans and technologies in its historical *and* biological specificity (cf. Whatmore, 1997). But do we want to be rid of the distinction between humans and natural non-humans altogether here? Do we really want to de-prioritize the values we have traditionally placed on human beings? As Soper (1986) has argued, humanism, as well as anti-humanism, has its political uses. Moreover, do we want to privilege 'relational ethics' over traditional 'individualized' ethics? As Birke and Michael (1997) note, there are certain issues (e.g. battery farming) where animal rights discourse – that is, an ethics concerned with individual animals – still seems indispensable. And as we have seen, even in Haraway's reworking and championing of the 'cyborg', there is an ambivalence wherein both anti-humanist and humanist, distributed and singularized political stances are expressed (Prins, 1995).

Here we begin to return to the question, formulated in the preceding chapter, as to 'who' or 'what' does the 'valuing', the dispensing of rights, or the fashioning of a relational ethics. The foregoing discussion, which raises the spectre of the limits of the efficacy of both rights discourse and hybrid discourse, is hinting at the relationality of the advocate of these rights, or the enunciator of these valuations, to the bearer of rights, or the entity being valued.

In the process of constructing the Hudogledog and exploring the grounds for its narration as a co(a)gent, I have been performing the God Trick, recounting from abstract, disemobodied space. But let us cast our minds back to the beginning of this chapter, to the vignette where a Hudogledog is encountered by my son as I push him along in his buggy. What is meeting here? It is two co(a)gents: the Hudogledog and the Dababug (Dababug = Da(ddy) + Ba(by) + Bug(gy)). The valuation of the Hudogledog by me in this encounter is specific to my location within the Dababug. This 'me' – let us call it MM – has a particularity, a situation, that shapes the process of valuation, that, in other words, partially affects what MM can say and do about the Hudogledog. Thus, MM as a part of the Dababug asks certain questions about the dog (is this a 'dangerous' breed? has this dog been trained properly to deal with sometimes meddlesome children?), about the human (is this someone who knows how to handle dogs in this sort of encounter?), and about the sort of dog-lead (will it extend too far and get tangled in the buggy?). Of course, MM is also drawing upon other stories (some of them exceedingly impoverished ones – cf. Hearne, 1986) in making this valuation, and in raising these sorts of questions. What the situatedness of these valuations should alert us to – and this is a key, if obvious, point – is their conditionality. As the remark about impoverished stories should indicate, the sorts of interaction (and the sorts of valuation) that were possible for the MM-of-the-Dababug were peculiar to a particular time and place. But this time and place incorporates, through sub-relationalities, the characteristics – the fragments of agency and identity – of other networks, not least those of the media with their sensationalist scare stories about dogs.

Now, the present reflections on the encounter between the Hudogledog and the Dababug have been couched in the vocabularies of the academy and have been partly realized through the medium of a computer. These reflections, the stories related here, are no less situated, no less relational, no less conditional, no less heterogeneously derived than the stories deployed by the MM-of-the-Dababug in its valuation of the Hudogledog. They are the partial product of another co(a)gent, the Acacomp (aca(demic) + comp(uter)). Perhaps, given the more extended networks of the Acacomp, these reflections – texts – will circulate more widely, be taken up by colleagues, perhaps even seem insightful. Their situatedness, however, does not diminish, it merely becomes, as the sociology of science has long documented, less obvious.

Yet, perhaps this contingency not only reflects the exigencies of the Acacomp, but incorporates a fragment of agency and identity that has come from the Dababug. To put this another way, what is the MM that is shared by these two co(a)gents – the Acacomp and the Dababug? Is there an order mediated by this MM as it passes between these co(a)gents? Is it the same MM, or does it change in the course of its trajectories? These questions are essentially about connections and the making of connections that extend between co(a)gents, about the passing on of fragments of agency and identity that make up the processes of sub-relationality. The issue of this passing – the nature of these 'little' semiotic and material flows and of their disposition in the processes of heterogeneous ordering and disordering – is addressed in the next, concluding, chapter.

7 Conclusion
Closings and openings

Introduction

In the four preceding 'empirical' chapters, there has been one figure that has, albeit tacitly, been a common feature. This is MM. Inserted in walking boots, this figure has pursued the sublime; cocooned in the car, this figure has practised one of the milder forms of road rage; attached to the television remote control, this figure has been a part of couch potato culture; as a pusher of buggy and baby, this figure has wrought judgement on humans and their canine companions. Seated before a computer, MM has attempted to craft a story about each of these, and now he attempts to write about the connections between them.

The status of MM is ambivalent. I/he/it has been both real and a fiction, both a fact and a fetish. That is to say, he has been a 'factish' (Latour, 1997). On the one hand, MM is an assumed, largely unproblematized, actor who has served loyally as a narrative linchpin for the preliminary vignette with which each of the four case study chapters begins. Yet, in three of those chapters, MM has been deconstructed: his role as a seeker-of-the-sublime, as a cason, or as a couch potato has been shown to be constituted through discourse and mundane technology, through the semiotic and the material. His co(a)gency has, it is hoped, been (always partially) laid bare.

As outlined in Chapter 1, the point of this common character was that we might ask how it is that, despite these varying co(a)gencies, we still apprehend the figure MM. Or rather, conversely, the goal was to set up a series of vignettes that were connected by MM's common presence, in order to explore what it means to see continuity across these co(a)gents – to see some form of ordering (and disordering) as we – and MM – move from co(a)gent to co(a)gent (and, clearly, here we must be mindful of the possibility that such dis/ordering is a partial artefact of the present writing, the present situation – see below).

In this chapter, I want to begin to theorize how we might think about these connections across co(a)gents, how we might see these as forms of ordering and disordering. I begin, then, with a brief summary of the preceding chapters, drawing out some of their key themes and commonalities. In the next section, I address the associations between the co(a)gents that featured in the case study chapters, focusing in particular on the figure of MM. After this, I elaborate some of the more general ways of thinking about these linkages, or sub-relationalities as I have called them above. I am especially keen to explore how what passes between co(a)gents is heterogeneous, that is, can include non-humans as well as humans. Finally, this leads me to reflect on how I have derived co(a)gents – how this process cannot be separated from the complex and oblique co(a)gency of MM as a 'writer'.

Summarizing

If Chapter 1 reviewed some of the key issues addressed by sociological approaches to technology with a view to identifying a number of aporias, Chapter 2 conveniently filled those spaces with a perspective derived from such scholars as Bruno Latour, Donna Haraway and Michel Serres. As such, the heterogeneity and distributedness of human relations to mundane technology were emphasized. Moreover, I began to sketch out how such technologies were implicated in the processes, at once semiotic and material, of ordering and disordering. This was illustrated in the next chapter where the roles of walking boots in ordering human relations with the environment (in particular, sublime or expressive, as well as scientific, relations), and, on occasion, disordering those relations, were explored. In addition, it was hoped that some small contribution was made to the analysis of human–environment relations (environmental sociology) as well as the sociology of the body. I noted at several points that these relations between humans and environment, mediated by mundane technologies such as walking boots, were thoroughly distributed. Thus, the walker-in-nature (or the seeker of the sublime) was seen to be enabled, materially and semiotically, by a mundane technology, which was itself constituted by other technologies, and by other relations between humans and humans, and humans and natures. The heterogeneous convolutions that were drafted in this chapter served as an initial illustration of the idea of the co(a)gent. The next chapter, in addition to extending fractionally the emergent field of the sociology of emotions, aimed to show how mundane technologies could be seen to be instrumental in the shaping of those emotions associated with road rage. Moreover, the chapter began to explore the way that certain co(a)gents could be formulated and judged, albeit it in an elementary and emergent way, in the discourse of particular groups. Chapter 5 took this a stage further, looking at how co(a)gents could be said to be 'formulated' and 'judged' not only through certain discourses but also heterogeneously through other co(a)gents. The couch potato was thus both discursively constructed (and valued) in a number of ways in popular culture, *and* heterogeneously constructed, 'surveilled' and disrupted by co(a)gents that were partially composed through what I called the 'coincidentalization of technologies'. This analysis of the couch potato was meant to suggest still more ways of thinking about the heterogeneous distributedness of the body. In Chapter 6, instead of looking for co(a)gents articulated in popular culture, I began to examine the possibility of actually contriving a co(a)gent – the Hudogledog. Through a series of metaphors – the black blob, the amoeba, the pseudopodium, fragments of agency and identity, sub-relationality – I attempted to outline a tentative and contingent vocabulary with which we could narrate the co(a)gent (such as the Hudogledog) as at once a distribution and a singularity.

The complementary aim was not only to raise the profile of animals in social thought, but also to consider how we might begin to value animal non-humans as aspects of co(a)gents.

The chapters on walking boots, the car and the remote control draw upon the generalized ethos of deconstructionism. The figures of the walker and the seeker of the sublime, of the road rager (cason, repmo), of the couch potato were subjected to an analysis that teased apart the discourses through which they are variously constituted, which resourced their seemingly unproblematic cogency as real entities. This is not new – it is common in the social sciences. The added twist, drawn from certain movements in science and technology studies, is to show that these resources are not simply social, cultural or linguistic but also include the non-human, specifically mundane technologies. Moreover, as I have stressed, these do not simply serve in the mediation of relations solely amongst humans. That is to say, these heterogeneous resources are also mobilized in mediating relations with the 'natural', variously construed in this book as the environment, the emotions, the body and animals, all of which are, in the process, themselves constructed (and, as such, the present work can be distinguished from some versions of studies in material culture – cf. Dant, 1999). However, these 'natures' are never 'wholly' constructed, they are never 'subaltern' by virtue of their constructedness – they too contribute to the processes of construction (of other natures, technologies and socials).

This 'will to deconstruction' has, nevertheless, been tempered by what might be dubbed a 'will to reconstruction' through which new 'figurations', as Haraway (1997) calls them, emerge. Haraway's brilliant figurations – crucially, the cyborg – are inherently ambiguous and multiform, capturing both the human and the non-human, the material and the semiotic, the emancipatory and the oppressive. Yet we have glimpsed figurations – albeit more mundane ones – in popular discourse: the emergent co(a)gents of road rage, the more fully-fledged co(a)gent of the couch potato. Moreover, these are, like Haraway's figurations, 'condensed maps of contestable worlds' (Haraway, 1997, p. 11). Thus, the couch potato signifies, on the one hand, a multiply wasted body and, on the other, a subcultural identity: it, in other words, is a site contested by various groupings (the moral guardians of youth, the practitioners of slacker culture, family members, the marketing executives of computers and TV stations, for example).

In the process of accounting for these co(a)gents various sub-disciplines have been traversed. As mentioned in Chapter 1, my aspiration was to practise a sort of infra-disciplinarity; the inevitable actuality is that I have performed a crypto-disciplinarity (most patently and jarringly evidenced in the minimal reference to the natural sciences). In Chapter 6, the concern with articulating the activities of the Hudogledog through a general, abstracted vocabulary (and here I follow in the fashion of ANT), or rather a sequence of metaphors, comprised a tentative and elementary attempt at sidestepping natural and social scientific disciplines, not by transcending or resolving their differences, but by 'bracketing' them. As noted above, these differences and disjunctions are not 'solved' logically, but reframed culturally, heterogeneously – it is a new paradigm, a sort of 'indiscipline' that hopefully suggests new ways of thinking about the social world that is heterogeneous (and which will, in its turn, no doubt be overcome by new figurations).

Now, the co(a)gents I have identified, that is to say, constructed, have one commonality, MM. This 'character' simultaneously emerges from them, but is also a figure that cuts across them, draws them together. In the next section, in order to pursue the issue of connection and continuity between these different co(a)gents in a little more detail, I address the status and function of this 'MM'.

The associations of MM

What is MM? It is clearly not a pure human (hence the switching between the pronouns 'I', 'he' and 'it'). It has been a common human figure that is thoroughly enmeshed in heterogeneous networks, and that, as a fragment of agency and identity, passes from network to network, co(a)gent to co(a)gent. The co(a)gents we have considered – the walker, the road rager and the couch potato – are connected by MM, but MM is not an intermediary in Callon's (1991) sense; that is, something – human or non-human – that can enable certain actors and networks and, in this case co(a)gents, to 'converge' and thus to become co-ordinated, integrated into a greater network, a larger, more durable co(a)gent. Insofar as they do converge, this is through the circulation of MM – but this is a very loose sort of convergence. As MM passes between them, he brings with him fragments of agency and identity from preceding co(a)gents, but the connections with subsequent co(a)gents are partial, for in the process of that movement MM changes: MM becomes altered, reshaped to the configuration of the new co(a)gent. MM is thus a 'string figure', and mediates sub-relationalities, as I've called them.

Therefore, MM carries certain material capacities and semiotic potentialities, some of which reflect his enmeshment in the preceding co(a)gents. Thus, his particular doings as a couch potato (for example, the frustrations of losing the remote) affect his doings as part of a car-person co(a)gent, which in turn affect his doings as a walker co(a)gent. The precise 'nature' of these influences will vary depending on the form of the doings of the particular co(a)gents 'out of' which MM 'emerges'. He is thus a carrier of the echoes of preceding co(a)gents, echoes that are released in each subsequent co(a)gency. At the same time, each co(a)gency absorbs or rebounds those echoes depending on its own circumstances.

From the perspective of the co(a)gent, MM is a constituent component that contributes a fragment of identity and agency that is variable. But there are also certain coherencies to MM, a certain intransigence. MM, in common with the prescriptions of certain technologies, the immutability of certain texts, the peculiar 'other worldness' of animals and the environment, is characterized by a number of consistent features, some corporeal, some semiotic. But this fixity is relative, contingent: it is partly realized through the co(a)gencies out of which MM emerges. On this score, then, MM does not simply and singularly 'move between', or 'hop across', co(a)gents: MM is itself a co(a)gent, at once distributed and singular, always already embroiled as a co(a)gent, always already emergent from, and entering into, co(a)gents. (That is to say, the sense of MM 'hopping across' co(a)gents is the upshot of the narrative conventions used here, most obviously the sequencing of vignettes.)

From the perspective of MM, this play of difference (fluidity) and sameness (fixity) is barely noticed, although sometimes it is, as when things go wrong (for instance, when an in-use body part or piece of technology or the environment is 'disobedient'). MM has available to it discourses that resource its sense of continuity. For example, MM is encumbered with something akin to the Western cultural baggage of sovereign individualism (for example, Abercrombie *et al.*, 1986; see also Freeman, 1993; Plummer, 1995). To hand are overarching stories about the individual, responsibility, the agency that enable him to narrate himself out of the shifts and changes that he undergoes in the process of these trajectories across co(a)gents. Of course, these stories are contestable and contested and, of course, these stories are heterogeneously constituted. Technologies too play their part in the articulation and dissemination of the sovereign, possessive individual, not only the subjectifying technologies of the psy complex (Rose, 1996, 1999) but also such technologies as surveillance machines (e.g. CCTV), person ordering machines (e.g. revolving doors), information processing machines (e.g. automatic cash dispensers), as well as the technologies we find as parts of our peculiar co(a)gents – the remote control, the car, the dog-lead (however, see Lury, 1998, for a discussion of the recent, possibly transformative, role of photographic technologies in the production of the 'individual'). Thus, for example, the ticket-operated turnstile serves heterogeneously in the reproduction of the juridical-corporeal individual: as Gomart and Hennion (1999) brilliantly show, and as I've been tacitly suggesting throughout this book, subjectivities, as well as objectivities, are heterogeneously constituted. The general point is that even this 'cultural baggage' is not distinct from the embroilment of humans in co(a)gents. It is one of the 'characteristics' imported into a co(a)gent from (a range of) others. Indeed, these technologies that serve in the perpetuation (and sometimes the undercutting) of the sovereign, self-possessed individual remind us that we should be circumspect in regard of abstracting something like 'cultural baggage'. As actor–network theory has taught us, these grand macro phenomena are resourced by, and realized in, the 'local'. Thus, macro entities, as seemingly indisputable as 'the market', are partly the local products (e.g. texts) of the discipline of economics that are put into circulation (cf. Callon, 1998a).

Now, this account of the trajectory of MM as it moves from co(a)gent to co(a)gent rests on a particular model of space and time. Time is linear and space is comprised of discrete localities. However, this is too simple, as Law (1999) stresses. Let us recall the co(a)gent, the couch potato. MM is associated with the television, the TV remote control and the sofa, but it is simultaneously a part of other co(a)gents that do not have a name: MM-sofa-coffee cup, MM-sofa-companion cat, MM-light bulb-remote control, MM-TV-partner and so on *ad infinitum*. As noted in Chapter 2, Button (1993) argues that actor–network theory's analytic sleight of hand is to pick and choose amongst the infinite array of possible associations. I have done this deliberately: in making such choices, the hope is to gain insights into otherwise unnoticed connections that make up heterogeneous ordering and disordering. The alternative configurations would yield other pathways than those that arose in the analysis of, for example, the couch potato. However, there is also the issue that some connections with MM are more partial than others, some configurations are less 'integrated' than others. Partiality is not an 'either/or' category then: some connections are 'looser', more labile (in the sense of slipping and changing) than others. All this suggests that we need to address the issue of the arbitrariness entailed in the composition of co(a)gents. I do this below.

Taking this multiplicity and partiality into account leads us to view space as fuzzy. MM occupies through these connections a strange topology: it is a fractal entity, being 'more than one and less than many' (Law, 1999, p. 12), at once a singularity and not a singularity, a multiplicity and not a multiplicity. The notion of 'trajectory' with its connotation of Cartesian space, of course, does not help us much in getting at this oxymoronic entity, but let me persevere with it for the moment. Perhaps we might think of MM as an old furry, frayed tennis ball with strands extending and entangling with the strands of all sorts of other tennis balls. Each entanglement – which, as ever, is semiotic and material – exerts a pressure on the tennis ball and distends it in various ways. Or, we might say that these linkages form threads, that is, capillaries or 'axons' through which pass materials and messages which, on arrival, may enable new extensions to be generated, and new connections to be made. Needless to say, the strands are multiply entangled. Further, they have differing strengths, differing adhesiveness, different ductilities. Some entanglements (see Callon, 1998a, 1998b) are tighter than others, some are more likely to snap than others. In all this connectedness, MM-as-a-discrete-entity, nevertheless, can still be regarded as lurking, somewhere in the interior of our distended tennis ball. So let us reduce this to a zero point – let us see only strands that cross over, are knotted at a point which is, as this metaphor hints, both a singularity and more than a singularity, more than one and less than many.

Now MM also moves, and that movement is intimately related to time. Even social scientists must nowadays think in terms of space–time or time–space (e.g. Thrift, 1996; Adam, 1990). The occupation of space, in my account of MM 'passing' through different co(a)gents, has so far been linear: MM 'hops' from co(a)gent to co(a)gent as from discrete locale to discrete locale. Yet, we might also see this movement as a form of Brownian motion, though of threads rather than particles. Different connections are strengthened or weakened in this motion. Time might be thought of as linear, as marking transition or evolution: the making of different connections, the absorption in different co(a)gents, transforms MM sequentially. But MM might also go through cycles of connections, rhythms of associations (recall the rhythmic pulse of the appearance of the Hudogledog). As such we might regard some patterns of connection, disconnection, reconnection as mediating a cyclical or homeostatic time. Moreover, some connections change at different rates: MacNaghten and Urry's (1998; Adam, 1998) talk of glacial and instantaneous time reflects large-scale, slow changes in the environment and super-fast changes wrought by new electronic media. Finally, some connections contribute to ordered patterns, while others serve in the precipitation of disorder – respectively, negentropic and entropic times. This rather ragged, and by no means discretely itemized, list of different times at the very most provides a sense that the linear time used so far is extraordinarily limited (cf. Lash *et al.*, 1998).

All this further complicates the view of 'MM passing' between co(a)gents. 'MM' is altogether more fluid (Mol and Law, 1994), and 'passing' now has a number of provisos and modifications, not least concerning space and time, attached to it. Moreover, although I have so far concentrated exclusively on 'MM passing' between and through such co(a)gents as walker, couch potato, cason and so on, I must not confine this 'movement' to humans alone; I want to make it clear that non-humans similarly 'pass'. I now consider these different 'passings' in a little more detail.

Quasi-usufruct and heterogeneity

In law, the term 'usufruct' refers to the right to enjoy something that legally belongs to another. From this thing one can derive all the profit or utility or advantage that it can yield, but only so long as one does not change its substance (an example familiar to many of us is the use of cutlery that comes with rented furnished accommodation). This, at least, is what complete or perfect usufruct is. Imperfect or quasi-usufruct refers to those instances where the thing would be of no use to the usufructuary if he or she did not change its substance by consuming or expending it in some way. In contrast to this definition, the social ecologist Murray Bookchin deploys a rather different version of usufruct: it is 'the freedom of individuals in a community to appropriate resources merely by virtue of the fact that they are using them. Such resources belong to the user as long as they are being used' (Bookchin, 1981, p. 50).

In the present case, I want to use the notion of quasi-usufruct to clarify the 'passing' of entities between co(a)gents, rather than property (and ownership, rights and duties), which passes between human individuals. However, there are fundamental differences between my own use of this term and that in law and of Bookchin. Firstly, the passing of entities facilitates not only functional use, but also enables expressive use. Secondly, it is not only practical non-humans that pass between co(a)gents, but signifying non-humans, 'natural' non-humans and also humans. Thirdly, these do not pass unaffected from co(a)gent to co(a)gent: it is not a matter of depletion; rather, their 'substance' is altered as they are partly reformed by each co(a)gent, taking up and transferring fragments of identity and agency. Fourthly, these passing entities do not leave from, and arrive at, fully formed individuals – rather they serve in the constitution of the sites of departure and arrival, the co(a)gents. Finally, what gets passed on is not necessarily what was picked up: a co(a)gent that might 'receive' (that is, be partially constituted with the arrival of) an entity belonging to one particular class of entities might subsequently 'pass on' an entity belonging to a rather different class (see below for an extended example).

This last difference is important. As we follow the connections between co(a)gents, what might tie them together, what might serve in the narration of an ordering, or rather a patterning, is not the movement of an entity that is identifiably the 'same', an entity such as MM. Sometimes it will be a human, sometimes a technology and sometimes a 'natural' non-human. In other words, as we move 'across' co(a)gents, what we see 'passing between' and 'connecting' them are different sorts of entities. But what does this patterning pertain to? For Serres, as we have seen, the circulation of a quasi-object serves in the continuing re-generation of the social order. For Bookchin, the usufructory circulation of objects fulfils not only individual needs, but also mediates the needs of the community. In these accounts, what is sought is some additional principle of social ordering, one ontological, the other political. But if one is concerned with heterogeneous ordering – the patterning of humans and technological and 'natural' non-humans – then the entities that circulate and trace out the patterns are themselves variable, heterogeneous. The movement of quasi-objects in the mediation of social ordering is conjoint with – that is, is reciprocally immersed in – the movement of humans in the mediation of material ordering. In sum, to detect patterns in the relations between co(a)gents, the 'tracers' we need to follow – the entities that move in between and tie co(a)gents together and thus 'trace' out the pattern – can be human, non-human, or mixtures of the two, and they can vary as one co(a)gent becomes associated with another.

A couch potato watches TV. The sunlight streams through the window. It is suddenly struck by a worry that it is wasting: it needs more exercise; it needs to take in nature; it needs to refresh itself in the face of something like the natural sublime. To get to that sublime it must drive – it becomes a cason. The roads to the sublime are full of traffic: it is angered, frustrated by the perceived slights of other drivers. It revs up at the traffic lights, and speeds whenever it has the chance. If there is clear road ahead, however short, the cason will accelerate to cover it. It tailgates. In the process, its exhaust emissions are increased. At the car park, it puts on its walking boots and sets off along a trail. On the way, in one of the old coppiced woods through which the seeker-of-the-sublime must pass, it notices that the foliage is tainted, that some trees seem to be dying. The temperature is high for the time of year and, as it walks, its feet begin to swell and what were comfortable boots become uncomfortable. After a curtailed but nevertheless painful walk, it returns to its car, again frustrated. It cannot wait to put its feet up on the sofa. With luck it will catch the natural history programme on the wildlife of the Amazon rainforest. It doesn't.

This rather strained vignette marks a series of sub-relationalities. Certainly, MM can be common to the three co(a)gents. But the connections proceed not simply through MM. The initial worry of the couch potato and its transformation into a cason is partly prompted by sunshine. The sunshine entails a fragment of agency and identity from the seeker-of-the-sublime. The cason's aggressive driving is partly prompted by the design of the car. The exhaust emissions contribute to the acid rain and global warming that detract from the sublime. The fumes entail fragments of agency and identity from the cason, which enter the seeker-of-the-sublime. The painful boots trigger a desire for a return to the sofa – another fragment of agency and identity of the seeker-of-the-sublime enters the couch potato, this time via the cason. What 'passes between' co(a)gents – what mediates sub-relationalities – are thus *both* humans and non-humans. Now, to be sure, there are differences that can be imputed to these mediators of sub-relationalities, and, as noted above, much scholarly work has gone into defining the differences between humans and non-humans (see also Ingold, 1988; Sheehan and Sosna, 1991). Yet I have not dwelled especially on these differences because the technologies, the natures, the humans that 'pass between' are not pure – they are heterogeneous and distributed co(a)gents. As I have attempted to argue throughout, the important thing is to define (and value) not humans or non-humans *per se*, but combinations of these in their relationality.

This all-too-neat circuit of sub-relationalities is, of course, all-too-partial: there are an infinite number of other links, other circuits, that could, in principle, have been traced. Further, this all-too-neat circuit has been enabled by a multitude of other co(a)gencies: for example, those that make up the specific locally encountered traffic and the host of many distant local traffics; those that serve in the production and circulation of the discourses of the bad couch potato and the natural sublime; those that mediate the movement and accumulation of greenhouse gases and standardized measures; and so on. In other words, if the limited connections I have traced here, and which signal the 'rolling transitions and transformations' of co(a)gents, are relatively short, and if the distances travelled 'between' co(a)gents are indeed small, they nevertheless encompass within them vast distances. The intricate, delicate transitions from couch potato to cason to seeker-of-the-sublime are not possible without the signs and materials that have been transported from afar (in space and time) and embodied in, for example, walking boots and remote controls, understandings of scenery and discourses of the individual, specific body techniques and relations of power, degraded habitats and technological design. But this long-distance transportation has proceeded through the local and the micro, moment by moment, linearly, cyclically, entropically, negentropically, quickly, slowly, through the intricate, delicate 'rolling transitions and transformations' of other co(a)gents that lead to our object or event of study. In these mundane co(a)gential moments, the world is knitted and knotted together. But it is also troubled: order and disorder intertwine. The vignette I have narrated above traces a linear story, but it is full of non-linearities; the story I tell seems ordered, but it is shot through with disorder. Quasi-objects and parasites abound, mediating and breaking up associations, excluding and introducing materials and signs, which generate new disorderings and orderings. The use I have made of co(a)gents allows us to begin to map – that is, narrate – a nexus of sub-relationalities mediated through the circulation of heterogeneous entities – 'angels' in Serres' terms, co(a)gents in mine – that simultaneously comprise consonances and dissonances, that make up and break up the seeming orderliness of everyday life.

A partial reprise

Let me take a step back at this point, and indulge in a moment of reiteration and re-contextualization. It should be clear by now that the notion of co(a)gency serves what we might call an '(a)methodological' purpose. I mean this in the broad sense (see Chapter 1) of allowing us to 'perform' the world in a particular way, that is, to narrate everyday life anew. It is a rough and ready tool for excavating usually unnoticed connections that constitute patterns that might suggest unforeseen orderings and disorderings. Co(a)gents are, as I have noted above, reifications, objectifications. This strategy runs counter to what I called above the 'will to deconstruction' that seems to prevail in some academic quarters, and in which there is a concern to focus not upon entities, but upon relations (e.g. Callon and Law, 1995), circulations (Latour, 1999a) or prepositions (Serres and Latour, 1995): the project is to dissolve entities into flows, to demonstrate how the product emerges out of the process.

Obviously, I too am concerned with these issues, but I am also interested in thinking about the points of departure and arrival, and the entities that mediate relations, which set off on their circulations. The co(a)gent is a tool for unpicking otherwise obscure relations and circulations by deriving and contriving other-wise obscure points of departure and arrival. If the common concern to map relationality connotes a sort of horror of nouns (that is, of reification), it is likely that the nouns that prompt these misgivings are commonplace ones – the traditional Western nouns that mediate our typical dualisms. My strategy – 'method' even – has been to coin new heterogeneous nouns to see what alternative relations, connections, might be revealed, to embark upon the development of uncommon verbs and prepositions.

Consequently, I have reified strange nouns in order to 'fluidify' relations and prepositions. It would seem, then, that reification does have its uses (see below). But, at the same time, we must be careful that such reification has not produced stories that are too neat, too secure, too 'impositional', that, in sum, end up occluding the fluidity of co(a)gents (cf. Law, 1994, 1999) that is supposed to be revealed. Of course, this sensitivity to the interwovenness of reification and fluidity echoes others' work, most notably the partial distinctions drawn between root and rhizome, and territorialization and deterritorialization by Deleuze and Guattari (1983, 1988; see also Latour, 1999b; Lee and Brown, 1994; Wise, 1997). There are also are powerful resonances, I have belatedly realized, with Whitehead's (1929) philosophy of the organism, not least in the uncanny resemblances between my 'co(a)gency' and 'sub-relationality' and his 'concrescence' and 'prehension').

Be that as it may, through the various vignettes presented here, I have attempted to unpack multiple and disparate co(a)gencies and sub-relationalities. In the process, I have found myself muddying disciplinary boundaries. The sequence of episodes in the above vignette could have been broken down into a series of sub-disciplinary objects of study – those of environmental sociology and environ-mental science, media studies and driver psychology for example. In the (inevitably compromised) attempt to practise hypo- or infra-disciplinarity, a number of different social scientific subdisciplines have been (all too lightly) traversed, most obviously the sociologies of emotion, the body, consumption, the environment, technology. But there are very many other specialisms within the social sciences that could have informed the case study chapters – rural sociology, sociology of the family, medical sociology, urban sociology – that have received no attention. And there are still other disciplines that could have enriched my stories: physics, chemistry, biology, geography. What notions such as co(a)gency and sub-relationality are meant to do – and I certainly cannot claim to have accomplished it here – is to weave these multiple aspects together, to navigate through the treacheries of what Serres calls the North-West Passage. This multiplicity is not about the attainment of some spurious comprehensiveness: these different disciplines do not contribute in some additive way to an account, for they cross-cut and, crucially, co-constitute one another (as Serres, 1982a, has demonstrated).

There is another point to make here. The obscurity of relations and circulations experienced in the transformations of co(a)gents raises the issue of the arbitrariness of co(a)gents. What goes with what to constitute a co(a)gent? Clearly, the co(a)gents I have deployed in this book are not arbitrary, they have some 'robustness' in the sense that they have been drawn from personal experience, from the media, from culturally available stereotypes, motifs and icons. Consequently, the sub-relationalities I have narrated are not especially novel or insightful. Arbitrariness *per se* is not a problem – it is a challenge to narrate odd, thrown-together co(a)gents that do not follow the sorts of recipes that characterize the co(a)gents I have exploited here. The adventure is to see whether these thrown-together co(a)gents yield new, interesting, unexpected sub-relationalities and patterns that contribute to, and draw upon, other networks, bigger string figures, grander hybrids, and thus illuminate in useful ways the associations, contingencies and coincidences used in these latter assemblages. As we might expect, there is no guarantee that the yield of insight will match the effort of invention.

My attempts at articulating a way of thinking about heterogeneity and distributedness, and my efforts to fashion some theoretical tools that might aid in this thinking, have been worked through a number of case studies. These case studies were, for good reasons (see Chapter 1), structured around personal anecdotes, and largely entailed unsystematic observations (a practice brilliantly exemplified in the modern period by Goffman, cf. Manning, 1992). However, the obvious shortcoming of this sort of approach is that much relevant material is simply missed. As noted, I have relied mostly on popular discourse in the derivation of the co(a)gents studied here. The point of moving beyond this, of embarking upon more observational studies of co(a)gents-in-action, for example, is not that this will provide a 'truer' picture. The gathering of more data and the accumulation of more detail *per se* should not be seen as increasing the 'accuracy' or 'rigour' of an account. Rather, what this more 'expansive' process of data collection can potentially do is 'nuance' an account, i.e. give it a more complex texture. In the process, 'one' – that is, the author – should be 'surprised'. In other words, such 'nuancing' should complexify the object of study, and point to yet more, and unexpected, sub-relationalities. The term 'surprise' should be seen as connoting a renewed relation to one's data, or, put more formally, one's co(a)gency with the object (the co(a)gent) of study has shifted, become reconfigured.

Space, time and politics

In the various stories that have littered this book, I have been wont to narrate in a 'God Tricky' way. That is to say, I have stood outside and above the array of phenomena, events, relations and, from a position of everywhere and nowhere, crafted (if that is the right term) a series of stories about the seeker-of-the-sublime, the enraged cason, the couch potato, the Hudogledog. And I have marshalled all these in order to unpack such abstractions as the 'co(a)gent' and 'sub-relationality'. However, at the same time, I have been present: the vignettes have indicated that I am not wholly separate from these phenomena, events, relations. The process of representing has been both ethereal and earthly.

The God Trick is, of course, about the divestment of situation and situatedness (Haraway, 1991a). Yet, despite the narrative injection of myself into the vignettes, I am still 'on the outside' doing the writing. In Chapter 6, I referred to the Acacomp (aca(demic) + comp(uter)) doing the writing of the Hudogledog and the Dababug. But what does this mean? To be sure, it implies a situation that can be unravelled to indicate some of the possible contingencies behind this work. At a prosaic level, one academic contingency might be the chronic shortage of research funding that necessitates an economically viable turn to texts as the main form of data. The computer – or rather, the internet – fortunately serves as a huge source of these texts. These aspects of the Acacomp can thus be said to condition, at the grossest of levels, the possibility of the present project.

However, the situation signified by this Acacomp is a *general* one. Should we not be explicating the situation of the *particular* Acacomp known as MM? But what would the dissection of such personalized hybridity accomplish? In various ways, such self-revelation might be used to perform contingency and modesty. Yet, this performance is conducted from 'beyond' – from another situation that, if it goes unexplicated, is itself immodest. If this situation (or location) of performance is explicated, that explication too becomes in need of explications and so on and so forth *ad infinitum*. The logic of this process is that of omni-science; it is in Haraway's words, 'transcendent and clean' (Haraway, 1997, p. 36), which brings us back to the God Trick. Haraway (1997) is thus surely right to argue that 'location is the always partial, always finite, always fraught play of foreground and background, text and context, that constitutes critical inquiry' (Haraway, 1997, p. 37). The modesty that derives from this 'finite and dirty' location is practical, it is aligned, it is committed – it is about 'modest intervention'. But it is also critically reflexive. Haraway is keenly aware that immodesty also has its part to play, as she demonstrates substantively when rebuking mainstream science studies scholars for their failure to engage with oppositional science studies, and formally in her immodesty about modesty.

One question that arises is: are we content to hold these two contrasting 'attitudes' (in the physical/corporeal, as well as cognitive, sense) of im/modesty in tension? It is certainly a tension that we find expressed in many fields where debates are conducted through such dichotomies as the real versus the constructed, the pure versus the hybrid, the essential versus the relational. We have already touched upon this terrain in relation to the politics of environmentalism and animal rights (which are themselves informed by like debates in feminist theory, e.g. Whatmore, 1997), and we can point to a similar terrain on which are conducted disputes over nationalism and cosmopolitanism (Cheah and Robbins, 1998), and anti-racism, multiculturalism and hybrid identity politics (Werbner and Modood, 1997; Cohen, 1999; Ratnum, 1999).

I have used the term 'terrain' quite deliberately. This is because it is a spatial metaphor – it is a space that can be traversed. To be sure it is a messy space – with positions cross-cutting, hybridizing, purifying and essentializing all over the place. Moreover, it is a space that can be surveyed: the messiness is inflated by the constant claims to have mapped out the terrain – to have sorted out and named the locations, ranked the positions, laid down the paths that connect them. Inevitably, such mapping claims become, in their turn, contested locations on the very terrain that was supposed to be mapped. Importantly, for our purposes, this messy spatiality is even messier when we begin to deal not only with positions made up of representations, discourses, and commonplaces, but with co(a)gencies, that is, where positions reflect not only the histories of cultural resources (e.g. the differing epistemologies of realism and relativism) but also the differing lineages of technologies and natures.

However, to this image of a messy spatiality we can add that of a messy temporality. Let me return to the Acacomp. As we have seen, the Acacomp is locationally messy, partly because it is not distinct from the co(a)gents it studies. Fragments of agency and identity 'from' these co(a)gents – the cason, the couch potato, for example – course through this Acacomp. These are not 'in' the Acacomp, like seams through a block of marble. They shift and interact in time, as well as spill out: they are tricky, or, rather, 'tricksterish'. Sometimes these interactions congeal into sustained, 'grammaticized' patterns; at other times they interfere with one another to produce eddies of uncertainty, disorder. But I have not put this in quite the right way. It is not that at certain times we have stable patterns of association, and at other times, there is disorder: these are not discrete times that can be arrayed, that is spatialized, along a time line. Rather, these sorts of interactional dynamics 'make' time – in Serres' terms, different times emerge from these different sorts of configurings (cf. S.D. Brown, 1999).

The politics implicated in these messy temporalities through which a co(a)gent such as the Acacomp emerges are messy too. They can reflect reifications (or grammaticizations) within the Acacomp – a certain 'closing down' of location and a 'certain halting' of time (or rather, flux) – through which the co(a)gent can become a political agent in the traditional sense. In this book, political agency was manifested, at least at the level of discourse, at a number of points. For example, there was the thematization of actors engaged in the making, and in the responsibilization of persons as singularized points of intervention (e.g. road ragers), while masking the heterogeneous and distributed roles of mundane technologies (e.g. cars). In addition, attempts were made to argue for different relational ways of valuing animals and environments wherein these are not romanticized, but regarded as steeped in, and steeping, human–technology relations, i.e. animals, environments and human–technology relations constitute mutual 'contexts', one steeped in one another. There is, then, nothing *a priori* in the notion of the co(a)gent that obviates a committed politics.

To reiterate, this committed politics is temporalised – it is emergent in the messy multiple connections and multiple times that make up the Acacomp-in-process. This is not a comfortable politics for there is no ultimate ground on which to base judgement and intervention. A final metaphor can perhaps help us come to grips with these convolutions of time, space and politics: if there is a politics to be derived from the idea of co(a)gency it is perhaps one of *agitation*. Agitation is a suitably complex term, managing to embrace the political, the physical and the epistemological. Firstly, it signifies a form of political intervention, that of keeping up the discussion and of stirring up public feeling. Secondly, it denotes constant movement in time and space – a generalized excitation – such that co(a)gents as political agents are not only always on the move, they are also in the process of flux, of becoming. Finally, agitation also means to be perturbed, to be perplexed: a co(a)gent should always be perplexed by and suspicious of, not least (but certainly not most) itself.

References

Abercrombie, N. (1996) *Television and Society*, Cambridge: Polity Press.

Abercrombie, N. Hill, S. and Turner, B. (1986) *The Sovereign Individual*, London: Allen and Unwin.

Adam, B. (1990) *Time and Social Theory*, Cambridge: Polity Press.

Adam, B. (1998) *Timescapes of Modernity*, London: Routledge.

Adams, C. (1990) *The Sexual Politics of Meat*, Cambridge: Polity/Blackwell.

Adams, D. and Lloyd, J. (1983) *The Meaning of Liff*, London: Pan and Faber & Faber.

Adams, J. (1995) *Risk*, London: UCL Press.

Akrich, M. (1992) The de-scription of technical objects. In: Bijker, W.E. and Law, J. (eds) *Shaping Technology/Building Society*, Cambridge, Mass.: MIT Press.

Akrich, M. and Latour, B. (1992) A summary of a convenient vocabulary for the semiotics of human and nonhuman assemblies. In: Bijker, W.E. and Law, J. (eds) *Shaping Technology/Building Society*, Cambridge, Mass.: MIT Press.

Allison, T.L. and Curry, R.R. (1996) Introduction: invitation to rage. In: Curry, R.R. and Allison, T.L. (eds) *States of Rage: Emotion, Eruption, Violence and Social Change*, New York: New York University Press.

Amsterdamska, O. (1990) Surely you are joking, Monsieur Latour! *Science, Technology and Human Values*, **15**, 494–504.

Appadurai, A. (1986) Introduction: commodities and the politics of value. In: Appadurai, A. (ed.) *The Social Life of Things: Commodities in Cultural Perspective*, Cambridge: Cambridge University Press.

Appadurai, A. (1990) Disjuncture and difference in the global cultural economy. *Theory, Culture and Society*, 7, 295–310.

Arendt, H. (1992) Introduction. In: Benjamin, W., *Illuminations*, London: Fontana Press.

Aries, P. (1962) *Centuries of Childhood*, Harmondsworth: Penguin.

Arksey, H. (1998) *RSI and the Experts: The Construction of Medical Knowledge*, London: UCL Press.

Arluke, A. (1988) Sacrificial symbolism in animal experimentation: Object or pet? *Anthrozoos*, **2**, 97–116.

Arluke, A. (1990) Uneasiness among animal technicians. *Laboratory Animal*, **19**, 20–39.

Arluke, A. and Sanders, C.R. (1996) *Regarding Animals*, Philadelphia: Temple University Press.

Ashmore, M. (1989) *The Reflexive Thesis: Wrighting Sociology of Scientific Knowledge*, Chicago: Chicago University Press.

Ashmore, M. (1993) Behaviour modification of a catflap: a contribution to the sociology of things. *Kennis en Methode*, **17**, 214–229.

Ashmore, M., Wooffitt, R. and Harding, S. (eds) (1994) Humans and others, agents and things. Special Issue of *American Behavioral Scientist*, **37** (6).

Baker, S. (1993) *Picturing the Beast: Animals, Identity and Representation*, Manchester: Manchester University Press.

Barnes, B. (1977) *Interests and the Growth of Knowledge*, London: Routledge and Kegan Paul.

Barnes, B. and Shapin, S. (eds) (1979) *Natural Order*, Beverly Hills: Sage.

Bate, J. (1991) *Romantic Ecology: Wordsworth and the Environmental Tradition*, London: Routledge.

Baudrillard, J. (1983) The ecstasy of communication. In: Foster, H. (ed.) *The Anti-aesthetic: Essays in Postmodern Culture*, Port Townsend: Bay Press.

Bauman, Z. (1991) *Modernity and Ambivalence*, Cambridge: Polity.

Bayley, S. (1986) *Sex, Drink and Fast Cars*, London: Faber and Faber.

Beck, U. (1992) *The Risk Society*, London: Sage.

Bendelow, G. (1998) Painful bodies: the role of the natural. Paper presented at the *British Sociological Association Making Sense of the Body Conference*, University of Edinburgh.

Bendelow, G. and Williams, S.J. (1998) Emotions, pain and gender. In: Bendelow, G. and Williams, S.J. (eds) *Emotions in Social Life: Critical Themes and Contemporary Issues*, London: Routledge.

Benton, T. (1993) *Natural Relations*, London: Verso.

Berg, A.-J. (1995) A gendered socio-technical construction: the smart house. In: Heap, N., Thomas, R., Einon, G., Mason, R. and Mackay, H. (eds) *Information Technology and Society*, London: Sage, pp. 74–89.

Berger, J. (1980) *About Looking*, London: Writers and Readers.

Berman, M. (1981) *The Reenchantment of the World*, Ithaca: Cornell University Press.

Bijker, W.E. (1995a) Sociohistorical technology studies. In: Jasanoff, S., Markle, G.E., Peterson, J.C. and Pinch, T. (eds) *Handbook of Science and Technology Studies*, Thousand Oaks, Calif.: Sage.

Bijker, W.E. (1995b) *Of Bicycles, Bakelite and Bulbs: Toward a Theory of Sociotechnical Change*, Cambridge, Mass.: MIT Press.

Billig, M., Condor, S., Edwards, D., Gane, M., Middleton, D. and Radley, A. (1988) *Ideological Dilemmas*, London: Sage.

Birke, L. (1994) *Feminism, Animals and Science: The Naming of the Shrew*, Buckingham: Open University Press.

Birke, L. and Michael, M. (1997) Rights, hybrids and their proliferation. *Animal Issues*, **1**, 1–19.

Birke, L., Brown, N. and Michael, M. (1998) The heart of the matter: animal bodies, ethics and species boundaries. *Society and Animals*, **6**, 245–261.

Bloor, D. (1976) *Knowledge and Social Imagery*, London: Routledge and Kegan Paul.

Boettger, O. (1998) *From Information Technology to Organising Information: An Interdiciplinary Study*. Unpublished PhD Thesis, Centre for Social Theory and Technology, Keele University.

Bookchin, M. (1981) *The Ecology of Freedom*, Palo Alto, Calif.: Cheshire Books.

Boothe, W.C. (1974) *A Rhetoric of Irony*, Chicago, Ill.: Chicago University Press.

Bourdieu, P. (1984) *Distinction*, London: Routledge and Kegan Paul.

Bowers, J. and Iwi, K. (1993) The discursive construction of society. *Discourse and Society*, **4**, 357–393.

Bowker, G.C. and Star, S.L. (1996) How things (actor-net)work: classification, magic and the ubiquity of standards. Internet Document: http://alexia.lis.uiuc.edu/~bowker/actnet.html

Bowler, P.J. (1992) *The Fontana History of the Environmental Sciences*, London: Fontana.

Boyne, R. (1998) Angels in the archive: lines into the future in the work of Jacques Derrida and Michel Serres. In: Lash, S., Quick, A. and Roberts, R. (eds) *Time and Value*, Oxford: Blackwell.

Brannigan, A. (1981) *Social Bases of Scientific Discovery*, New York: Cambridge University Press.

Brown, N. (1998) *Ordering Hope: Representations of Xenotransplantation – an Actor/Actant Network Theory Account.* Unpublished PhD Thesis, School of Independent Studies, Lancaster University.

Brown, N. (1999) Xenotransplantation: normalizing disgust. *Science as Culture*, **8**, 327–355.

Brown, S.D. (1999) The theology of translation: Michel Serres. Unpublished manuscript.

Buber, M. (1970) *I and Thou*, New York: Scribner's.

Budiansky, S. (1994) *The Covenant of the Wild*, London: Weidenfeld and Nicolson.

Burningham, K. (1995) Attitudes, accounts and impact assessment. *The Sociological Review*, **43**, 100–121

Burningham, K. and O'Brien, M. (1994) Global environmental values and local contexts of action. *Sociology*, **28**, 913–932.

Button, G. (1993) The curious case of the vanishing technology. In: Button, G. (ed.) *Technology in Working Order: Studies in Work, Interaction and Technology*, London: Routledge.

Callon, M. (1986a) The sociology of an actor-network: the case of the electric vehicle. In: Callon, M., Law, J. and Rip, A. (eds) *Mapping the Dynamics of Science and Technology*, London: Macmillan.

Callon, M. (1986b) Some elements in a sociology of translation: domestication of the scallops and fishermen of St Brieuc Bay. In: Law, J. (ed.) *Power, Action and Belief*, London: Routledge and Kegan Paul.

Callon, M. (1991) Techno-economic networks and irreversibility. In: Law, J. (ed.) *A Sociology of Monsters*, London: Routledge.

Callon, M. (1998a) Introduction: the embeddedness of economic markets in economics. In: Callon, M. (ed.) *The Laws of the Markets*, Oxford: Blackwell.

Callon, M. (1998b) An essay on framing and overflowing: economic externalities revisited by sociology. In: Callon, M. (ed.) *The Laws of the Markets*, Oxford: Blackwell.

Callon, M. and Latour, B. (1981) Unscrewing the big Leviathan. In: Knorr-Cetina, K.D. and Mulkay, M. (eds) *Advances in Social Theory and Methodology*, London: Routledge and Kegan Paul.

Callon, M. and Latour, B. (1992) Don't throw the baby out with the Bath school: a reply to Collins and Yearley. In: Pickering, A. (ed.) *Science as Practice and Culture*, Chicago, Ill.: The University of Chicago Press.

Callon, M. and Law, J. (1982) On interests and their transformation: enrolment and counter-enrolment. *Social Studies of Science*, **12**, 615–625.

Callon, M. and Law, J. (1995) Agency and the hybrid *collectif*. *The South Atlantic Quarterly*, **94**, 481–507.

Carruthers, P. (1993) *The Animals Issue*, Cambridge: Cambridge University Press.

Cheah, P. and Robbins, B. (eds) (1998) *Cosmopolitics: Thinking and Feeling Beyond the Nation*, Minneapolis: University of Minnesota Press.

Cockburn, C. and Ormrod, S. (1993) *Gender and Technology in the Making*, London: Sage.

Cohen, P. (ed.) (1999) *New Ethnicities, Old Racisms?* London: Zed Books.

Collingwood, R.G. (1960) *The Idea of Nature*, New York: Galaxy.

Collins, H.M. (1981) Stages in the empirical programme of relativism. *Social Studies of Science*, **11**, 3–10.

Collins, H.M. (1985) *Changing Order*, London: Sage.

Collins, H.M. and Yearley, S. (1992a) Epistemological chicken. In: Pickering, A. (ed.) *Science as Practice and Culture*, Chicago, Ill.: The University of Chicago Press.

Collins. H.M. and Yearley, S. (1992b) Journey into space. In: Pickering, A. (ed.) *Science as Practice and Culture*, Chicago, Ill.: The University of Chicago Press.

Costall, A. (1995a) Socializing affordances. *Theory and Psychology*, **5**, 467–482.

Costall, A. (1995b) Psychology and the pet owners. Paper presented at the *British Psychological Society Annual Conference*, London.

Coulter, J. (1986) Affect and social context: emotion definition as a social task. In: Harre, R. (ed.) *The Social Construction of Emotions*, Oxford: Blackwell.

Cowan, R.S. (1987) The consumption junction: a proposal for research strategies in the sociology of technology. In: Bijker, W.E., Hughes, T.P and Pinch, T. (eds) *Social Construction of Technological Systems*. Cambridge, Mass.: MIT Press.

Cowan, R.S. (1997) *A Social History of American Technology*, New York: Oxford University Press.

Cox, G. and Ashford, T. (1998) Riddle me this: the craft and concept of animal mind. *Science, Technology and Human Values*, **23**, 425–438.

Croll, E. and Parkin, D. (1992) Cultural understandings of the environment. In: Croll, E. and Parkin, D. (eds) *Bush Base: Forest Farm – Culture, Environment and Development*, London: Routledge.

Cronon, W. (1996) Introduction: in search of nature. In: Cronon, W. (ed.) *Uncommon Ground: Rethinking the Human Place in Nature*, New York: Norton.

Crook, S. (1998) Minotaurs and other monsters: 'everyday life' in recent social theory. *Sociology*, **32**, 523–540.

Crossley, N. (1995) Body techniques, agency and intercorporeality: on Goffman's relations in public. *Sociology*, **29**, 133–149.

Cunnington, P. and Lucas, C. (1967) *Occupational Costume in England from the 11th Century to 1914*, London: Adam and Charles Black.

Cunnington, P. and Mansfield, A. (1969) *English Costume for Sport and Outdoor Recreation from 16th to 19th Centuries*, London: Adam and Charles Black.

Cussins, C. (1996) Ontological choreography: agency for women in an infertility clinic. In: Berg, M. and Mol, A. (eds) *Differences in Medicine*, Durham, N. Carolina: Duke University Press.

Cussins, C. (1997) Elephants, biodiversity and complexity: Amboseli National Park, Kenya. Paper presented at *Actor–Network Theory and After Conference*, Keele University.

Damon, M. (1997) Angelology: things with wings. In: Gibian, P. (ed.) *Mass Culture and Everyday Life*, London: Routledge.

Dant, T. (1999) *Material Culture in the Modern World*, Buckingham: Open University Press.

Davison, C., Davey-Smith, G. and Frankel, S. (1991) Lay epidemiology and the prevention of paradox: the implications of coronary candidacy for health promotion. *Sociology of Health and Illness*, **13**, 2–19.

Day, A. (1996) *Romanticism*, London: Routledge.

De Certeau, M. (1984) *The Practice of Everyday Life*, Berkeley, Calif.: University of California Press.

Deleuze, G. and Guattari, F. (1983) *Anti-Oedipus: Capitalism and Schizophrenia*, London: Athlone Press.

Deleuze, G. and Guattari, F. (1988) *A Thousand Plateaus: Capitalism and Schizophrenia*, London: Athlone Press.

Derrida, J. (1976) *Of Grammatology*, Baltimore and London: Johns Hopkins University Press.

Derrida, J. (1978) *Writing and Difference*, London: Routledge and Kegan Paul.

Derrida, J. (1982) *Positions*, London: Athlone Press.

Dickens, P. (1992) *Nature and Society*, Hemel Hempstead, Herts: Harvester Wheatsheaf.

Dobson, A. (1990) *Green Political Thought*, London: HarperCollins.

Donald, C. (ed.) (1994) *Top Tips: From the 'Letterbocks' Pages of Viz*, London: John Brown.

Donald, C. (ed.) (1995) *Top Tips 2*, London: John Brown.

Doran, C. (1989) Jumping frames: reflexivity and recursion in the sociology of science. *Social Studies of Science*, **19**, 515–531.

Douglas, M. (1966) *Purity and Danger*, London: Ark.

Douglas, M. (1987) *How Institutions Think*, London: Routledge and Kegan Paul.

Douglas, M. and Isherwood, B. (1979) *The World of Goods: Towards an Anthropology of Consumption*, Harmondsworth: Penguin.

Dryzek, J.S. (1997) *The Politics of the Earth: Environmental Discourses*, Oxford: Oxford University Press.

Edwards, D. (1996) *Discourse and Cognition*, London: Sage.

Elam, M. (1999) Living dangerously with Bruno Latour in hybrid world. *Theory, Culture and Society*, **16**, 1–24.

Eliade, M. (1964) *Shamanism: Archaic Techniques of Ecstasy*, London: Penguin Arkana.

Elias, N. (1939/1994) *The Civilizing Process*, Oxford: Blackwell.

Elias, N. (1995) Technization and civilization. *Theory, Culture and Society*, **12**, 7–42.

Fairclough, N. (1992) *Discourse and Social Change*, Cambridge: Polity.

Falk, P. (1995) Written in the flesh. *Body and Society*, **1**, 95–105.

Featherstone, M. (1991) *Consumer Culture and Postmodernism*, London: Sage.

Fiddes, N. (1992) *Meat: A Natural Symbol*, London: Routledge.

Fineman, J. (1989) The history of the anecdote: fiction and fiction. In: Veeser, H.A. (ed.) *The New Historicism*, New York: Routledge.

Fleck, L. (1979) *Genesis and Development of a Scientific Fact*, Chicago, Ill.: Chicago University Press.

Flick, U. (1995) Social representations. In: Smith, J.A., Harré, R. and Van Langenhove, L. (eds) *Rethinking Psychology*, London: Sage.

Flink, J.J. (1988) *The Automobile Age*, Cambridge, Mass.: MIT Press.

Foucault, M. (1979) *Discipline and Punish*, Harmondsworth: Penguin.

Foucault, M. (1981) *History of Sexuality, Vol. 1*, Harmondsworth: Penguin.

Franklin, A. (1999) *Animals and Modern Cultures: A Sociology of Human–Animal Relations in Modernity*, London: Sage.

Freeman, M. (1993) *Rewriting the Self: History, Memory, Narrative*, London: Routledge.

Friedel, R. (1994) *Zipper: An Exploration in Novelty*, New York: Norton.

Furhman, E.R. and Oehler, K. (1987) Discourse analysis and reflexivity. *Social Studies of Science*, **16**, 293–307.

Garfinkel, H. (1967) *Studies in Ethnomethodology*, Cambridge: Polity Press.

George, S. (1998) Fast castes. In: Millar, J. and Schwarz, M. (eds) *Speed – Visions of an Accelerated Age*, London: The Photographers' Gallery and the Trustees of the Whitechapel Art Gallery.

Gergen, K.J. (1991) *The Saturated Self*, New York: Basic Books.

Gibson, E.E. (1979) *The Ecological Approach to Visual Perception*, Boston: Houghton Mifflin.

Giddens, A. (1984) *The Constitution of Society*, Cambridge: Polity.

Giddens, A. (1990) *Consequences of Modernity*, Cambridge: Polity.

Giddens, A. (1991) *Modernity and Self-identity*, Cambridge: Polity.

Gifford, D. (1990) *The Farther Shore: A Natural History of Perception*, London: Faber & Faber.

Gilbert, G.N. and Mulkay, M. (1984) *Opening Pandora's Box: A Sociological Analysis of Scientists' Discourse*, Cambridge: Cambridge University Press.

Gomart, E. and Hennion, A. (1999) A sociology of attachment: music amateurs, drug users. In: Law, J. and Hassard, J. (eds) *Actor Network and After*, Oxford and Keele, Blackwell and the Sociological Review.

Gray, C.H., Mentor, S. and Feguera-Sarriera, H.J. (1995) Cyborgology: constructing the knowledge of cybernetic organisms. In: Gray, C.H. (ed.) *The Cyborg Handbook*, New York: Routledge.

Green, J. (1995) *The Macmillan Dictionary of Contemporary Slang*, 3rd edition, London: Macmillan.

Grint, K. and Gill, R. (eds) (1995) *The Gender-Technology Relation: Contemporary Theory and Research*, London: Taylor & Francis.

Grosz, E. (1993) Merleau-Ponty and Irigaray in the flesh. *Thesis Eleven*, **36**, 37–59.

Grove-White, R. and Michael, M. (1993) Nature conservation: culture, ethics and science. In: Burgess, J. (ed.) *People, Economies and Nature Conservation. Proceedings of a Conference held at University College London* (25 November 1992), University College London: Ecology and Conservation Unit, Discussion Paper No. 60.

Guattari, F. (1984) *Molecular Revolution: Psychiatry and Politics*, Harmondsworth: Penguin.

Guyer, P. (1997) *Kant and the Claims of Taste*, 2nd edition, Cambridge: Cambridge University Press.

Hacking, I. (1986) Making up people. In: Heller, T.C., Sosna, M. and Wellberg, D.E. (eds) *Reconstructing Individualism*, Stanford, Calif.: Stanford University Press.

Hagman, O. (1994) The Swedishness of cars in Sweden. In: Sorensen, K.H. (ed.) *The Car and Its Environments*, Brussels: ECSC-EEC-EAEC.

Hannigan, J.A. (1995) *Environmental Sociology: A Social Constructionist Perspective*, London: Routledge.

Harari, J.V. and Bell, D.F. (1982) Introduction. In: Serres, M., *Hermes: Literature, Science, Philosophy*, Baltimore, Md.: Johns Hopkins University Press.

Haraway, D. (1989) *Primate Visions*, London: Routledge and Kegan Paul.

Haraway, D. (1991a) *Simians, Cyborgs and Nature*, London: Free Association Books.

Haraway, D. (1991b) The actors are cyborg, nature is coyote, and the geography is elsewhere: postscript to 'cyborgs at large'. In: Penley, C. and Ross, A. (eds) *Technoculture*, Minneapolis, Minn.: University of Minnesota Press.

Haraway, D. (1992a) The promises of monsters: a regenerative politics for inappropriate/d others. In: Grossberg, L., Nelson C., and Treichler, P.A. (eds) *Cultural Studies*, New York: Routledge.

Haraway, D. (1992b) Other worldly conversations; terran topics; local terms. *Science as Culture*, **3**, 64–99.

Haraway, D. (1994) A game of cat's cradle: science studies, feminist theory, cultural studies. *Configurations*, 2, 59–71.

Haraway, D. (1995) Cyborgs and symbionts: living together in the New World Order. In: Gray, C.H. (ed.) *The Cyborg Handbook*, New York: Routledge.

Haraway, D. (1997) *Modest_Witness@Second_Millennium.FemaleMan.Meets_OncoMouse: Feminism and Technoscience*, London: Routledge.

Hargrove, E. (1992) *The Animal Rights/Environmental Ethics Debate: The Environmental Perspective*, New York: State University of New York Press.

Harrison, C. and Burgess, J. (1994) Social constructions of nature: a case study of conflicts over Rainham Marshes SSSI. *Transactions of the Institute of British Geographers*, **19**, 291–310.

Harrison, R.P. (1996) Toward a philosophy of nature. In: Cronin, W. (ed.) *Uncommon Ground: Rethinking the Human Place in Nature*, New York: Norton.

Harvey, D. and Haraway, D. (1995) Nature, politics and possibilities: a debate and discussion with David Harvey and Donna Haraway. *Environment and Planning D: Society and Space*, **13**, 507–527.

Hastrup, K. and Olwig, K.F. (1997) Introduction. In: Olwig, K.F. and Hastrup, K. (eds), *Siting Culture: The Shifting Anthropological Object*, London: Routledge.

Hearne, V. (1986) *Adam's Task: Calling Animals by Name*, London: Heinemann.

Hebdidge, D. (1979) *Subcultures: The Meaning of Style*, London: Methuen.

Heft, H. (1989) Affordances and the body: an intentional analysis of Gibson's ecological approach to visual perception. *Journal for the Theory of Social Behaviour*, **19**, 1–30.

Heritage, J. (1984) *Garfinkel and Ethnomethodology*, Cambridge: Polity Press.

Hess, D.J. (1995a) *Science and Technology in a Multicultural World*, Columbia: Columbia University Press.

Hess, D. (1995b) On low-tech cyborgs. In: Gray, C.H. (ed.) *The Cyborg Handbook*. New York: Routledge.

Hetherington, K. (1999) From blindness to blindness: museums, heterogeneity and the subject. In: Law, J. and Hassard, J. (eds) *Actor Network and After*, Oxford and Keele, Blackwell and the Sociological Review.

Hubak, M. (1996) The car as a cultural statement: car advertising as gendered socio-technical scripts. In: Lie, M. and Sorensen, K.H. (eds) *Making Technology Our Own? Domesticating Technologies into Everyday Life*, Oslo: Scandinavian University Press.

Hughes, T.P. (1983) *Networks of Power: Electrification in Western Society, 1880–1930*, Baltimore: Johns Hopkins University Press.

Ingold, T. (ed.) (1988) *What is an Animal?* London: Unwin Hyman.

Ingold, T. (1992) Culture and the perception of the environment. In: Croll, E. and Parkin, D. (eds) *Bush Base: Forest Farm – Culture, Environment and Development*, London: Routledge.

Ingold, T. (1993) The temporality of the landscape. *World Archeology*, **25**, 152–174.

Jasper, J. and Nelkin, D. (1991) *The Animal Rights Crusade*, New York: Free Press.

Kendall, G. and Michael, M. (1997) Politicising the politics of postmodern social psychology. *Theory and Psychology*, 7 (1), 7–29.

Knorr Cetina, K.D. (1981) *The Manufacture of Knowledge: An Essay on the Constructivist and Contextual Nature of Science*, Oxford: Pergamon.

Knorr Cetina, K.D. (1997) Sociality with objects: social relations in postsocial knowledge societies. *Theory, Culture and Society*, **14**, 1–30.

Kopytoff, I. (1986) The cultural biography of things: commoditization as process. In: A. Appadurai (ed.) *The Social Life of Things: Commodities in Cultural Perspective*, Cambridge: Cambridge University Press.

Kultgen, J. (1982) Saving you for real people. *Environmental Ethics*, **4**, 59–67.

Lamvik, G.M. (1996) A fairy tale on wheels: the car as a vehicle for meaning within a Norwegian subculture. In: Lie, M. and Sorensen, K.H. (eds) *Making Technology Our Own? Domesticating Technologies into Everyday Life*, Oslo: Scandinavian University Press.

Lash, S. and Urry, J. (1987) *The End of Organized Capitalism*, Cambridge: Polity Press.

Lash, S. and Urry, J. (1994) *Economies of Signs and Space*, London: Sage.

Lash, S., Quick, A. and Roberts, R. (1998) Introduction: millenniums and catastrophic times. In: Lash, S., Quick, A. and Roberts, R. (eds) *Time and Value*, Oxford: Blackwell.

Latour, B. (1987a) *Science in Action: How to Follow Engineers in Society*, Milton Keynes: Open University Press.

Latour, B. (1987b) Enlightenment without critique: a word on Michel Serres' philosophy. In: Phillips, A. (ed.) *Contemporary French Philosophy*, Cambridge: Cambridge University Press.

Latour, B. (1988a) The politics of explanation – an alternative. In: Woolgar, S. (ed.) *Knowledge and Reflexivity: New Frontiers in the Sociology of Knowledge*, London: Sage.

Latour, B. (1988b) *The Pasteurization of France*, Cambridge, Mass.: Harvard University Press.

Latour, B. (1990) Drawing things together. In: Lynch, M. and Woolgar, S. (eds) *Representations in Scientific Practice*, Cambridge, Mass.: MIT Press.

Latour, B. (1991) Technology is society made durable. In: Law, J. (ed.) *A Sociology of Monsters*, London: Routledge.

Latour, B. (1992) Where are the missing masses? A sociology of a few mundane artifacts. In: Bijker, W.E. and Law, J. (eds) *Shaping Technology/Building Society*, Cambridge, Mass.: MIT Press.

Latour, B. (1993a) *We Have Never Been Modern*, Hemel Hempstead: Harvester Wheatsheaf.

Latour, B. (1993b) *On Technical Mediation: The Messenger Lectures on the Evolution of Civilization*, Cornell University, Institute of Economic Research: Working Papers Series.

Latour, B. (1994) Pragmatogonies: a mythical account of how humans and nonhumans swap properties. *American Behavioral Scientist*, **37**, 791–808.

Latour, B. (1995) The 'pedofil' of Boa Vista: a photo-philosophical montage. *Common Knowledge*, **4**, 142–187.

Latour, B. (1996a) *Aramis, or the Love of Technology*, Cambridge, Mass.: Harvard University Press.

Latour, B. (1996b) On interobjectivity. *Mind, Culture and Activity*, **3** (4), 228–245.

Latour, B. (1997) A few steps toward an anthropology of the iconoclastic gesture. *Science in Context*, 10, 63–83.

Latour, B. (1998) To modernise or ecologise? That is the question. In: Braun, B. and Castree, N. (eds) *Remaking Reality: Nature at the Millennium*, London: Routledge.

Latour, B. (1999a) On recalling ANT. In: Law, J. and Hassard, J. (eds) *Actor Network and After*, Oxford and Keele, Blackwell and the Sociological Review.

Latour, B. (1999b) *Pandora's Hope: Essays on the Reality of Science Studies*, Cambridge, Mass.: Harvard University Press.

Latour, B. and Johnson, J. (1988) Mixing humans with non-humans? Sociology of a few mundane artefacts. *Social Problems*, **35**, 298–310.

Latour, B. and Strum, S. (1986) Human social origins: oh please, tell us another story. *Journal of Social and Biological Structures*, **9**, 169–187.

Latour, B. and Woolgar, S. (1979) *Laboratory Life: The Social Construction of Scientific Facts*, London: Sage.

Law, J. (1987) Technology and heterogeneous engineering: the case of Portuguese expansion. In: Bijker, W.E., Hughes, T.P. and Pinch, T. (eds) *Social Construction of Technological Systems*, Cambridge, Mass.: MIT Press.

Law, J. (1991a) Introduction: monsters, machines and sociotechnical relations. In: Law, J. (ed.) *A Sociology of Monsters*, London: Routledge.

Law, J. (1991b) Power, discretion and strategy. In: Law, J. (ed.) *A Sociology of Monsters*, London: Routledge.

Law, J. (1994) *Organizing Modernity*, Oxford: Blackwell.

Law, J. (1999) After ANT: complexity, naming and topology. In: Law, J. and Hassard, J. (eds) *Actor Network and After*, Oxford and Keele, Blackwell and the Sociological Review

Leahy, M.P.T. (1994) *Against Liberation: Putting Animals in Perspective*, London: Routledge.

Lee, N. and Brown, S. (1994) Otherness and actor network: the undiscovered continent. *American Behavioral Scientist*, **37**, 772–790.

Lemonnier, P. (1993) Introduction. In: Lemonnier, P. (ed.) *Technological Choices: Transformation in Material Culture since the Neolithic*, London: Routledge.

Lie, M. and Sorensen, K.H. (1996) Making technology our own? Domesticating technologies into everyday life. In: Lie, M. and Sorensen, K.H. (eds) *Making Technology Our Own? Domesticating Technologies into Everyday Life*, Oslo: Scandinavian University Press.

Lowe, P. and Goyder, J. (1983)*Environmental Groups in Politics*, London: George Allen and Unwin.

Lury, C. (1996) *Consumer Culture*, Cambridge: Polity.

Lury, C. (1998) *Prosthetic Culture*, London: Routledge.

Lykke, N. (1996) Between monsters, goddesses and cyborgs: feminist confrontations with science. In: Lykke, N. and Braidotti, R. (eds) *Between Monsters, Goddesses and Cyborgs: Feminist Confrontations with Science, Medicine and Cyberspace*, London: Zed Books.

Lynch, M. (1985) *Art and Artifact in Laboratory Science*, London: Routledge.

Lynch, M. (1988) Sacrifice and transformation of the animal body into a scientific object: laboratory culture and ritual practice in the neurosciences. *Social Studies of Science*, **18**, 265–289.

Lynch, M. (1993) *Scientific Practice and Ordinary Action: Ethnomethodology and Social Studies of Science* Cambridge: Cambridge University Press.

Lynch, M. and Collins, H.M. (1998) Introduction: humans, animals, machines. *Science, Technology and Human Values*, **23**, 371–383.

Lyon, M.L. (1998) The limitations of cultural constructionism in the study of emotion. In: Bendelow, G. and Williams, S.J. (eds) *Emotions in Social Life: Critical Themes and Contemporary Issues*, London: Routledge, pp. 39–59.

MacKenzie, D. (1990) *Inventing Accuracy*, Cambridge, Mass:. MIT Press.

MacNaghten, P., Grove-White, R., Jacobs, M. and Wynne, B. (1995) *Public Perceptions and Sustainability*, Preston: Lancashire County Council.

MacNaghten, P. and Urry, J. (1998) *Contested Nature*, London: Sage.

Manning, P. (1992) *Erving Goffman and Social Theory*, Cambridge: Polity.

Mansfield, A. and Cunnington, P. (1973) *Handbook of English Costume in the 20th Century, 1900–1950*, London: Faber and Faber.

Marsh, P. and Collett, P. (1986) *Driving Passion: The Psychology of the Car*, London: Jonathan Cape.

Martin, E. (1998) Anthropology and cultural study of science. *Science, Technology and Human Values*, 23, 24–44.

Mauss, M. (1985) A category of the person: the notion of person; the notion of self. In: Carrithers, M., Collins, S. and Lukes, S. (eds) *The Category of the Person*, Cambridge: Cambridge University Press.

Melucci, A. (1989) *Nomads of the Present*, London: Hutchinson Radius.

Mennell, S. (1989) *Norbert Elias: Civilization and the Human Self-Image*, Oxford: Blackwell.

Mennell, S. (1995) Comment on technicization and civilization. *Theory, Culture and Society*, 12, 1–5.

Merchant, C. (1980) *Death of Nature: Women, Ecology and the Scientific Revolution*, London: Harper and Row.

Merleau-Ponty, M. (1968) *The Visible and the Invisible*, Evanston, Ill.: Northwestern University Press.

Mialet, H. (1999) Do angels have bodies? *Social Studies of Science*, 29, 551–581.

Michael, M. (1996) *Constructing Identities: The Social, the Nonhuman and Change*, London: Sage.

Michael, M. (1997) Inoculating gadgets against ridicule. *Science as Culture*, 6, 167–193.

Michael, M. (1998) Between citizen and consumer: multiplying the meanings of the public understanding of science. *Public Understanding of Science*, 7, 313–327.

Michael, M. (1999) Walking talking boots: mediating relations between natures, cultures and bodies. Paper presented at the *Sociality/Materiality – The Status of the Object in Social Science Conference*, Brunel University.

Michael, M. (in press) These boots are made for walking . . . : mundane technology, the body and human–environment relations. Special Issue of *Body and Society* (eds J. Urry and P. MacNaghten).

Michael, M. and Birke, L. (1994) Animal experimentation: enrolling the core set. *Social Studies of Science*, 24, 81–95.

Michael, M. and Grove-White, R. (1993) Talking about talking about 'nature': nurturing 'ecological consciousness'. *Environmental Ethics*, 15, 33–47.

Michael, M. and Kendall, G. (1997) Critical thought and institutional contexts: a reply to Gergen's 'on the poly/tics of postmodern psychology'. *Theory and Psychology*, 7, 37–41.

Michael, M. and Still, A. (1992) A resource for resistance: affordance and power-knowledge. *Theory and Society*, 21, 869–888.

Midgley, M. (1978) *Man and Beast*, Hassocks: Harvester.

Midgley, M. (1983) *Animals and Why They Matter*, Harmondsworth: Penguin.

Millar, J. and Schwarz, M. (1998) Introduction – speed is a vehicle. In Millar, J. and Schwarz, M. (eds) *Speed – Visions of an Accelerated Age*, London: The Photographers' Gallery and the Trustees of the Whitechapel Art Gallery.

Miller, D. (1995) Consumption as the vanguard of history. In: Miller, D. (ed.) *Acknowledging Consumption*, London: Routledge.

Mol, A. and Law, J. (1994) Regions, networks and fluids: anaemia and social topology. *Social Studies of Science*, 24, 641–671.

Molloy, E. (1997a) Product Profile Analysis (PPA). Paper presented to the *ERP Environment Eco-management and Auditing Conference*, UMIST, Manchester.

Molloy, E. (1997b) Social, ethical and environmental accounting: integrating values into management. Paper presented to the *ERP Environment Business Strategy and the Environment Conference*, University of Leeds.

Morley, D. (1992) *Television, Audiences and Cultural Studies*, London: Routledge.

Morley, D. (1995) Television: not so much a visual medium, more a visible object. In: Jenks, C. (ed.) *Visual Culture*, London: Routledge.

Morse, M. (1994) What do cyborgs eat? Oral logic in an information society. In Bender, G. and Druckrey, T. (eds) *Culture on the Brink: Ideologies of Technology*, Seattle: Bay Press.

Mort, M. (1995) *Building the Trident Network: A Study of the Enrolment of People, Knowledge and Machines*. Unpublished PhD Thesis, School of Independent Studies, Lancaster University.

Mort, M. and Michael, M. (1998) Pain and unemployment: phantom intermediaries in the durability of a sociotechnical network. *Social Studies of Science*, **28**, 355–400.

Moscovici, S. (1981) On social representations. In: Forgas, J.P. (ed.), *Social Cognition*, London: Academic Press.

Moscovici, S. (1984) The phenomenon of social representations. In: Farr, R.M. and Moscovici, S. (eds) *Social Representations*, Cambridge: Cambridge University Press.

Muecke, D.C. (1969) *The Compass of Irony*, London: Methuen.

Muhlhausler, P. and Harre, R. (1990) *Pronouns and People: The Linguistic Construction of Social and Personal Identity*, Oxford: Blackwell.

Mulkay, M. (1979) *Science and the Sociology of Knowledge*, London: Allen and Unwin.

Mulkay, M. (1985) *The Word and the World*, London: Allen and Unwin.

Mulkay, M. (1988) *On Humour*, Cambridge: Polity Press.

Myerson, G. and Rydin, Y. (1996) *The Language of Environment: The New Rhetoric*, London: UCL Press.

Newton, T. (1996) Agency and discourse: recruiting consultants in a life insurance company. *Sociology*, **30**, 717–739.

Norman, D. (1988) *The Psychology of Everyday Things*, New York: Basic Books.

Noske, B. (1989) *Humans and Other Animals*, London: Pluto Press.

Noske, B. (1992) Animals and anthropology. In: Hicks, E.K. (ed.) *Science and the Human–Animal Relationship*, Amsterdam: SISWO.

Nye, D.E. (1994) *American Technological Sublime*, Cambridge, Mass.: MIT Press.

O'Brien, F. (1967) *The Third Policeman*, London: Flamingo.

O'Connell, J. (1993) Metrology: the creation of universality by the circulation of particulars. *Social Studies of Science*, **23**, 129–173.

O'Connell, S. (1998) *The Car in British Society: Class, Gender and Motoring 1896–1939*, Manchester: Manchester University Press.

Ong, W. (1982) *Orality and Literacy*, London: Methuen.

Passmore, J. (1974) *Man's Responsibility for Nature*, London: Duckworth.

Penley, C. and Ross, A. (1991) Cyborgs at large: interview with Donna Haraway. In: Penley, C. and Ross, A. (eds) *Technoculture*, Minneapolis: University of Minnesota Press.

Pepper, D. (1996) *Modern Environmentalism: An Introduction*, London: Routledge.

Pfaffenberger, B. (1992a) Social anthropology of technology. *Annual Review of Anthropology*, **21**, 491–516.

Pfaffenberger, B. (1992b) Technological dramas. *Science, Technology and Human Values*, **17**, 282–312.

Pickering, A. (1995) *The Mangle of Practice: Time, Agency and Science*, Chicago and London: University of Chicago Press.

Pinch, T. J. and Bijker, W. E. (1984) The social construction of facts and artefacts: or how the sociology of science and the sociology of technology might benefit each other. *Social Studies of Science*, **14**, 399–441.

Plummer, K. (1995) *Telling Sexual Stories: Power, Change and Social Worlds*, London: Routledge.

Prins, B. (1995) The ethics of hybrid subjects: feminist constructivism according to Donna Haraway. *Science, Technology and Human Values*, **20**, 352–367.

Radley, A. (1990) Artefacts, memory and a sense of the past. In: Middleton, D. and Edwards, D. (eds) *Collective Remembering*, London: Sage.

Ratnum, N. (1999) Chris Ofili and the limits of hybridity. *New Left Review*, **235**, 153–159.

Reed, P. (1989) Man apart: an alternative to the self-realization approach. *Environmental Ethics*, **11**, 53–69.

Ribbens, J. and Edwards, R. (eds) (1997) *Feminist Dilemmas in Qualitative Research: Public Knowledge and Private Lives*, London: Sage.

Richards, E. and Ashmore, M. (1996) More sauce please! The politics of SSK: neutrality, commitment and beyond. *Social Studies of Science*, **26**, 219–228.

Ritvo, H. (1987) *The Animal Estate: The English and Other Creatures in the Victorian Age*, Cambridge, Mass.: Harvard University Press.

Roberts, R.H. and Good, J.M.M. (eds) (1993) *The Recovery of Rhetoric*, Charlottesville: University Press of Virginia.

Rose, H. (1993) Rhetoric, feminism and scientific knowledge: or from either/or to both/and. In: Roberts, R.H. and Good, J.M.M. (eds) *The Recovery of Rhetoric*, Charlottesville: University Press of Virginia.

Rose, N. (1996) *Inventing Our Selves: Psychology, Power and Personhood*, Cambridge: Cambridge University Press.

Rose, N. (1999) *Powers of Freedom*, Cambridge: Cambridge University Press.

Rosen, P. (1993) The social construction of mountain bikes: technology and post-modernity in the cycle industry. *Social Studies of Science*, **23**, 479–513.

Rosen, P. (1995) *Modernity, Postmodernity and Socio-Technical Change in the British Cycle Industry and Cycling Culture*. Unpublished PhD Thesis, School of Independent Studies, Lancaster University.

Rosengren, A. (1994) Some notes on the male motoring world in a Swedish community. In: Sorensen, K.H. (ed.) *The Car and Its Environments*, Brussels: ECSC-EEC-EAEC.

Rowland, B. (1973) *Animals with Human Faces*, Knoxville: University of Tennessee Press.

Russell, S. (1986) The social construction of artefacts: a response to Pinch and Bijker. *Social Studies of Science*, **16**, 31–46.

Sachs, W. (1984) *For Love of the Automobile*, Berkeley: University of California Press.

Sachs, W. (1998) Speed limits. In: Millar, J. and Schwarz, M. (eds) *Speed – Visions of an Accelerated Age*, London: The Photographers' Gallery and the Trustees of the Whitechapel Art Gallery.

Samuel, A. (1996) *Science as Practice: Conserving Scotland's Natural Heritage*. Unpublished PhD Thesis, School of Independent Studies, Lancaster University.

Sanders, C.R. (1990) Excusing tactics: social responsiveness to the public misbehavior of companion animals. *Anthrozoos*, **4**, 82–90.

Sanders, C.R. (1992) Perceptions of intersubjectivity and the process of 'speaking-for' in canine–human relationships. Paper presented at the *International Conference on Science and the Human–Animal Relationship*, Amsterdam.

Sanders, C.R. (1993) Understanding dogs: caretakers' attributions of mindedness in canine–human relationships. *Journal of Contemporary Ethnography*, **22**, 205–226.

Sanders, C.R. (1995) Killing with kindness: veterinary euthanasia and the social construction of personhood. *Sociological Forum*, **10**, 195–214.

Sanders, C.R. and Arluke, A. (1993) If lions could speak: investigating the animal–human relationship and the perspectives of nonhuman others. *The Sociological Quarterly*, **34**, 377–390.

Sarbin, T. (1986) Emotion and act: roles and rhetoric. In: Harre, R. (ed.) *The Social Construction of Emotions*, Oxford: Blackwell.

Scarry, E. (1985) *The Body in Pain: The Making and the Unmaking of the World*, New York: Oxford University Press.

Scott, P., Richards, E. and Martin, B. (1990) Captives of controversy: the myth of the neutral science researcher in contemporary scientific controversies. *Science, Technology and Human Values*, **15**, 474–494.

Serpell, J. (1986) *In the Company of Animals*, Oxford: Blackwell.

Serres, M. (1982a) *Hermes: Literature, Science, Philosophy*, Baltimore, Md.: Johns Hopkins University Press.

Serres, M. (1982b) *The Parasite*, Baltimore, Md.: Johns Hopkins University Press.

Serres, M. (1991) *Rome: The Book of Foundations*, Stanford, Calif.: Stanford University Press.

Serres, M. (1995a) *The Natural Contract*, Ann Arbor, Mich.: Michigan University Press.

Serres, M. (1995b) *Genesis*, Ann Arbor, Mich.: Michigan University Press.

Serres, M. (1995c) *Angels: A Modern Myth*, Paris: Flammarion.

Serres, M. (1997) *The Troubadour of Knowledge*, Ann Arbor, Mich.: Michigan University Press.

Serres, M. and Latour, B. (1995) *Conversations on Science, Culture and Time*, Ann Arbor, Mich.: Michigan University Press.

Shapin, S. (1991) Science and the public. In: Olby, R.C. Cantor, G.N. Christie, J.R.R. and Hodge, M.J.S. (eds) *Companion to the History of Modern Science*, London: Routledge and Kegan Paul.

Sheehan, J.J. and Sosna, M. (eds) (1991) *The Boundaries of Humanity: Humans, Animals, Machines*, Berkeley, Calif.: University of California Press.

Short, J.R. (1991) *Imagined Country: Society, Culture and Environment*, London: Routledge.

Shotter, J. (1984) *Social Accountability and Selfhood*, Oxford: Blackwell.

Silverstone, R. (1994) *Television and Everyday Life*, London: Routledge.

Silverstone, R., Hirsch, E. and Morley, D. (1992) Information and communication technologies and the moral economy of the household. In: Silverstone, R. and Hirsch, E. (eds) *Consuming Technologies*, London: Routledge, pp. 15–31.

Simmell, C. (1999) *Traffic Calming: A Study of Contestation Between Lay and Expert Groups in the Construction of Risk-related Knowledges*. Unpublished PhD Thesis, School of Independent Studies, Lancaster University.

Singer, P. (1970) *Animal Liberation*, London: Jonathan Cape.

Singleton, V. and Michael, M. (1993) Actor-networks and ambivalence: general practitioners in the cervical screening programme. *Social Studies of Science*, **23**, 227–264.

Slater, D. (1997) *Consumer Culture and Modernity*, Cambridge: Polity.

Slater, D. (1998) Trading sexpics on IRC: embodiment and authenticity on the internet. *Body and Society*, **4**, 91–117.

Smart, K. (1990) The 'devil dog' debate. Unpublished manuscript.

Smart, K. (1993) *Resourcing Ambivalence: Dogbreeders, Animals and the Social Studies of Science*. Unpublished PhD Thesis, School of Independent Studies, Lancaster University.

Smith, J.W. and Turner, B.S. (1986) Constructing social theory and constituting society. *Theory, Culture and Society*, 3, 125–133.

Soper, K. (1986) *Humanism and Anti-Humanism*, London: Hutchinson.

Soper, K. (1995) *What is Nature?* Oxford: Blackwell.

Sorensen, K.H. (1994) Introduction. In Sorensen, K.H. (ed.) *The Car and Its Environments*, Brussels: ECSC-EEC-EAEC.

Sorensen, K.H. and Sorgaard, J. (1994) Mobility and modernity: towards a sociology of cars. In: Sorensen, K.H. (ed.) *The Car and Its Environments*, Brussels: ECSC-EEC-EAEC.

Spierenberg, P. (1984) *The Spectacle of Suffering*, Cambridge: Cambridge University Press.

Star, S.L. (1991) Power, technologies and the phenomenology of conventions: on being allergic to onions. In: Law, J. (ed.) *A Sociology of Monsters*, London: Routledge.

Stenien, J.M. (1994) Controlling the car: a regime change in the political understanding of traffic risk in Norway. In Sorensen, K.H. (ed.) *The Car and Its Environments*, Brussels: ECSC-EEC-EAEC.

Strathern, M. (1991) *Partial Connections*, Savage, Md.: Rowman and Littlefield.

Strathern, M. (1992) *After Nature*, Cambridge: Cambridge University Press.

Strathern, M. (1996) Cutting the network. *Journal of the Royal Anthropological Institute (New Series)*, 2 517–535.

Strum, S. and Latour, B. (1988) Redefining the social link: from baboons to humans. *Social Science Information*, **26**, 783–802.

Szerszynski, B. (1996) On knowing what to do: environmentalism and the modern problematic. In: Lash, S., Szerszynski, B. and Wynne, B. (eds) *Risk, Environment and Modernity*, London: Sage.

Tallmadge, J. (1981) Saying you to the land. *Environmental Ethics*, 3, 351–363.

Tenner, E. (1996) *Why Things Bite Back: Predicting the Problems of Progress*, London: Fourth Estate.

Tester, K. (1991) *Animals and Society*, London: Routledge.

Thoits, P.A. (1989) The sociology of emotions. *Annual Review of Sociology*, **15**, 317–342.

Thoits, P.A. (1990) Emotional deviance: research agendas. In: Kemper, T.D. (ed.) *Research Agendas in the Sociology of Emotions*, Albany, NY: SUNY Press.

Thomas, E.M. (1993) *The Hidden Life of Dogs*, London: Weidenfeld and Nicolson.

Thomas, K. (1984) *Man and the Natural World*, Harmondsworth: Penguin.

Thorne, T. (1990) *Bloomsbury Dictionary of Contemporary Slang*, London: Bloomsbury.

Thorngate, W. (1984) Recursive adaptation, stopping rules and ironies of computing. *Journal of Social Issues*, 40, 145–153.

Thrift, N. (1996) *Spatial Formations*, London: Sage.

Traweek, S. (1988) *Life Times and Beamtimes. The World of High Energy Physicists*, Cambridge, Mass.: Harvard University Press.

Turner, B. (1992) *Regulating Bodies*, London: Routledge.

Turner, B. (1994) Preface. In: Falk, P., *The Consuming Body*, London: Sage.

Turner, B. (1996) *The Body and Society*. 2nd edition, London: Sage.

Urry, J. (1990) *The Tourist Gaze*, London: Sage.

Urry, J. (1995) *Consuming Places*, London: Routledge.

Urry, J. (1999) Automobility, car culture and weightless travel: a discussion paper (draft). Department of Sociology, Lancaster University, http://www.lancaster.ac.uk/sociology/soc008ju.html.

Vestby, G.M. (1996) Technologies of autonomy? Parenthood in contemporary 'Modern Times'. In: Lie, M. and Sorensen, K.H. (eds) *Making Technology Our Own? Domesticating Technologies into Everyday Life*, Oslo: Scandinavian University Press.

Virilio, P. (1977/1986) *Speed and Politics*, New York: Semiotext(e).

Virilio, P. (1995) *The Art of the Motor*, Minneapolis: University of Minnesota Press.

Wajcman, J. (1995) Feminist theories of technology. In: Jasanoff, S., Markle, G. E., Peterson, J. C. and Pinch, T. (eds) *Handbook of Science and Technology Studies*, Thousand Oaks, Calif.: Sage.

Wallace, A.D. (1993) *Walking, Literature and English Culture: The Origins and Uses of Peripatetic in the Nineteenth Century*, Oxford: Clarendon Press.

Wallis, R. (ed.) (1979) *On the Margins of Science*, Keele: Keele University Press.

Warner, C.T. (1986) Anger and similar delusions. In: Harre, R. (ed.) *The Social Construction of Emotions*, Oxford: Blackwell.

Weldon, S. (1998) *Runway Rhetorics and Networking with Nature: A Study of Scientific Expertise in Environmental Impact Assessment*. Unpublished PhD Thesis, School of Independent Studies, Lancaster University.

Werbner, P. and Modood, T. (eds) (1997) *Debating Cultural Hybridity*, London: Zed Books.

Whatmore, S. (1997) Dissecting the autonomous self: hybrid cartographies for a relational ethics. *Environment and Planning D: Society and Space*, **15**, 37–53.

White, D.G. (1991) *Myths of the Dog-Man*, Chicago: Chicago University Press.

White Jr., L. (1962) *Medieval Technology and Social Change*, Oxford: Clarendon Press.

White, S.K. (1994) *Edmund Burke: Modernity, Politics, and Aesthetics*, Thousand Oaks, Calif.: Sage.

Whitehead, A.N. (1929) *Process and Reality*, Cambridge: Cambridge University Press.

Whitehouse, A. (1993) *Joyriding – Policy, Law and Probation Practice*, University of East Anglia, Norwich: Social Work Monographs.

Whitelegg, J. (1997) On a highway to hell. *Times Higher Education Supplement*, 7 March 1997, p. 22.

Williams, R. (1973) *The Country and the City*, London: The Hogarth Press.

Williams, S.J. (1998) Modernity and the emotions: corporeal reflections on the (ir)rational. *Sociology*, **32**, 747–769.

Williams, S.J. and Bendelow, G. (1998a) Introduction: emotions in social life – mapping the sociological terrain. In: Bendelow, G. and Williams, S.J. (eds) *Emotions in Social Life: Critical Themes and Contemporary Issues*, London: Routledge.

Williams, S.J. and Bendelow, G. (1998b) In search of the 'missing body': pain, suffering and the (post)modern condition. In: Scambler, G. and Higgs, P. (eds) *Modernity, Medicine and Health*, London: Routledge.

Winner, L. (1985) Do artifacts have politics? *Daedelus*, **109**, 121–136.

Winner, L. (1993) Upon opening the black box and finding it empty: social constructivism and the philosophy of technology. *Science, Technology and Human Values*, **18**, 362–378.

Wise, J.M. (1997) *Exploring Technology and Social Space*, Thousand Oaks, Calif.: Sage.

Woolgar, S. (ed.) (1988a) *Knowledge and Reflexivity*, London: Sage.

Woolgar, S. (1988b) *Science: The Very Idea*, Chichester: Ellis Horwood.

Woolgar, S. (1991) Configuring the user: the case of usability trials. In: Law, J. (ed.) *A Sociology of Monsters*, London: Routledge.

Woolgar, S. (1992) Some remarks about positionism: a reply to Collins and Yearley. In: Pickering, A. (ed.) *Science as Practice and Culture*, Chicago, Ill.: The University of Chicago Press.

Wynne, B.E. (1992) Misunderstood misunderstanding: social identities and public uptake of science. *Public Understanding of Science*, 1, 281–304.

Wynne, B.E. (1996) May the sheep safely graze? A reflexive view of the expert-lay divide. In: Lash, S., Szerszynski, B. and Wynne, B. (eds) *Risk, Environment and Modernity*, London: Sage.

Yearley, S. (1991) *The Green Case*, London: HarperCollins.

Yearley, S. (1996) *Sociology, Environmentalism, Globalization: Reinventing the Globe*, London: Sage.

Index